Veils of Separation

Finding the Face of Oneness

RABIA ERDUMAN

Library of Congress Card Number: 00 093470

ISBN 0-9705260-9-1

The author gratefully acknowledges permission to reprint
the poem by Rumi, "Out beyond ideas of wrongdoing and
rightdoing," from *Open Secret* translated by Coleman Barks
with John Moyne. Originally published by Threshold Books,
151 Emerald City Way, Watsonville, CA 95076.

"When the mind is at peace . . ." by Layman P'ang,
translated by Stephen Mitchell, from *The Enlightened Heart:
an anthology of sacred poetry*, edited by Stephen Mitchell.
Copyright © 1989 by Stephen Mitchell. Reprinted
by permission of HarperCollins Publishers, Inc.,
10 East 53rd Street, New York, N.Y. 10022-5299.

Printed in Canada by Hignell Printing, Inc.
Set in Korinna
Editor: Ann West
Design & Typography: K Bryson
Cover Illustration: Melissa Lofton

This book is dedicated to

my mother and father for giving me life, my spiritual teachers Osho and Jeru Kabbal for showing me the path, and my mentors Jeanne Brown-Hopkins, Hugh Milne, and David Quigley for providing the tools.

CONTENTS

Acknowledgments vi

Foreword by Stephen Mitchell vii

Introduction ix

The Beginning: BABLA MEETS WHITE SWAN 1

Chapter 1: BABLA'S FIRST INSIGHTS IN LIFE. 5

    Ram-Man: Learning to Laugh
    Contented Sage: Bonding With Rabia, the Adult Self
    Inner Guides: Eternal Friend, Alan, Black Panther, and Maya
    Mountain Man: The Outer World
    One-Eyed Eagle, Mother Hen, Scared Rabbit,
       and Black Witch: Clearing the Past
    Higher Self: Accepting What Is

Chapter 2: THE ALCHEMIST
    Inner Beings, Inner Guides, Worlds Within Worlds 35

    Butterfly, Madwoman, and Birdie: The Exotic Land
    Inner Beings: Changing From the Inside
    Tantrika, the Nun, and the Slut: A New Perspective
    The Nun: Making a Wise Choice
    Loretta: Learning to Receive
    Eric: Letting Go of Hopelessness
    Fireball: Rage Comes out of the Cage
    Greedy Rich Man: Misusing Power
    Two Priestesses: Uniting Earth and Sky
    Miriam: Giving Love
    Worlds Within Worlds: Delving Into the Depths
    Golden Queen: Enjoying Abundance
    Ms. Romantic: Opening to Intimacy

Chapter 3: THE HEALING JOURNEY
    Outer Beings, Inner Guides 79

    Otter: The Dance of Us
    Lion Woman and Deer Lady: The Beauty of Friendship
    The Vultures: Facing Fear and Judgment
    Fuzzy Brown Bear: The Joy of Self-Acceptance
    Humangus: Power of Wisdom
    The Witch in the Cave: Fear in the Heart

The Witch's Journey: Finding Courage
Little Knight: True Identity
The Needle: Mending the Heart
Cheng Li and Wise Owl: Dragon Wisdom
Wondering Magician: Understanding Self-Doubt
Lost & Found Man: Who Am I?
Eagle Feather and Hawk Feather: Balancing Opposites
Wondering Magician and the Witch: Words With Meaning
Return of the Vultures: Love, Fear, Anger, and Avoidance
Return to Lost & Found Man: Duality Versus Unity
Oracle: Abiding in Truth
Mountain Lion: Losing the Heart
Frozen Man and Gayland: Ice in the Heart
The World of Silence: True Connection
Deer Woman: Maturing

Chapter 4: THE PLACE BEYOND PARADISE 145
Dolphin and Emanuella: Unveiling the Longing
Manuel: Meeting the Inner Man
Flute Player and Eric: The World of Relationships

Chapter 5: HEALING CIRCLE 159
Healing Circle: The Beings Meet
Birthing of Oracle: Back to Oneness
The Witch's Heart: The Garden of Self-Love
Kiwi: Delighting in Who We Are
Lost & Found Man: Uncovering the True Name
Ax-Woman, Mermaid, and Little Seashell: The Inner Woman
Blue Swan: Returning to Essence
Unloved Phoenix: The World of Separation
Mountain Lion and Batwoman: Restoring the Lionheart
Armadillo: Ready to Trust
The Wizard in the Pumpkin and Black Man: Healing the Split
Wondering Magician: Lifting the Curse
Eelprince: The Secret Beyond All Secrets

Chapter 6: FINISHING TOUCHES 223
Humangus: The World of the Eagle
Lion Woman and Cheng Li: Exploring Elements, Orbs, and Organs
Peace With the Vultures: In Our Hearts, We Are One

The End: DISSOLVING THE VEILS OF SEPARATION 237
Afterword by Jodi Korpi 242
About the Author 243

Acknowledgments

I am deeply grateful to Svarna Wilkens, Gaye Russell-Bruce, and Paul Fridlund, without whose emotional and practical support this book would not have been written.

Special thanks to my editor Ann West, who helped me in so many ways that words cannot describe. She kept gently pushing me through my fears and overwhelm, encouraging me with her knowledge, experience, and open heart.

I extend my gratitude to Kedron Bryson, who prepared the layout and design, for her diligence and precision. She gave me the final courage to publish this book.

I am most grateful to the artist Melissa Lofton, who created the cover and the inserts, for being her beautiful self, and so easy to work with.

I am grateful to Gwyneth Cravens for her encouragement. Her seeing me as an author helped me see myself as one.

I am grateful to Jenny D'Angelo for the initial editing.

I thank Don Panec for his invaluable suggestions.

Many thanks to Cheryll Daniel and Jodi Korpi for their final proofreading.

I am appreciative of all the "Outer Beings" mentioned in the book. Without their presence in my life, there would be no story.

And, much Love to Jodi Korpi for standing by me in spirit and heart.

Foreword

My friend Rabia Erduman's *Veils of Separation* is a journey through the landscapes of the inner life. She calls it a fairy tale, though it seems to me not so much a fairy tale as an allegory, a modern, female *Pilgrim's Progress*. But unlike Christian's journey to salvation, Babla's is a tantric journey to an integrated self. By the end of the book, all the disparate fragments of the self have merged into a sense of spiritual wholeness.

It takes courage to enter our own interior. But what is the alternative? "If you bring forth what is inside you," the Gospel of Thomas says, "what you bring forth will save you. If you don't bring forth what is inside you, what you don't bring forth will destroy you." Even the first step into the interior can be daunting. As Arjuna says in the *Bhagavad Gita*:

> The mind is restless, unsteady,
> turbulent, wild, stubborn;
> truly, it seems to me
> as hard to master as the wind.

Inside, there may be nothing that we can see but chaos, a Mad Hatter's tea party with insane or repulsive parts of the self running totally out of control. There may be dozens, hundreds in our cast of characters. Wisdom at this point means simply taking a look. Later, wisdom may mean letting the characters have their say. Each character saves us because it is included and attended to, like a neglected child who finally feels heard.

Still later in the journey, the dramas begin to fade. The cast of characters thins out. The inner landscape becomes clear. Until finally there is nothing to be integrated. There is no inside or outside, nothing we can point to as self or non-self. There is only what appears before our eyes in its brief, luminous presence. This pen moving across the white page. This cup of tea on the table. This breath.

~ Stephen Mitchell

Out beyond ideas of wrongdoing and rightdoing,
there is a field. I'll meet you there.

When the soul lies down in that grass,
the world is too full to talk about.
Ideas, language, even the phrase *each other*
doesn't make any sense.

Rumi (1207–1273)

Translated by Coleman Barks
with John Moyne

Introduction

V*eils of Separation* was birthed from a strong sense of "needing" to write a book. I didn't necessarily *want* to, yet the urge to write was so present that I decided to follow it. The idea of a serious spiritual book wasn't appealing because so many wonderful books already exist. But, the possibility of a fairy tale with a deeper message brought a smile to my face, and my creativity started to flow.

Fairy tales engage the subconscious mind with their nonlinear, visual language. Milton Erickson, a great hypnotherapist, used to tell clients stories that seemed to have nothing to do with their actual situation, yet their issues would disappear. When working with deep-set patterns, the power of metaphor is indeed a welcome tool.

The main Truth of this book is that there is no separation, only Oneness. When we go beyond the physical appearance of the body into subtler energies inside, we find that everyone is made of the same substance. I call this *radiance*. By contrast, separation is created out of fear, shame, anger, and self-negating thought patterns we believe to be true. These, then, form the "veils" that hide our Essence. When two people meet, their veils often interact, rather than their true beings.

Each of us, depending on our upbringing, has a different set of veils. This story has many characters to show the multitude of ways a person might be split. Because everyone is unique, there are also countless ways to dissolve the veils of separation and come home.

Approach this book as a series of doorways to lasting transformation, allowing a profound opening inside that moves toward wholeness. As a map to personal change, each story contains easy yet powerful exercises pointing to breakthroughs in consciousness. This shift can continue in dreams and in quiet reflection as well.

On the spiritual path, I have learned that self-discovery doesn't have to be a struggle. A fairy tale, more than any other format, shows that lifting our veils can be joyful and effortless. That is, separation is but an illusion. Whether we experience it or not, we are forever sitting, moving, breathing in an infinite Field of Ecstasy. Finding the face of Oneness, we experience this Ecstasy as ourselves!

Love, Rabia
10. 28. 2000, Pacific Grove, California

Characters

The Child Selves, Inner Children: Babla, Fireball

Rabia: The Adult Self

Inner Beings: Ms. Romantic, Loretta (the Victim), Eric the Cynic, the Nun, Inner Judge, Miriam (the Rescuer), the Slut, Mermaid, Ax-Woman, Little Seashell, Mr. Money, Slimy Joe, Emanuella (Inner Woman), Manuel (Inner Man)

Inner Guides: Higher Self, Eternal Friend, Alan (Inner Mate), Maya, Black Panther, Zak, Amazon Woman, Wise Owl, Cheng Li, Golden Queen, Tantrika

Outer Guides: White Swan, Eagle, Hawk

Outer Beings Babla meets prior to the Healing Circle: Ram-Man, all the Outer Beings in Contented Sage's cave, Mountain Man, Madwoman, the Alchemist, Otter, Lion Woman, Deer Lady, Vultures, Dolphin, Flute Player

Outer Beings of the Healing Circle: Humangus the Giant/little boy, Wondering Magician, Kiwi the Fuzzy Brown Bear/Fetus, the Witch in the Cave/Frozen Man/Gayland, Unloved Phoenix, Lost & Found Man, Wizard in the Pumpkin/Black Man, Armadillo, Blue Swan, Oracle/Lion Cub/Panther/Isabella/Feather, Eelprince/little eel, Mountain Lion/Batwoman

Outer Beings who meet the Witch in the Cave: Little Knight, Little Fairy, Mermaid, the dog M

Humangus's Inner Guides: Old Man, Old Woman, Inner Mate

Kiwi's Inner Guides: Zoran (Inner Mate)

Oracle's Inner Guides: Daniel, Amanda, Miranda

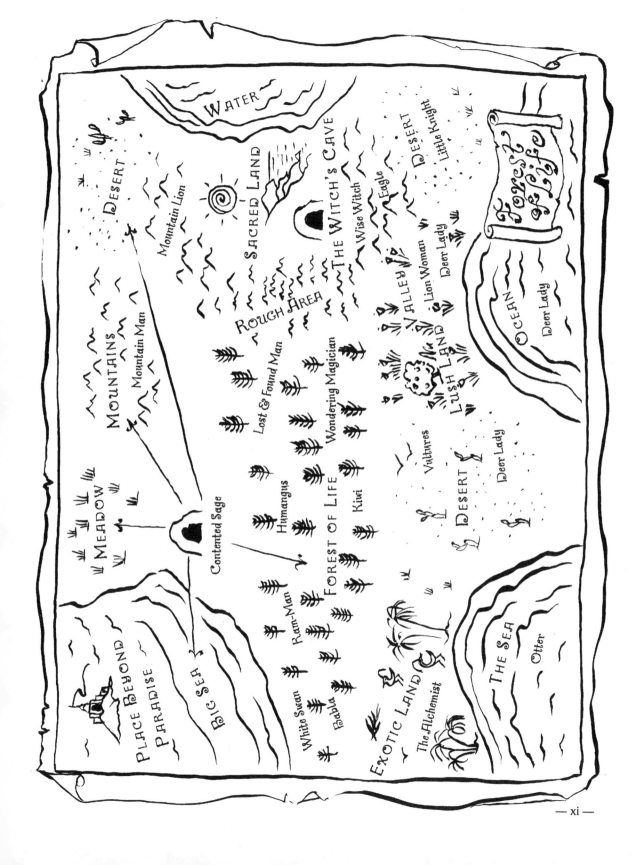

the beginning

babla meets white swan

BABLA MEETS WHITE SWAN

Once upon a time there was a four-year-old girl with curly blond hair and big blue eyes. She was called Babla. She lived in the Forest of Life with no real home. All the comings and goings in the forest, all the strange sounds were very confusing to her. Loving and giving, she would have given away her very clothes if someone had asked for them. And yet, she wasn't happy. Most of the time she was so scared and lost that she felt like a tiny mouse in a maze looking for cheese—running from one potential happiness to another, never getting anywhere. Often, when she was smiling and taking care of others, she would think how unfair life was. Here she was so loving and so giving, with hardly any reward for it, yet feeling as miserable as ever. But somehow, she couldn't stop giving.

"Oh, well," she thought. "I guess being loving and giving is my nature. So, what can I do?"

One day, as she sat huddled in a corner with her Teddy and little Leo, hiding from the big cruel world and sure that nobody cared about her, Babla heard the sound of wings. When she looked up, she saw a big white swan flying towards her—graceful, powerful, and free.

The amazing bird landed smoothly in front of Babla and looked deeply into her eyes. Babla stared back in awe. She couldn't understand what was in the swan's eyes, but something soothing and calming came into her being. Gradually, she started to relax, taking some deep breaths.

White Swan told Babla about the Place Beyond Paradise, where Beings loved each other and treated each other equally no matter what their type, age, or size; where they laughed and cried together and celebrated life. "Only by living fully can you find true happiness," said the beautiful creature.

Babla wanted to know more about this place. How could she get there?

White Swan offered her a ride. As Babla climbed onto its back, she felt soft, white feathers brush against her arms and legs. "These aren't just soft swan feathers," she thought. "Their special touch goes way beyond my skin, right to my bones."

When Babla was safely seated, White Swan took off, gliding high into the sky. After flying for what seemed like a lifetime, the two drifted down and started floating on the Big Sea. Flying in the air had been wonderful for Babla.

The infinite sky had helped her little heart open. As she breathed deeply, her whole chest began to feel spacious from the inside.

Coming down to float on the Big Sea was a totally different experience. White Swan was moving in total harmony with the water, and the rhythm of the sea created a gentle rocking for Babla. After a while, as the soothing motion spread into her body, she started smiling, then giggling, then laughing—with no reason at all. She felt waves of joy moving through her.

Then White Swan took off into the air again, and Babla felt the laughter enter her heart. It was as if all of her body were laughing.

At last they came to the Place Beyond Paradise. White Swan was right. The Beings here had an inner glow about them that Babla had never seen before. Babla started to cry and laugh with them. At the end of tears laughter appeared, and at the end of laughter there were tears. After a while, however, she had moments where the crying and laughing stopped, and she was silent. At those times, the whole world seemed different to her; the colors were more vibrant, and nature seemed more alive.

One day, White Swan announced that it was time to leave this wonderful land. Babla must now put the things she had learned there into practice. Babla climbed onto the swan's back and they easily took off, heading back to where they had first met.

When they arrived in the forest, Babla climbed down and nestled close to her friend. White Swan looked deeply into her eyes, gently touched her forehead, and said, "Remember one thing: surrender to Love. Never surrender to another Being; surrender only to Love. I'll be with you and I love you." From its wing feathers, the white bird took out a small golden key on a chain and put it around Babla's neck. With a nod, the swan took off, its enormous wings carrying it higher and higher. For a while, it made circles and spirals around Babla, then finally flew away.

Babla was speechless. She didn't know what to make of this all, yet something had changed. Somehow her heart was feeling lighter. "Surrender to Love, surrender to Love," she repeated, touching the key around her neck. "I wonder what it means."

I.
babla's first insights in life

RAM-MAN: Learning to Laugh

Time passed. Babla was still unhappy and often scared, yet never as deeply as before she had met White Swan. One day, sitting in the corner of the forest that life had given her, feeling that her lot was unfair, she couldn't stand it any longer.

She called out loud, "White Swan, I need your help!" After a moment's silence, she heard the sound of wings coming closer. When she looked up, she saw the beloved bird preparing to land.

"I'm here, Babla."

Babla cried in anguish, "Oh, White Swan! I want to understand what 'surrender to Love' means. I feel so confused."

White Swan looked deeply into Babla's eyes. It could have been for a moment or for an eternity. For Babla, time stopped. At last, the awesome bird responded. "You need to find the Contented Sage and be with him for a while. Before you can surrender to Love, you must understand his teaching. I love you. I'm always here for you."

And Babla knew that what White Swan had said was true. For the first time, she knew how Love felt. This sweet fragrance coming into her was real Love, indeed.

The swan's beak moved into what could be called a smile, and Babla felt a wing touch her heart. Then, off it flew, circling above the stunned little girl, lifting higher and higher into the sky.

Babla's mind, now as empty as the clear blue sky, allowed just one statement to come through. "One day, I'll be able to fly with you, White Swan." Although she couldn't fully understand it yet, she had tapped into a wise part of herself.

Babla got up from her corner of life to search for Contented Sage. She walked at random, thinking of White Swan's words and asking people she met on the path to find this Being. Nobody seemed to know.

Not sure what else to do, she decided to focus on White Swan's parting words: "I love you." When she took these words and the sweet fragrance that came along with them into her heart, they seemed to warm her. This made her feel calm and peaceful, and she liked it.

One day Babla met Ram-Man, who was half ram and half man. He had four strong legs, the trunk of a man, two beautiful horns, and very green eyes that sparkled. She asked him about Contented Sage.

To her surprise, Ram-Man answered, "Oh, yes. I know how to find him. His place is right on my way. Why don't you jump on my back and I'll give you a ride."

And that's what Babla did. It was so wondrous to ride on Ram-Man. When they stopped to rest at the end of each day, he taught her things he had learned in his travels. He showed her how to have fun, smile at the sun, talk to the moon, pick flowers, and chase after birds. Laughter was important in his life.

One morning, Ram-Man said, "At the end of this day, we will arrive at Contented Sage's home. I very much enjoyed giving you a ride." And Babla told him that she had enjoyed everything he had taught her.

As the sun sank in the sky, they came to an intersection; one path was going into a forest, one path into a meadow, one into the desert, one into the mountains, and a fifth path was going into the sea. Right at the intersection was a huge stone cave. Ram-Man pointed ahead. "Contented Sage lives here. I need to continue my journey into the forest. Be well."

They gave each other a long hug. As Babla approached the cave, Ram-Man waved one last time and disappeared into the forest.

CONTENTED SAGE: *Bonding With Rabia, the Adult Self*

The cave had a wooden door. Babla knocked. It opened and a smiling woman said, "Welcome," and let Babla in.

The cave was bigger than it had seemed from the outside. It was full of all kinds of little Beings: girls, boys, wolf cubs, bunnies, fawns, baby fairies, cherubs, lion cubs, young birds, and many other Beings, and even some that Babla had never seen before.

Everyone was gathered around a small, thin man with long black hair and a long beard. Even though his hair and beard were black, the man seemed ageless. He wore a long, simple robe and sat quietly, enveloped in what seemed like eternal peace. "That's why he is called Contented Sage," thought Babla.

She sat at the back of the space, wondering what would to happen next. Soon the Sage started to speak. He talked about something Babla had never heard before—the "Adult Self." Babla listened.

The Sage said, "The Adult Self is the part of us in touch with reality. This part knows that inner and outer resources are available to handle anything that comes along. However, the Child Self is often lost in fear, shame, sadness, or anger from unresolved memories in the past. These emotions can cloud one's perception of reality. For example, when the Child Self is afraid, it doesn't necessarily mean something is happening in that moment to threaten the Child's survival. But, something could be happening to *remind* the Child Self of an old, scary memory. Thus, the fear is coming from the past memory, not from the Now."

It was difficult for Babla to understand all of this. "The Adult Self is very loving and understanding," the Sage told them. "He or she is also strong and capable of taking care of the Child Self—to meet its survival needs, to nurture it, to accept it unconditionally.

"Even though the Adult Self is a grown-up Being, it is not a parent; it never judges or criticizes the Child Self. This part is more like a friend you can trust and count on."

"Wow!" thought Babla. "Do I have an Adult Self, too? I hope so. It sure would make life a lot easier if I did."

Contented Sage waved his hand to one of his assistants, a tall blond woman with long, beautiful hair and a flowing, pale blue dress. With a loving expression on her face, she got up to open the door. All kinds of Adult Selves entered the cave. Adult gnomes, fairies, men and women, lions and lionesses, huge grown-up wolves, big deer, as well as grown-up flowers and plants were, one by one, coming in, looking for their Child Selves.

Babla saw a curly, dark-blond-haired woman dressed in off-white tights and a dark blue tunic coming toward her. When this pretty woman was closer, Babla could see long lashes above her big blue eyes, deep as the sea.

"Just like my eyes," she thought. Then she realized that these were her own eyes—her eyes in a grown-up body, which was so much stronger than her little body.

"Are you my Adult?" Babla asked in a faint, disbelieving voice.

"Yes," the woman replied. "I am your Adult Self. My name is Rabia. I am very happy to meet you at last. May I give you a hug?"

Babla was so speechless that all she could do was nod her head 'yes.' Rabia took her into arms that were strong and soft at the same time. Babla was sure the Adult would be leaving soon to do things that surely were more important than holding a little girl. But Rabia stayed and stayed and stayed.

After a long time, tears started rolling down Babla's cheeks. This really surprised her because she hadn't cried in such a long time and thought she would never cry again. Meanwhile, her Adult Self was still holding her, making comforting sounds to let Babla know that her tears were welcome.

The tall woman in the blue dress came over with tissues to wipe away the tears. Then Babla saw the tiny wings on her back.

The woman smiled. "I am the Fairy Princess, Babla. I'm glad to see your tears. My Child Self also shed many tears, before she remembered how to smile again. I am happy that you're with us."

Contented Sage told all the Adult Selves to take their Child Self by the hand and go for a walk, to show them the world from the adult perspective.

As Babla walked through the cave door holding Rabia's hand, she could sense the warmth and strength from this big hand. It felt very comforting. For a second, Babla glimpsed that somehow, from this moment on, her life would never be the same.

INNER GUIDES: *Eternal Friend, Black Panther, and Maya*

Babla and Rabia stayed with Contented Sage for a long time. Every day, Babla learned more about her Adult—how strong and capable Rabia really was, that she could be trusted and counted on. All these things, at first only the Sage's words, were becoming her own experience.

Babla soon realized she was much less afraid of life, knowing that she wasn't alone. To have a friend like Rabia, who not only loved her but was always available, was such a relief. Whenever Babla ran to Rabia with some fear or worry, the Adult seemed to find a way to make it go away, or at least seem less scary. She started to enjoy being with the Adult Self, who hugged her a lot.

One day, Contented Sage told all the Child Selves that they were going on a journey. They all got dressed accordingly, ready to leave the cave.

It was a beautiful day, warm and sunny, just perfect for a journey. As the group walked out of the cave, the Sage asked everyone to choose one of the paths around them.

Babla chose the meadow with the green grass and little yellow flowers. She loved to watch the breeze move the grass this way, then that way.

After a while on this path, she saw someone in the distance. As this person came closer, Babla could see it was a young man with straight blond hair, almost shoulder length. He had light blue eyes and wore clothes like Robin Hood's—light brown tights and a matching tunic with long sleeves and a V-neck. The man had an open face with a smile on it. He walked up to her and took her hands into his.

"Hi, Babla," he said in a gentle but strong voice. "I am Eternal Friend. Contented Sage sent you on this journey to meet me. I am an Inner Guide."

Babla could feel in her bones that she could trust this man. "What is an Inner Guide?" she asked.

"It is the wise and compassionate aspect of a Being. I live inside Rabia, just like you do. I assist her in making the best possible choices in her life. My sole purpose of existence is to help you and Rabia find true happiness and deep fulfillment in life. I am always available. You can call on me with or without a reason at any time. I have deep insights to share with both of you."

Eternal Friend started touching Babla's blond curls with a gentleness she had never felt before. She took a deep breath of relief and melted into his arms. They stood there for a long time.

Then Eternal Friend asked Babla whether she had any questions or needs before she had to return to the cave for lunch.

Babla asked why she wasn't being rewarded for the things she did for other Beings. "I always thought one must be loving and giving, but it doesn't make me feel any better. I still feel lost and lonely," she confessed.

Eternal Friend nodded with understanding. "This is because you are not loving and giving to yourself. The first step is to love yourself. When you fill yourself with your own love, after a while it will start spilling out, just like a very full cup. That extra love you can give to other Beings.

"When you are empty and try to give to someone else, you will still feel empty afterwards. But when you are full and give only what is spilling out from you, you will be left full," he explained.

"Then, whether the Being you give to appreciates it or not won't matter. Giving out of feeling empty is depleting; giving out of fullness is its own reward." Eternal Friend gave Babla a final hug. Babla knew she would see him again.

On the way back, Babla was sure the grass was greener, and the yellow flowers somehow had become more yellow. She didn't quite understand the meaning of his words, yet they felt soothing and relaxing to her little heart.

Rabia was waiting for her in the cave and seemed delighted to hear about Babla's journey. She told her all about Eternal Friend, and Babla's Adult was glad to see her so satisfied.

One day, the Sage announced another journey. When the Child Selves went outside, they were surprised to see lots of puffy clouds of different colors on the ground right in front of the cave.

Contented Sage, with a smile on his face, told everyone to choose a cloud and to sit or lie in it. Babla chose a pink cloud and climbed aboard; it was puffy and soft and comfortable. The Sage gave a signal, and all the clouds started lifting up into the air. Soon, Babla's cloud left the others and rose higher and higher in the clear blue sky.

After some time of drifting in the air, the cloud started to slow down. Babla opened her eyes just as her cloud was entering a cloud city. Everything here was made out of clouds, in all different colors.

When Babla's cloud stopped, she got off and couldn't believe her eyes. She was in front of a castle made out of pure white clouds. The sparkle and brilliance of this made her eyes blink; it was almost too much to take in.

White cloud steps led to a big gate. At the entrance, Babla was met by a winged Being dressed in white, who pointed her in the direction she was to go.

Babla took a deep breath as she entered the castle. A long hallway stretched in front of her. She walked slowly to one end and found herself facing a huge, white double door made out of clouds. As she approached the door, it opened by itself, and Babla entered a white room filled with windows.

In total contrast to all this white, a young woman in a long, grass-green dress stood right in the middle of the room. Babla admired her curly black hair and green eyes.

She came forward to greet Babla. "Hi, I am Maya, the Cloud Princess. Just like Eternal Friend, I am one of your Inner Guides. I am very happy that we've met today. Whenever you are confused about something, come here and we will look into the crystal ball."

In one corner of the room, a huge crystal rested on a cloud table. "I am often confused," said Babla, as Maya led her to the sphere. "I'm still unhappy at times, and I don't know what to do with my life."

"Look into the ball now," suggested Maya.

As Babla did so, the clouds in the globe cleared away and a tree became visible. It had a few roots, a strong trunk, many branches, and no leaves or blossoms. The image suddenly changed; it was still the same tree, this time with strong roots going very deep into the earth. A cover of green leaves and big peach-colored blossoms made it so that one could barely see the branches.

"It seems like the first tree is me at this moment, and the second is what I could become," gasped Babla, not hiding her excitement.

"That is very true," said Cloud Princess. "The journey from the first tree to becoming the second one will lead you into different adventures, different lessons, different understandings. Some of them will be easier than others. Always remember, though, that what you are doing is becoming the second tree."

When it was time for Babla to return to the cave, Maya gave her a big hug and said she could come back any time. Babla left, feeling content.

In time, Babla learned to accept the other Child Selves. Even though some of them looked and acted very different, she realized that all of them were on the same journey to find their roots and their blossoms.

One of the Child Selves she liked a lot was Clown. He wore funny clothes covered with ruffles, and his face was painted with bright, shiny colors. But his eyes spoke to Babla about pain and sorrow. She detected a bitter silence in them. During their time in the cave, Clown showed Babla his real face.

Another Child Self Babla enjoyed was a small brown bird whose wings were broken. She tried to flap them and fly with the other birds, but it didn't work. The Adult brown bird came every day to do some repair work on her tiny wings. Babla often talked to this bird. Her sweet voice was as soft as her feathers and her gentle brown eyes spoke to Babla about patience.

Then there was Little Witch. One side of her face was active, the other side was silent. As the two became friends, Little Witch talked to Babla about other worlds where she had traveled. Babla had always believed that hers was the only world, so this was a strange idea. Were there really worlds within worlds within worlds forever?

Babla trusted her friend, yet she wasn't quite sure how much she could believe her. Then one day, Little Witch took Babla into one of these other worlds. Even though it was not at all familiar, it felt just as real. She was intrigued. After this visit, everything Babla looked at in her own world seemed to have more depth to it.

There was also a tiny fairy Babla spent time with. They would go for walks and Babla would marvel at her delicate wings. One day while sitting in the cave, Babla looked at her fairy friend and saw colors all around her—pale blue and pale green enveloped her body. Babla didn't know what to make of this, so she told her friend what she saw.

The little fairy smiled and explained that everyone has colors around them, but one has to look through different eyes to see them. Babla was surprised.

Later, when she asked Eternal Friend, he said, "Some day you will understand, Babla. For now, focus on the roots of your tree. The main purpose of your time with the Sage is to strengthen the roots of your tree. Everything else will follow."

One day, the Sage asked them to prepare for another journey. As they left the cave, he said, "You are to go into the forest. Before long, you will come to an intersection. A sign saying 'Jungle' will point toward one of the paths. Take that path into the jungle and see what happens."

Babla went into the forest and found the sign. She had never been in a jungle before and soon realized it was quite different from a forest. It seemed dense and unpredictable, yet strangely exciting. The incredible sounds she was hearing were almost overwhelming.

Then she heard a very specific sound—footsteps were coming closer. "Oh my!" Babla thought. "Are there more than two feet walking?" Not knowing what else to do, she sat on the jungle floor and waited.

From behind one of the gnarled trees emerged a black panther, walking straight toward her. He came very close, almost nose to nose. Babla felt her legs quiver. But looking into his green eyes, she saw enormous power and deep wisdom.

"I am Black Panther with Green Eyes," he announced. "I am your Animal Guide. If you are ever lost in the Jungle of Life, call on me. I am here to teach you about power. Those who use power without wisdom can create a lot of trouble for themselves and others."

Babla was very excited to have this huge cat as her guide. "May I touch your fur?"

Black Panther turned so Babla could pet his black, shiny coat. She was amazed, because it was soft and coarse at the same time.

Black Panther answered Babla's unasked question: "To be soft and coarse, gentle and strong is the nature of all things. If something is only soft, the coarseness is hiding behind it; if something is only strong, the gentleness is hiding. To be sure something is real, look to see whether it contains both." He told Babla they would continue to see each other, and he would teach her more every time.

Hugging this huge cat good-bye was a wonderful experience; Babla felt she had taken on some of his raw animal strength. As she walked back to the cave, she felt stronger, more confident, and more connected to the earth.

Contented Sage came one day to suggest that it was time for everyone to again leave the cave. They were to go out into the world and use the tools they had received from him.

It was an exciting day and it was a sad day. Babla liked the idea of going out to explore. At the same time, she was sad to say good-bye to her friends. The Child Selves all hugged each other and then departed, hand in hand with their Adult Selves.

Standing outside, Rabia suggested they journey to the mountains, and Babla agreed. Taking a deep breath, Babla started walking toward the mountain path, Rabia by her side.

MOUNTAIN MAN: The Outer World

Babla and Rabia traveled into the mountains for quite some time. They walked by themselves as well as with others. Finally, they came to the top of a mountain. The climb had been steep and they were tired. At the very top, they came upon a man chopping wood beside a cabin. A goat stood nearby, watching.

The man heard their footsteps and turned around. Babla thought, "What a hard man." Steel blue eyes pierced through his defined, angular face.

"Hi," he said, smiling. "Welcome to my kingdom. I am Mountain Man, and this is my goat. For as long as I can remember, he has been with me. We seem to be inseparable."

Suddenly, his voice changed and his eyes became softer. "I've been waiting for you." He turned to Babla. "The birds told me you were coming. I haven't had guests for a long time. I hope you'll stay awhile."

"Babla has some things to learn from you, Mountain Man. We will both stay," Rabia said just as the goat started to make loud, high-pitched complaints.

"Oh," laughed Mountain Man. "Don't pay any attention to him. He's so used to having me all to himself, I think he is jealous. He'll get used to you being here."

They all entered the cabin to have dinner and to rest.

Days, weeks, months went by. Babla was enjoying the fresh air of the mountains. Mountain Man was very friendly to Babla; he stroked her hair and told her nice things. But mostly he was busy. Sometimes he had to chop wood or fix the cabin or go down the mountain to get supplies. And, he had to take care of the goat, which was the worst thing of all for Babla.

At first, the goat had been quiet. As time passed, however, he got louder and louder, needing more and more attention. Many times, right when Mountain Man was stroking Babla's hair and saying nice things, the goat would come into the cabin and stand between them, demanding attention. By the time he had talked to the goat, given him some water, and calmed him down, Mountain Man would be too tired to spend more time with Babla.

Nevertheless, Mountain Man was a good teacher, and Babla learned about the mountains, how to chop wood and make a fire. Sometimes her fire would go out and he would show her how to light it again. She enjoyed her time with him very much, as long as the goat wasn't interfering.

She tried to make friends with the goat—to feed him, pet him, talk to him—but the goat was one of the most stubborn Beings she had ever met. He would eat only what Mountain Man had given him and wouldn't allow anyone else to come close.

Babla became more and more frustrated and unhappy. Finally, she realized that she had lost her connection to Rabia and her Inner Guides, and asked for help. She told them that her heart was closing down and that she was afraid. As a group, they decided it was time to go back to Contented Sage and be given more tools.

When Babla went to say good-bye, Mountain Man's eyes looked sad. "I wish you well," he said. "It is the same with all my guests. They enjoy being here at first, but no one can get along with my goat. Before long, they all leave. I will miss you."

Babla felt sad, too. She really loved Mountain Man, yet she knew she had to leave. Under these circumstances, she couldn't be happy. They parted, knowing that they would always love each other.

ONE-EYED EAGLE, MOTHER HEN, SCARED RABBIT, AND BLACK WITCH: Clearing the Past

Babla and Rabia went down the mountain and stopped in amazement; the cave was hardly visible now. Huge, tall trees with red trunks had grown all around, making it impossible to see from the outside.

They found the entrance, nonetheless, and were warmly welcomed by the Sage. He was pleased to see Babla back, ready for her next lesson.

The Fairy Princess was the only one Babla knew from her first visit. She came to Babla one day and asked, "Would you like to play with my Child Self? She gets lonely at times."

A shy fairy girl was standing next to Fairy Princess, half hiding behind her long dress. At first sight, Babla liked this tiny golden fairy. Her name was Raindrop. From that moment on, Babla and Raindrop spent countless hours together—talking, playing, helping each other out of difficult situations, and developing a deep friendship.

There came a day when Contented Sage told Babla that she was ready to clear her past. For this, she must go back and face it. She had to stand right in front of it. She would look at it until there was nothing left to see. When she realized the past didn't exist, she would live totally in the moment. He told her that this clearing was to begin in the cave.

Fairy Princess guided Babla into the very back of the cave where it was quite dark. They stood in front of an old, wooden door with a sign on it: "The Past." Fairy Princess wished Babla good luck and left. With hesitant fingers, Babla opened the door and stepped through it. Just like that, she found herself outside on a bright and sunny day.

"This can't be that bad," she thought. "Maybe my past is already pretty clear."

She could see a peaceful meadow with some trees around it. Under one of the trees, there was a small rabbit and a hen. As Babla approached them, she saw the hen brushing the rabbit's fur with her feathers.

"Hi," said Babla when she was close enough to be heard. "I'm Babla."

"Hi," the hen welcomed her. "I am Mother Hen and this is Scared Rabbit. Have you come to clear your past?"

"So you know, already?" asked Babla, wide-eyed. "But I don't see anything to be cleared. Everything looks so peaceful here."

Mother Hen sighed. "Yes," she said, "it looks that way. But things aren't always the way they seem. You will soon realize that yourself. I will help you as much as I can, yet certain things you have to clear without my help."

When she was done brushing Scared Rabbit, she came over and started arranging Babla's hair. Babla realized that Mother Hen loved to be a mother. Her touch was so nurturing and loving that Babla closed her eyes and leaned against Mother Hen to rest a bit.

But, in a moment's flash, everything changed. A huge bird flew right above them, zooming down toward Scared Rabbit. Scared Rabbit froze in terror as the bird started sinking his sharp beak into her flesh—in and out, in and out—until blood flowed.

Mother Hen, busy with Babla's hair all this time, finally interfered. "All right, my dear," she said calmly, "that's enough now. Here's your dinner."

She gave the attacker his dinner and went over to clean Rabbit's wounds, dry up the blood, and put on a bandage. The big bird finished his dinner, praised the taste of the food, kissed Mother Hen good night, and went to sleep.

Babla was shocked. Mother Hen sat down next to Scared Rabbit and looked sadly at Babla. "That was One-Eyed Eagle. He lives with us. When he looks at the world with his seeing eye, he's wonderful to be around. He brings us food, makes lots of jokes, and is helpful in every way.

"When he looks at the world through his blind eye, though, watch out! He hurts us, gets very unhappy, and is terribly rigid and angry. Mostly he knows when to stop. But sometimes I have to stop him."

"Oh my," protested Babla. "Can't I just leave you all here and go back to the cave?"

"I'm afraid not," was Mother Hen's answer. "You need to learn not to be influenced by his blind eye. You must always stay in your heart, no matter whether he is using his good eye or the blind one. Not only that, you also need to teach this to Scared Rabbit."

For the first time, Babla's attention went to Rabbit, who was scared, all right. She was trembling all over with fear.

"Why didn't you run and hide?" asked Babla.

"Where to?" replied Scared Rabbit. "He can find me anywhere."

This rabbit seemed unlike others Babla had met. "Look at those eyes," thought Babla. Behind the fear in Rabbit's velvety brown eyes, she saw something else—a vastness, a depth, that was very attractive. Babla searched for other differences: her fur was brown.

Seeing Babla looking at her, Scared Rabbit gave a sigh. "Yes," she said despondently, "because I have brown fur instead of gray, the other rabbits won't play with me. Mother Hen is the only one who accepts me the way I am."

"I can't see anything wrong in being a brown rabbit instead of a gray one," said Babla. "White Bird and Contented Sage have both said it's not what's outside that counts. It's not about how you look, but what's inside. I'm sure you could be a happy brown rabbit."

"Really?" Scared Rabbit perked up, her soft eyes more hopeful. "I'd never thought of that."

One-Eyed Eagle was still sound asleep, which meant Babla had some time before having to deal with him. She decided to try something. She started telling Rabbit about her Inner Guides, how she had found them, and how helpful they had been.

Rabbit was now jumping up and down with excitement. "That's exactly what I need. Please, help me find one for myself!"

Babla decided to give it a try. She told Rabbit to walk to the middle of the meadow where a Guide would come to meet her.

Just as Scared Rabbit reached the center, the sky shifted. Babla looked up to see a huge Angel, all in white, float down and land in front of Rabbit. His beautiful wings were shimmering with the colors of the rainbow. They stood in awe of the Angel's presence.

"Weren't you looking for a Guide?" asked the Angel, an amused smile on his face.

"How can you be my Inner Guide?" wondered Scared Rabbit. "You are so beautiful!"

"And so are you," said the Angel, looking deeply into her eyes. "Actually, I am not your Inner Guide," he continued, breaking the silence. "I am an Outer Guide. That is, I spend time with other Beings and protect them as well. I've waited for you to call me for a long time. And now, here I am."

Mother Hen and Babla looked at each other. Both knew that Scared Rabbit would never be the same again.

The Angel held Scared Rabbit's paw and walked with her toward the trees. There they talked, surrounded by the shimmering white light of Oneness.

It was time for Babla to go back to the cave, so she said good-bye to Mother Hen and left. However, she knew she still had to face One-Eyed Eagle.

In the cave she met a baby bull who wanted to play. He offered her a ride on his back. This was fun at first, but without warning the bull began to rage and threw her off his back. Babla was badly ruffled and felt hurt. She was contemplating never trusting any bulls again when Contented Sage asked her to join the Sacred Circle.

They all sat in a big circle, closed their eyes, and listened to silence. It seemed boring at first, just sitting doing nothing, but soon the energy started to shift.

Babla felt a door open that she didn't even know was inside of her. She heard White Swan's voice: "When you feel like you are open and you still get hurt, you weren't really open."

Babla was puzzled. What did this mean? When she later asked the Sage, he said, "To be open means that you know there is actually no past. You are fully in the moment, responding to every situation with freshness. You have memories, but you don't have a past. Some of these memories we call 'unfinished.' They cling to you, clouding your mind. To feel hurt means you have been experiencing a present situation through the filter of old, unpleasant memories. If you were really open, without these memories clouding you, you would have made a different decision. It all takes practice."

Babla was eager to get back to the memories and transform more of them—when the time was right.

The Sacred Circle met every day for a long time. Soon Babla started making friends with some of the other Beings in it. One of them was Confused Witch, and everyone called her "Fusy". She was very lovable, but her head was disconnected from her body and was always floating ahead at a speed impossible to follow. Her head kept forgetting that it was part of a body.

At times during the Sacred Circle, her head would slow down and arrange itself on the body in full alignment. During these times, Fusy would become present to the moment, her heart wide open, with nothing confused about her. Her blue eyes looked deeply into others and she could tell them the Truth. Babla learned that when Truth was told from a place of clarity, it never hurt.

Babla also liked Butterfly. She had earth colors on her wings—shades of brown, gold, orange, green, tan. She looked so pretty. Her right wing was crippled, though. She could still fly, but she had to stop and rest a lot.

Whenever the Sage played music in the cave, Butterfly would lift up and start dancing in the air, spiraling throughout the entire cave. One day, as she was flying outside, strengthening her right wing, an archer shot her with a pink arrow very close to her heart. A few inches higher and Butterfly would have been no more. Babla and some friends carried her into the cave. She was deeply hurt. It took a long time for her wound to heal. Babla visited her every day and told her stories or simply sat quietly, holding her wing. She loved Butterfly with all her heart and was glad her friend was still alive.

And then there was Patient Wanderer. He was a young man with steady blue eyes who always carried a wooden staff.

When Babla was lost in fear or sadness, it was he who came over and gave her a long hug. He would stay with her, hugging her with great patience, until all her fear or sadness melted away.

As they sat in the Sacred Circle day after day, each Being needed fewer and fewer words. A deep meeting was happening in the silence. Babla realized that it was safe to open her heart and be with the other Beings.

One day, Contented Sage told Babla it was time to go into the memories again. Babla was excited to meet Mother Hen and Scared Rabbit, but she wasn't quite sure about One-Eyed Eagle.

At the door, she saw that the sign "The Past" had been replaced with "Memories." She went through the opening and was astonished by what she encountered. The sky was all black. Thunder and lightning were striking down with a force Babla had never experienced before. A woman dressed in black— with long robes, a black hat, and a nose like a beak—was beating Mother Hen with a broom.

Babla ran toward them shouting, "Mother Hen, Mother Hen, I'm here to help you!"

The woman in black, seeing Babla, sat on her broom and darted up into the air. "Just wait, little one," she cackled. "I'll get you one of these days." Then, she was gone, and the sky cleared.

Mother Hen brushed herself off. She looked at Babla with loving eyes. "That was Black Witch," she explained. "For as long as I can remember, she's been coming here regularly to beat us up. She is very mean and has no heart."

"And you have so much of it," mused Babla.

"Yes," came the answer. "Watching Black Witch year after year, I decided not to be like her. So, no matter what happens around me, I keep my heart open."

Babla was troubled. "Why do you have to get hurt like this?"

Sadness filled Mother Hen's eyes. "I don't know what else to do," she replied. "I don't know how to protect myself from Black Witch and One-Eyed Eagle and keep my heart open at the same time. If you have any ideas, please tell me."

Babla sat on the ground, thinking. Then she said, "I think I have to ask my Guides for help." She started calling Eternal Friend, Maya, and Black Panther. Usually, other living Beings couldn't see her Inner Guides. But as they appeared, Mother Hen could see them easily, which amazed Babla.

Out of the woods appeared Scared Rabbit with Angel still holding her paw. However, Rabbit couldn't see the Inner Guides, so Babla explained who they were and what they looked like.

Eternal Friend was talking now. "You are not strong enough yet to face One-Eyed Eagle," he said, "so start with Black Witch. She is not as harmful as she looks. Because she seems so scary, you see, nobody looks any closer.

"In order to face her, you have to understand some things about the power of black. There is the black of darkness, and there is the black of light. Black Witch is coming from the black of darkness. Black Panther, however, belongs to the black of light.

"Black power can be faced successfully only by black power," he continued. "No other kind of power will transform it. If your intention is to kill her black power, you will be serving the black of darkness. If your intention is to transform her black power, then you belong to the black of light, which in turn will protect you from any harm."

"How do I know where my power is coming from?" asked Babla.

It was Maya who answered this time. "It all has to do with your heart," she said. "If you are using your power directly, it tends to hurt others. If you bring it to your heart first and then let it out, it will bring Truth to any situation. Black Panther will teach you."

Babla was relieved. "I knew I could count on you, Inner Guides," she said with gratitude. "Let's get going. I don't want Black Witch to hurt Mother Hen any more." Mother Hen looked at her with deeply loving eyes.

Eternal Friend told Babla to lie on Black Panther. As the panther sat on the ground, his liquid body stretched out. Babla climbed on him and arranged her little body on his back.

Black Panther just breathed in and out normally. After a short time, Babla started feeling the immense power in her Animal Guide. He was totally relaxed, and at the same time he was ready for action. Babla felt the panther directing his power into her body. She tried to keep herself open to receive it as best she could.

Eventually, Eternal Friend asked her to come down. Now, she was to sit facing Mother Hen, with both of their hearts touching in a sweet and loving hug. Or so it seemed at first.

A few moments into the hug, however, Babla started feeling a stronger outpouring of Love from Mother Hen's heart into hers. She had to take several deep breaths just to keep her own heart open wide enough to receive it. When she remembered White Swan's Love, her heart opened more easily. At last, she could feel Black Panther's power and Mother Hen's Love merging inside her—strength that was soft, Love that was firm.

After what seemed an eternity, Maya gently asked them to separate. Babla was now ready to face Black Witch. She was even eager.

As Mother Hen prepared dinner, the sky darkened suddenly and thunder and lightning came upon them. Looking up, they saw Black Witch on her broom bolting toward them cackling. As she descended, she took her broom and went for Mother Hen, her eyes bloody with rage.

Then, mysteriously, she stopped. Something was different; Mother Hen wasn't ducking this time. Hearing the sound of feet, Black Witch turned to see Babla running toward her. The witch was so used to everyone fleeing that she was caught totally off guard.

Babla positioned herself between Black Witch and Mother Hen, her arms crossed in front of her chest, her legs wide apart, looking directly at the witch. Black Witch opened her mouth but nothing came out. Her eyes were like yellow beads, glaring at Babla as if hypnotized.

"What now?" thought Babla. She knew that this energy in and around her was Black Panther's power, and it had stopped the witch. But what was the next step? What about transformation?

Just as she asked the question, Babla felt her heart moving. It was as if an inner gate had opened and Love began pouring out to Black Witch—Love in the colors of the rainbow. First, it surrounded the witch completely. Then, slowly and quietly it penetrated into her, its strength breathtaking.

Babla realized that the power of the panther was holding Black Witch in place so that the Love of Mother Hen could do its magic. Meanwhile, the rainbows were swirling over Black Witch, making it impossible to see what was happening.

Babla sat down on the ground. As the colors subsided, her mouth flew open in disbelief: An old woman with short gray hair was sitting in a rocking chair knitting a sweater. She wore a dark blue dress with a white flower print. Her wrinkled face looked peaceful. The only thing that reminded Babla of Black Witch was her beak-shaped nose.

The woman looked up with a smile in her eyes. "I'm almost finished with this sweater. Whomever it fits best can have it. Then I'll make two more."

Babla turned around to see Mother Hen coming toward them carrying a tray with four tall glasses, Scared Rabbit next to her.

"It's a warm day today," said Mother Hen, pleasantly. "Here is some lemonade for all of us."

"You must have read my mind," replied the old woman. "Thank you so much."

While Babla was drinking her lemonade, Mother Hen whispered into her ear. "You did it, Babla. Black Witch is totally transformed."

"Isn't it amazing?" sighed Babla. "It's hard to believe, but here it is for all to see. I couldn't have done it without your Love." Satisfied, Babla said good-bye to her friends and returned to the Sage's cave. She had learned an unforgettable lesson about power and Love.

HIGHER SELF: Accepting What Is

In the cave, Babla continued to listen and learn. Contented Sage often came in and talked. All the Child Selves would sit on the laps of their Adult Selves and listen. Babla didn't always understand what he meant and hoped that Rabia did, yet just being there with the Sage was calming and peaceful. At those times, she was afraid of nothing. She felt very safe and taken care of with Rabia's strong and loving arms around her and the soothing voice of the Sage flowing into her ears and trickling down into her body.

The day arrived when Contented Sage asked them to get ready for another journey. When all the Child Selves walked out of the cave, they were to walk on the different paths around the cave. It was a beautiful day, so Babla chose the path next to the meadow. Everything was so green and sparkly.

In the distance, she saw someone coming. When she recognized Eternal Friend, she ran into his arms and he held her a long time. He told Babla that he was going to take her to her Higher Self.

"Higher Self," he explained, "is the part of you with no fear. It is both male and female, and it lives in Truth. Your Inner Guides and your Adult are a bridge between you and Higher Self. Once you know your Higher Self, you can access it any time you want. And remember, in the Higher-Self realm, there is no judgment, no comparison, and no duality."

Hand in hand, they continued walking until they turned a corner. Babla stepped back, eyes and mouth wide open. Right in front of them was a white temple. Even though it seemed to be white, it was really shining like a prism. Babla was mystified by where these colors were coming from. They walked up the steps to the temple entrance, and Eternal Friend told Babla that he would wait for her there.

Entering the temple, Babla saw a figure dressed in a simple, long white robe sitting in the middle of a large room. The figure had gray hair, but no face. Babla sat next to Higher Self, not knowing what else to do.

Higher Self, taking her hand, started speaking. "In reality, I don't have a body. I am pure light. If I showed myself to you in my pure Essence, it would be difficult for you to connect with me. I've taken on this physical form so that you have something to see and touch. That I have no face will remind you of my true Nature.

"A key lesson for you in this time is to find your enthusiasm. In your attempt to help and please others, you let yourself be influenced by them and give up too soon.

"Your Guides and I will help you find your lost enthusiasm and keep it no matter what is happening around you. I love you."

The presence of Higher Self was so enormous, so strong and yet so loving, so golden. It reached into a pocket and gave Babla a heart-shaped black stone to wear as a pendant.

Thanking Higher Self for the gift, Babla put the talisman around her neck along with White Swan's golden key, and then got up to leave. She joined Eternal Friend at the top of the stairs, and together they started walking back to the cave.

"Now that you've met your Higher Self and received the black pendant," he said, "you can face One-Eyed Eagle."

Babla knew that she would soon go back into the memories to look Eagle in the eye.

Back in the cave, Contented Sage introduced the Child Selves to something called "the Now." For this, the Child Selves and the Adult Selves needed to work closely together. It was not easy for Babla to understand what this meant, and she hoped Rabia would know.

Babla didn't have long to wait. Rabia took her out into the beautiful gardens at the back of the cave, where there was a huge oak tree. Rabia asked the tree, "What do you understand?"

To Babla's amazement, the tree answered, "Nothing. There is nothing to understand. There is only Being."

Rabia asked again, "Tree, how do you survive?"

And the tree said, "My roots collect water from the earth, the earth provides the nurturing I need, the sunlight gives me other kinds of nurturing, and the air does the rest."

"Is that all?" exclaimed Babla. "There is nothing to understand, and everything for survival is already provided! Then there is no reason to ever be afraid."

"Exactly," replied Rabia. "There is no reason to be afraid, little one."

Babla felt her jaw relax; she hadn't even realized that it was tense. She followed Rabia into the garden. They stopped periodically, and Rabia asked her questions, such as What do you see right now? What do you hear right now? What do you smell right now? What do you sense right now?

The Adult Self had Babla close her eyes and open her mouth. She put something in Babla's mouth and asked, "What do you taste right now?" It was sweet and juicy. Babla guessed correctly that it was a grape. She had never tasted a grape like this before!

While Babla was answering these questions, she felt that something inside of her was changing. What was it? Her muscles were more relaxed, her breath had deepened, she was highly aware of everything all around. She felt her feet firmly on the ground. Even though she was the Child Self, she was maturing in some way.

She shared these experiences with Rabia, who smiled and said, "Great. You and I are connecting more deeply. My experience of the Now is becoming your experience, too. When the Sage talks about "being in the Now," he means experiencing what is happening right now instead of being lost in memory. When old memories don't carry a charge any longer, the energy held captive in them is freed, and life is experienced more fully."

Listening to Rabia, looking into deep blue eyes that were exactly like her own, Babla felt dizzy for a moment. Then something powerfully strange began to happen; she started merging with Rabia.

For just a moment, there was only one Self, one Being, one Breath.

Then, she was again looking at Rabia's deep blue eyes. "What happened?" asked Babla.

Rabia smiled. "You just experienced being totally in the Now. There was no separation. You and I became one."

"It was so nice to be one with you," sighed Babla. "Why can't we do it all the time?"

"Because," replied the Adult, "our journey to clear the emotionally charged memories isn't finished yet. As long as we believe in the past, these memories will keep us in separation. We can't be one completely. And yet, we will experience Oneness more and more as we go along."

"When we are one, will I disappear?" Babla wanted to know.

"Yes and no," was Rabia's answer. "Your form as the Child Self will disappear, but your energy and your qualities such as spontaneity, joy, innocence, and intuition will be integrated with my strength, resourcefulness, and ability to be in the Now. Nothing will be lost."

"Hm," said Babla, contemplating what this meant. "Then what?"

"Then," answered Rabia, "we'll merge with our Higher Self. That seems to be the end of our journey as far as I understand. The main thing is to take one step at a time, to see where it takes us. And, above all, we can have fun doing it."

Babla spent some time in the cave trying to figure out how all this worked, until one day Contented Sage came in to give another talk. Babla loved sitting on Rabia's lap while listening to the Sage, even though she didn't understand everything.

Looking around in his peaceful, calm way, the Sage started by saying, "Always expect the unexpected. If you try hard to figure things out, you can forget that life is a Mystery. It is important to be aware of how certain things that happened in 'the past' still make you unhappy or unfulfilled today. But, even as you go into these memories to transform them, always keep a sense of the Mystery."

Listening to Contented Sage this time gave Babla a sense of awe. Life seemed to be something wonderful to be explored. After the talk, Rabia took Babla by the hand and led her to the door of the memories. They both knew Babla was ready to rendezvous with One-Eyed Eagle.

Babla went through the door. It was the same peaceful scene. Mother Hen was washing clothes, and Scared Rabbit was watching her, talking. Babla had never seen Scared Rabbit so animated. At the edge of the meadow where the forest began, Angel also was watching. Everyone was pleased to see Babla. Mother Hen wanted to know whether she had any clothes that needed washing.

"I'm here to look Eagle in the eye," said Babla.

"I know," replied Mother Hen, as she kept on washing.

Scared Rabbit spoke up. "I'm sick and tired of being scared all the time," she complained. "The more time I spend with Angel, the more I realize how incredible life can be. But whenever One-Eyed Eagle is around, I feel as scared as ever. It's as if he puts a spell on me!" Tears of frustration filled her eyes.

"Spells can be broken, dear," said Mother Hen. "It is all about timing and the right tools. Babla has been gathering the tools, and this seems to be the right time to use them.

"I've been enjoying my time with the old woman who used to be Black Witch," she continued. "She is so sweet and easygoing now. To be honest, I could use a change with Eagle, too."

"Great!" Babla was overjoyed. "Then we're all ready." At that moment, the shadow of a big bird crept over them. They looked up and saw One-Eyed Eagle circling high in the sky.

Babla's heart jumped. "Oh dear," she thought. "Am I really ready for this?"

From the corner of her eye, she saw Scared Rabbit's Angel stand up in watchful silence. Next to him was Black Panther, Eternal Friend, and Maya. Eternal Friend was pointing toward her chest. Babla looked down and remembered the black, heart-shaped stone from Higher Self. She sighed with relief; she was not alone.

One-Eyed Eagle came down. Babla realized that he was peering at the world through his blind eye, emanating a strong visionless power. This time he went for Babla.

Just as the attacker was sinking his beak into her flesh, Babla heard Black Panther's voice in her ear. "Black power, Babla. Remember, black power." Babla felt the panther's power come into her. She stood erect, legs wide apart, arms at her side, looking Eagle directly in the eye.

The fierce bird stopped and eyed her in mild surprise. He started to laugh. "You little worm," he taunted. "Do you really believe you have the power to stop me? I will show you who the boss is here."

He went for her even more ferociously. And Babla, glancing toward Mother Hen and Scared Rabbit, saw them hold their breath. "Speak, Babla," Eternal Friend suggested calmly. "Try to gain some time."

Babla opened her mouth, not knowing what would come out. Much to her surprise, her own voice uttered words that seemed to be coming directly from Eternal Friend. This was most eerie to the little girl.

She heard herself say, "Who do you think you are, Blind Eagle? All you can do is attack helpless creatures. That doesn't say much for your power."

Stopping in mid-action, Eagle looked around. Yes, Mother Hen, Scared Rabbit, and this little girl did seem pretty helpless. She was right. "Well," he retorted, "I'm not Blind Eagle. I'm One-Eyed Eagle."

"As far as I'm concerned," Babla heard herself say, "you are blind. And so is anyone else who attacks others to gain power. What is the use of your good eye anyway?"

And, with that, the big bird sat down to figure this out. Upon remembering his seeing eye, however, he had switched his vision and was looking at everyone lovingly.

"I really love Mother Hen," he declared. "And, I've tried to take care of you and Scared Rabbit the best I can. I don't understand why you aren't happy."

Now it was Maya who was speaking through Babla. "Eagle, do you know what you do when you switch to your blind eye?"

"No," pondered the bird. "I've never thought of that. I can't imagine being much different, though."

They looked at each other in dismay. Clearly, no transformation was possible as long as Eagle stayed with his seeing eye .

"So why not switch to your blind eye and show us?" Mother Hen pitched in.

"Oh no!" thought Babla. "Now what?"

As soon as Eagle looked through his unseeing eye, he again became a mean, terrible bird of prey, not because he was hungry but because he was blinded to the Truth within himself.

He started attacking Mother Hen this time. Babla's hand went to her heart in panic, not knowing what to do. In desperation, she touched the stone that hung from her neck.

"Higher Self!" she shouted. "I need your help!"

The deep voice of Higher Self spoke from its place of eternal wisdom. "Show him his own Truth," suggested Higher Self.

Perplexed, Babla wondered about Eagle's Truth. She heard Rabia's voice say, "Look at his beautiful feathers, Babla, his strong presence, his commitment to Mother Hen, his ability to heal sick people with just a touch of his wing, his clear focus in life, and his connection to his own Higher Self. Please remind him of these things."

Babla went over to Eagle, right in the middle of his attack. She began stroking his feather and One-Eyed Eagle stopped, startled.

"I love your feathers," she said softly. "They are so smooth and so strong at the same time. I've heard that the touch of your wings heals the sick. I also know that sometimes your Higher Self speaks directly to you. Moreover, you have great love for Mother Hen, don't you?"

"Hm." Eagle thoughtfully cocked his head. "I do love Mother Hen. And I'm not sure why I'm attacking her right now."

He moved away from the disheveled Mother Hen and looked around, confused. Then, his blind eye fixed on Babla. He began screaming at the top of his lungs.

"I know you. You're trying to trick me," he yelled. "But I am more clever than you are. You can't get the best of me. I'll show you!"

He turned his back to them all and froze. Strong visionless energy was pulsating from his frozen body, creating waves of tension. The entire meadow sank into a poignant silence. Even Mother Hen wasn't able to do the things she normally did. This was more than she could handle. She turned her back, hiding her emotions.

Babla was at the end of her wits, too. "What now?" she thought. "I need help."

After a long moment of not knowing, she heard wings flapping. Babla looked up and saw White Swan spiraling right above her.

"Life is not a problem to be solved; it is a Mystery to be lived," her friend offered before gracefully disappearing in the sky.

"Well then," said Babla to herself, "rather than trying to solve this problem, I'll just live the Mystery."

After Babla talked to Mother Hen and Scared Rabbit, all three decided to do just that. They started to play and have fun, do things together, relax, take care of themselves and each other, creating a wonderful time full of sparkling moments.

Whenever they thought of One-Eyed Eagle or came close to where he sat, still frozen, they sent him Love. They imagined a bubble of pink light floating from their hearts to surround his body. In time, they saw a slight movement in his feathers, especially when the wind was blowing. His breath became audible. Eagle was thawing out. Gradually, movement returned to his wings and legs, and finally to the rest of his body.

At last, he started turning toward them. There was a smile on his face, and—yes—he was looking through both of his eyes! The three friends looked at each other in utter disbelief.

Eagle came over to Mother Hen and held her in his strong wings. "I'm sorry," he said. "I'm so sorry."

Leaning against her beloved big bird, Mother Hen let go. The emotions trapped in her heart for so many years started rolling down her cheeks in the form of tears. They all stood together for a long time. Babla, gazing at Eagle's eyes, saw deep wisdom in them. She sat on the ground, knowing that she had learned her own lesson.

"Rest now, Babla," Maya whispered in her ear. "You need to rest now. There is one more thing to do before you can go back to the cave. You need to help Scared Rabbit transform."

Babla closed her eyes. She rested very deeply. When she was fully replenished, she went over to Scared Rabbit.

Chewing on some grass, Scared Rabbit looked at Babla through soft brown eyes. There was no fear left in them. Eagle's transformation seemed to have broken the spell.

"I've spent my entire life in fear of him," said Rabbit. "Now that things have changed, what am I going to do?"

"We shall find you a new life's purpose," replied Babla. "Why don't we ask your Angel?"

They went to Angel, who with deep compassion and Love offered a solution: "Where I come from, rabbits with brown fur are considered sacred. They are sensitive and wise and are meant to be teachers of sacred things. Being so intuitive, they have a lot to give to the gray rabbits. When you fully acknowledge that you are a brown rabbit, you can embody these beautiful qualities. Your life's purpose is to be a Sacred Rabbit."

Babla and Brown Rabbit went dancing in the meadow after hearing Angel's heartfelt words. Babla wasn't surprised, though; from the first time she had looked into Rabbit's eyes, she knew they held something special. Her work here was done.

After saying good-bye to Sacred Rabbit, Mother Hen, and Eagle, she left the realm of memories and went back to the cave.

Babla was glad to rest and be nurtured. She played with other Beings until Contented Sage told her it was time to leave the cave and study with the Alchemist. Happy and sad at the same time, Babla bid farewell to her beloved friends. She had no idea where to look for the Alchemist, but she had no doubt she would find him.

II.
the alchemist

*inner beings, inner guides,
worlds within worlds*

BUTTERFLY, MADWOMAN, AND BIRDIE:
The Exotic Land

Babla left the cave and traveled far. She went through forests and valleys, climbed up mountains, and jumped across rivers. Finally, quite exhausted, she sat down and decided she needed help.

"Please," she shouted into the air, "I need help to find the Alchemist." Immediately, a butterfly flew by and landed on her leg. Babla couldn't believe her eyes. "Butterfly!" she said smiling. "You are my friend from the Sage's cave. I've never met another butterfly with such wondrous colors on its wings."

"Thank you for recognizing me, Babla. I've still not fully recovered from the archer's arrow. But I made it here to help you. Find Madwoman, she will lead you to the Alchemist."

"Thank you," said Babla gratefully. "I'm so happy to see you. What are you going to do about your wound?"

"I'm off to see White Swan and rest at the Place Beyond Paradise," was Butterfly's cheerful answer. They hugged each other with deep affection and went their own way.

Babla continued her journey, asking birds and animals she happened to meet where she could find Madwoman. Following their lead, she at last arrived at a large hut, built exactly in between a tropical jungle and a flat, dry desert. The contrast of terrain was overwhelming to Babla.

Babla knocked on the door and was greeted by a woman with a shawl over her shoulders. At the sight of Babla, she laughed out loud. She laughed and laughed, then she stopped. Next, she started crying. She cried and cried and cried. Then she stopped. There was a quiet look in her eyes now, a deeply silent, peaceful look.

"You must be Madwoman," said Babla, a bit cautious yet curious.

"Yes," was the reply. The woman motioned for Babla to enter. After hearing Babla's story, Madwoman agreed to help her find the Alchemist. In return, she wanted Babla to show her the way to Contented Sage.

When Babla agreed, Madwoman directed her to the Exotic Land with Exotic Birds where the Alchemist lived. After explaining how to find the Sage's Cave, Babla said good-bye to Madwoman and resumed her journey.

After traveling all day, Babla's feet were aching. She plopped on the ground, tired and hungry.

"If I'm supposed to get to the Alchemist in one piece, I'll need some assistance," she murmured to herself. Out of exhaustion, she fell asleep right then and there.

When she woke up, a big white bird was standing in front of her. Babla blinked and said, "Well, hi. Who are you?"

"You can call me Birdie. I'm here to carry you to the Exotic Land. Don't you remember asking for help? Here I am."

Babla's mouth dropped open in amazement. Bravely, she climbed aboard Birdie and they took off. She enjoyed gliding in the air on this big bird.

Before long, Birdie landed and Babla could see a gate with a sign above it: "The Exotic Land with Exotic Birds." Babla thanked Birdie, and the bird told her to call when she wanted to leave this place. Knowing that Birdie would carry her wherever she wanted to go, Babla felt very warm in her heart.

INNER BEINGS: Changing From the Inside

After the bird left, Babla went through the gate and started looking around. This definitely was an exotic place; all over the land were animals and birds she had never seen before. But, where was the Alchemist?

Over there, that must be him. It had to be him, even though Babla had never seen an alchemist. The man walking toward her was wearing a dark purple robe made from a shiny material decorated with gold embroidery. He had the funniest hat—one moment it would be flat like a piece of gold and the next it would turn a greasy gray. Babla later learned this was lead.

The man's arms and hands stretched out as if he were playing the piano. He moved his hands in thin air, yet piano music was happening! Babla looked and looked to be sure there was no piano nearby, but the music arose right from the man's hands. At the sight of the bewildered girl, the man stopped and smiled—and the music stopped, too.

"Hi," he said. "I am the Alchemist. I don't remember seeing you before. You must have just arrived."

"Yes." Babla admired his clear, light blue eyes. "I am Babla. I'm supposed to learn some things from you."

The Alchemist nodded, somewhat amused. "Don't look only at appearances," he grinned. "What you see in my clothes, my hat, and my hands is just a show. The real Alchemy happens inside. Outer Alchemy without Inner Alchemy is worthless. Come, I will introduce you to my other students, and they'll help you get settled. Then you can start learning about Inner Alchemy."

Babla's stay at the Exotic Land was very exciting. One of the most astonishing things she learned was that other Beings besides herself were a part of Rabia. They were called Inner Beings.

One day, the Alchemist guided her down some steps into a room with a big round table. Sitting around it were folks she had never met.

"These are some of Rabia's Inner Beings," he said. "Alchemy is about creating a happy Inner Family. I will support you from my realm, even though I won't be physically with you." After explaining to everyone that Babla was Rabia's Child Self, he left the room.

At the head of the table, she saw a stern-looking man dressed in a black robe. Babla didn't like him very much.

"I am Inner Judge," said the man. "You'd better be a good girl or I will make you feel guilty. I am very powerful."

Babla felt small and scared.

"And as far as Rabia is concerned," Inner Judge added, "she needs to find a good man, get married, settle down, and forget about this spiritual path and independency business. All a woman is good for is to be subservient. She should stick to being a loving mother and a good wife."

Then there was a young man all dressed in green—tights, tunic, and boots—sitting in a chair with his feet on the table.

"I am Eric, the Cynic." His flat voice droned on, "You'd better tell Rabia that relationships won't work for her in this life. She might as well stop trying. Why even bother?" His brown eyes were equally dull.

There was a commotion on the other side of the table. A voluptuous young woman wearing a provocative red dress stood up. With a toss of her flowing black hair, she said lustily, "I am the Slut. All I want is a man—any man with a hard penis will do."

Babla's cheeks turned bright red with embarrassment. "This can't be true," she thought. "I'm sure I am in the wrong room. These must be someone else's Inner Beings, not Rabia's."

Then she heard Eternal Friend's gentle but firm voice in her ear. "This is the right room and these are Rabia's Inner Beings. To make it easier for you, I'll join in."

The door opened. Eternal Friend walked in and sat beside Inner Judge. Babla breathed a sigh of relief; she was grateful to see her Guide. At least now there was somebody in the room who loved her.

Another woman stood up to introduce herself; she was dressed in a black habit. "I am the Nun," her controlled voice rang out. "I agree with Eric. One can't be spiritual and have a long-term, committed relationship at the same time. Rabia has chosen to be on a spiritual path in this life, so she has no business with men."

Sporting a smirk, Eric nodded in agreement. Almost immediately, Babla heard the sound of tears. She turned to see a middle-aged black woman with graying hair, slumped on one of the chairs, sobbing.

"I am Loretta," she said through her tears. "I'm the Victim. It's not only that I don't deserve a relationship, I don't deserve anything. I shouldn't even be sitting at this table with all of you."

Yet another woman stood up. She had wavy brown hair and remarked in a hurried voice, "I am Miriam and I love to give. I have to find a man I can give my love to."

Above the table was a teenage girl suspended in a fluffy cloud. She looked down to the others and introduced herself. "I am Ms. Romantic. I'm waiting for my Knight in Shining Armor. He will come to rescue me from all the bad things in the world. We'll be walking on the beach, hand in hand, forever."

Babla was totally confused. She had already met Rabia, Higher Self, and her Guides—Eternal Friend, Maya, and Black Panther; and she knew White Swan was around somewhere. She was very happy with her life. Why couldn't these Beings be just as happy?

Babla was just about to despair when the door opened again and a tall, strong woman stood in the doorway, legs wide apart. She had straight, dark brown hair nearly to her waist and sparkly brown eyes. She wore only a leopard skin, carried a spear in one hand, and was barefoot.

"I am Amazon Woman, one of Rabia's Inner Guides," said a strong, firm voice. "I am the Inner Warrior. I am here to protect her, to make sure no harm comes to her or Babla." Amazon Woman helped herself to one of the empty chairs at the table. Babla immediately liked her confident, reassuring manner.

Still another woman stood up. "I am Tantrika," she said. "I know that sensuality and sexuality are the roots of true spirituality. Spirituality, in the way I feel it, is all inclusive. Every aspect of Rabia is welcome. She can be fully spiritual and also have a sexual, sensual, healthy relationship with a man. A relationship with the right attitude thus becomes a path to Truth."

Tantrika's words warmed Babla's heart, even though she couldn't quite understand all of what they meant. It felt just like a flowing river on a warm, sunny day.

Next, a young man entered through the door. He had curly blond hair and warm blue eyes. He looked comfortable in jeans and t-shirt and came over to sit right next to Babla.

"I'm Alan," he said lovingly. "I am Rabia's Inner Mate. I am also an Inner Guide." Turning to Babla, he added, "If you would like to sit in my lap, I would love to hold you."

Climbing onto his lap, Babla asked, "What is an Inner Mate?"

Alan smiled. "I help Inner Beings understand relationships with the other sex. They might have confusion and misunderstanding about how to relate to an outer mate. If so, this would make it difficult for Rabia as an Adult to have a healthy, satisfying relationship. I'm here to teach about masculine energy so that she can be with an outer mate in a fulfilling way, as part of her spiritual path, and *with the support* of the Inner Beings. As the Inner Mate, I also love the Inner Child, and I would love to be a friend to you, Babla."

Babla was beaming. "I like you," she said. "But you've chosen a tough job. Some of the Inner Beings are very mean and nasty. They're not going to like you."

"I don't need them to like me to do what I need to do." Alan smiled warmly.

Babla took a deep breath. She leaned against Alan's strong chest and felt her body relax. From the comfort of Inner Mate's lap, the whole world somehow seemed much simpler than it had a few minutes ago.

When the door opened again, Babla saw Rabia, Maya, and Black Panther. She knew everything would be fine. Closing her eyes, she relaxed even deeper.

Her Adult and her Guides certainly would be strong enough to take care of these eccentric Inner Beings.

Rabia began talking to Inner Judge. When Babla looked at him, she realized that he acted like a puppet. Even though he was talking to Rabia, he didn't quite seem alive. He was saying the same phrases over and over.

At that moment, Inner Judge moved his legs in a way that his long robe lifted and exposed his ankles. Babla saw a heavy metal chain clasped at his right ankle. When she showed it to Alan, he smiled and made a gesture to Eternal Friend. Babla knew that Inner Guides didn't need words; they could communicate with each other in some way she didn't understand.

Eternal Friend got up and pointed at the chain. The Judge was perplexed, not having noticed it before. When they all followed the chain, they found that it split in two, one end going an image of Black Witch, the other to an image of One-Eyed Eagle. Recognizing this, Eternal Friend explained:

"This chain has bound you for a long time, Inner Judge, reflecting your life through the attitudes of Black Witch and One-Eyed Eagle. Thus, you have pre-judged how Babla should behave, which isn't necessarily appropriate any longer. Remember, her life is very different today than when she was living with them. Now, Babla is more in tune with Rabia and us, the Inner Guides, who have a much better sense of what is good for her. Moreover, Black Witch has turned into a peaceful old woman, and Eagle has found his wisdom. Even they wouldn't go back to their outworn attitudes."

Inner Judge was speechless. Being a man of logic, he couldn't deny that Eternal Friend's words made sense. Hesitantly, he agreed to have the chain removed. Black Panther slowly moved toward him and placed the chain between his teeth. With one quick snap, his ankle was freed.

A reverent silence filled the room. Inner Judge faced Eternal Friend, then Rabia. Finally, he leaned back in his seat.

"Well," he said with a hint of dejection. "I've spent my whole life trying to protect Babla. I thought that as long as I made sure she obeyed the rules, she would be safe. These rules seem terribly outdated now, and Rabia and you Inner Guides are fully qualified to guide her. It seems that I've lost my job. Perhaps there's no place for me in Babla and Rabia's life. Maybe I should just leave."

Listening to these words, Babla realized how Inner Judge wanted her to be safe. He wasn't mean after all. "I could actually grow to like him," she thought.

She heard Eternal Friend talking to the Judge. "No," he said. "Babla and Rabia still need you, but not in the same capacity as before. Let's redefine your purpose. Tell me your qualities."

Inner Judge straightened up in his chair. A spark had come into his eyes. "Well," he said with conviction, "as a judge I know how to make decisions, how to discriminate for everyone's well-being. That is, I have a good overview of situations and am very organized. I also have a clear mind and an excellent memory. I know how to listen without judgment. I'm fair."

"That's a lot," Rabia said with a chuckle. "These are all characteristics I need in my daily life. I would welcome your help. But I would like to change your name to "Modern Judge" to remind you of the transformation you've just gone through. Does everyone agree?"

All Inner Beings and Inner Guides started clapping joyously. Alan seconded the idea that, in order to make such a decision, everyone had to agree. This way, when the decision was made, everybody would support it. This sounded good to Babla. First, he suggested, it was time for a break—and everyone readily agreed.

TANTRIKA, THE NUN, AND THE SLUT: A New Perspective

When they came back from the break, Babla wondered what would happen next. As they sat down, she assumed her place on Alan's lap. The Nun stood up; she bore a grim look, her lips tight and eyes stern.

"No matter how modern Inner Judge becomes, it is still not okay for Rabia to have a relationship because she's on a spiritual path. And it's my job to keep her on it."

"I don't deserve anything anyway," Loretta pitched in.

The atmosphere in the room was thick and heavy. The Slut rose to confront the Nun. She didn't agree at all. "I love men," she argued. "I don't care a bit about spirituality. Besides, you just think you are spiritual! If it were left up to you, Babla would be growing up in a nunnery, totally shut off from the world. I am not going to let that happen. Watch me carefully; when I turn on my sex-appeal, Rabia can't resist wanting to be sexual with a man. And, there goes your so-called spirituality."

With these words, the Slut turned on her glow and the entire room turned orange—deep, vibrant orange with red and yellow streaking through.

The Nun's eyes nearly fell out in utter horror. Desperate, she petitioned the Inner Guides. "You must do something," she begged, "otherwise the Slut will take over, and Babla and Rabia will be lost forever. I can't take this any longer. I can't breathe."

Maya, smiling, gestured to the Slut to turn down her sex-appeal. It was Tantrika who finally spoke. Looking at the Slut and the Nun, she said, "You both have a point. Yes, Rabia is on a spiritual path. Just the same, her spiritual path starts with her sexuality. One of Rabia's lessons in this life is to help the two of you become good friends."

"Over my dead body," spat the Slut, hands on her hips and her voice shrill.

The Nun, horrified by this idea, was trembling. At last she found her voice. Trying to sound calm, she said, "No way," almost stuttering. "I won't have anything to do with this impossible creature, who . . . who doesn't even know how to dress properly. If you don't listen to me, she'll be the downfall of us all."

Watching these two women as they stood across from each other, Babla saw that they were opposites in every way: their clothes—baggy and black versus tight and crimson; their fingernails—short and dull versus long and polished; their hair—shaved and covered versus dark and sexy; their faces—plain and pale versus brightly made up.

"Aren't they both extreme?" she asked, turning to Alan.

"Exactly. One of Rabia's main lessons in this life is to bring her extremes into balance. The Nun and the Slut are two such extremes."

"Are there others?" Babla wanted to know.

"Yes," said Alan. "For example, Inner Man and Inner Woman, Mr. Money and Slimy Joe are extremes. But they will come later. She has to deal with these two first."

"How?" Babla asked. "They both seem quite stubborn and stuck in their ways."

"Well, they have been—until now, that is. But, they've never faced each other like this before. They've never sat in a circle with Inner Beings and Inner Guides and expressed their opinions. This is where the Mystery of Life takes over. I can't tell you how it will happen, yet I know that somehow, in facing each other and by staying with their truth, without compromising, a transformation will take place. Everyone will be happier afterward." Alan's blue eyes were sparkling.

Babla realized that suddenly the quality of the air had changed. A sweet fragrance wafted through the room, and rays of golden-white light beamed from above. Without so much as a whisper, everybody watched the rays gradually take the form of Higher Self. To Babla, it felt as if the size of the room had doubled. She could breathe more deeply and easily. Her curious bright eyes never stopped looking at Higher Self.

The figure came closer and sat at the head of the table. The Slut and the Nun also sat down. The room filled with an expansive, yet strong presence— unconditional Love and compassion. Everyone could feel this all-inclusive Essence.

Higher Self broke the hushed mood. "One of the most challenging tasks for all earth Beings is to embrace opposites. When you are into duality, right and wrong, the Slut and the Nun are both right and wrong. This so-called problem cannot be solved while you are in it; you have to rise above the situation to see its roots. Then, the issue simply disappears. Let us all consider this seeming problem between the Nun and the Slut from a more expanded view."

Everyone, with the exception of the Slut and the Nun, began to float above the table, looking down from a new perspective. Even Ms. Romantic, floating on her cloud and daydreaming, was captivated.

"Wow!" said Amazon Woman. "It's like a scale. Both sides are equally strong. The scale will stay perfectly in balance as long as these two stick to their extreme beliefs."

"Yes," replied Higher Self. "Even though it looks like they are opposites, they actually are working together to keep everything the same. As long as they hold on to their different positions, nothing can move."

Hearing these words, both the Nun and the Slut jumped up, very annoyed. "What?" they screamed at the same time. "I am working together with her? No way! She is my arch enemy."

Silence . . . . They looked at each other, stunned. Amazon Woman and Higher Self were right. Just by hating each other with equal strength, they were keeping Rabia stuck. In this place, she couldn't be with a man in a satisfying way, nor could she thoroughly follow her spiritual path.

"Well," said the Nun, softening a bit. "Let's talk about this."

"Yes," admitted the Slut. "I want what's best for Rabia and Babla. If my behavior is keeping them stuck, then I'm willing to change. But, I need the Guides' help."

"Me, too," added the Nun.

Everybody came back down to sit at the table; except Ms. Romantic, who resumed her daydreaming.

"What needs to be done next?" Amazon Woman asked.

"We have to travel to another world to find the roots of this opposition," advised Higher Self.

"You mean, go to one of the worlds within this one?" Babla's ears had perked up.

Higher Self nodded yes. "I will leave you now. You can handle this without my assistance. Call if you need help and I will reappear."

The form of Higher Self first dissolved into golden-white rays of shimmery light, then into thin air—or so it seemed to Babla.

"Where did it go?" she asked Alan.

"Back to Essence. The form and the formless are one, and emptiness is fullness and fullness is emptiness." Babla didn't have any idea what this meant and knew Alan wasn't expecting her to understand. Somehow, it just sounded and felt wonderful.

THE NUN: Making a Wise Choice

It was time to journey into another world. The Nun, Rabia, Babla, Alan, Amazon Woman, and Eternal Friend all wished to find out about this other world within their world. It seemed to hold the root cause for the Nun's rigid beliefs about Rabia's spiritual path. This promised to be a long journey, so they took plenty of food. They left early in the morning and traveled all day and all night. When Babla got tired, Alan took her on his shoulders so she could rest.

The next morning, the adventurers found themselves facing a forest; Babla looked at the sight in surprise—this wasn't like any other forest she had ever seen. Although the trees were huge, they looked old and gnarly. And at the same time, they seemed timeless. There was a mysterious glow all through the forest. The air was still, but a misty smoke circled the trees as if there was a breeze. It was so strange.

When she asked Alan about it, he said this was the Forest of Time; once they went into it, they could go to the different worlds within this world.

Just as they entered the forest, the Nun took over leading the group. Babla was next in line. Deep in the forest, strange events began to take place. Babla couldn't believe her eyes when she saw the Nun becoming younger. Her clothes were changing and her headdress disappeared. Now Babla could see long blond hair, reaching down to her waist, that was held back with a pretty blue bow. As the Nun's black robe vanished, Babla saw the Nun in a perky, light blue dress with white flowers, ruffles, and lace.

Babla turned to Alan and whispered, "This is unbelievable. She looks about 15 or 16 years old."

"She is 16. You're right," Alan replied.

The Nun stopped in front of a big door carved into a giant tree trunk. She opened it and went in with the others following. They went down some steps, then stopped in front of another door.

When the Nun opened this door and took a step in, Babla was stunned. They were in a castle. She could see huge crystal chandeliers hanging from high ceilings. Almost everything inside was made of dark wood, heavily carved. "I bet these people are rich," she thought. Servants scurried from room to room; people looked very busy.

Babla asked Alan why nobody was noticing them; they all were going about their business as if Babla's group wasn't there.

Alan said that the people in this castle couldn't see them. "We are invisible, unless we want to be seen."

They moved to what looked like a library. The walls were covered with shelves of books. The Nun was talking to a middle-aged woman and man, both formally dressed. The woman was wearing a fluffy, dark brown gown with lace and ruffles and her hair was swept up; she seemed very impatient. The man, acting a bit softer, was patting the Nun gently on her back.

"It will be okay," he said. "I'm sure you will be happy. I know you don't like that he is much older than you, but I think it is good. He's more experienced and can teach you how to do things the right way. He is a good man, you know. He'll make a good husband. He is rich and he has a beautiful estate. You will be well provided for. All he asks is that you bear his children."

"And besides," the woman added, "by marrying him you will help us enormously. Your father lost some money gambling, so having a wealthy son-in-law will help our situation. This is how all girls feel; I didn't want to marry your father at first, but now I'm glad I did."

"But I'm only 16," protested the Nun. "None of my friends are married yet. I don't even like him. He's almost my father's age."

"Now, now," said the woman, growing impatient. "You know we love you, dear daughter. We wouldn't insist on it if this weren't good for you. Tomorrow, when he comes to propose formally, I want you to be very nice. It's past your bedtime. Go to bed now and don't think about this any more."

Sullen and disappointed, the Nun left the library and went upstairs to her bedroom where her maid was waiting to undress her. The maid, only a few years older than she, was gentle and kind.

"If you were forced to marry someone you didn't like, what would you do?" asked the girl.

"I would run away to the nunnery," replied the maid. "That's what my cousin did five years ago. Since then, none of the girls in my family have been forced to marry someone they didn't like."

"Why didn't her parents just take her back?" asked the Nun.

"Because," said the maid, "a nunnery is more powerful than the parents. Once you are in the nunnery, not even the King could get you out if you didn't want to leave."

Feeling desperate, the Nun made her decision. The maid told her how to get to the closest nunnery, which was a full night's walk away. By the time her parents realized what had happened, she would be safely there. The maid got her some food and water from the kitchen, and gave her an old cloak to disguise her identity. Then the Nun went to the nunnery to avoid marriage.

Sitting in the Nun's bedroom, Babla conferred with her Adult Self and her Inner Guides.

"So this is why the Nun is so opposed to men and marriage! What are we going to do now?" She was starting to understand the Nun's extreme position.

"We need to find where the Nun has gone," said Eternal Friend.

They left the castle, walking through the tree door. Retracing her steps in the forest, they soon came upon the Nun in her usual attire and headpiece, sitting on a log waiting for them. As they gathered around, Babla realized something was different about her now; it was her eyes! They reflected a sparkle of wisdom and understanding she had not seen before.

"So," asked Eternal Friend, "what have you learned?"

The Nun was in deep thought. "Well, this explains a lot. No wonder I carry hatred toward men and marriage and believe that spirituality can be expressed only as a nun and in no other way. I can see the rigidity of it now."

"In that other world we just visited, becoming a nun was a wise choice," said Amazon Woman. "When you look at Rabia's life in this world now, however, would you still make the same choice?"

The Nun lifted her head up higher. "No. Rabia's life today is multifaceted, like a diamond; it can include more than one view of reality. So, maybe the Slut and I can have different ideas and serve Rabia in a beautiful way, enhancing her life and her Essence."

There was a penetrating silence in the Forest of Time as the Nun's habit disappeared. She now wore a long maroon dress, her hair draped lightly over her shoulders.

Babla melted into an indescribable feeling of relaxation, deeply connected to the group, safe and content beyond anything she had known ever before.

LORETTA: Learning to Receive

Leaving the forest, the group returned to the sanctuary of Inner Beings. As the Nun took her seat, the Slut watched in amazement. Everyone could see the transformation in the Nun; her entire demeanor was softer and more flowing.

"Indeed, there is a time for Rabia to sit in meditation and be disciplined about her spiritual growth," the Slut conceded.

"And, there is a time for Rabia to let go of all discipline and enjoy herself, enjoy her sexuality and sensuality, enjoy being with a man," added the Nun, smiling.

Tantrika stood up, went to them and put her hands on their shoulders. Her intense presence was the focus in the room.

Looking at the trio, Babla felt a powerful energy, almost like electricity going out from Tantrika's hands into the Nun and the Slut. Both looked up at Tantrika, their eyes glowing with a warm, peaceful light.

Amazon Woman spoke the necessary words so that all Inner Beings could understand what was happening. "Tantrika is the bridge between them," she said. "She can teach the Slut and the Nun how to be sexual and sensual, to fully enjoy it, yet how not to stop there. She knows that sexuality and sensuality are the seeds of true spirituality. For Rabia to live a deeply satisfying life, the Nun and the Slut need to stay connected and work together. Tantrika will teach them how."

After a brief moment, the Inner Beings began celebrating the new friendship developing between these two women. They felt that as the Slut and the Nun spent more time with Tantrika, more joy would fill Rabia's life. Everyone felt connected and inspired.

Except Loretta. She remained serious and tense with her head hanging down, not looking at anyone. Rabia asked her what was happening.

In a teary voice, Loretta wept, "I definitely don't deserve to sit at this table with you. If I'm here at all, I should be doing something, like scrubbing the floors or cleaning the windows. I can't just sit here and do nothing. I need to be useful to exist."

Babla couldn't understand. Why couldn't Loretta enjoy herself like the others?

"Because she is stuck in another world inside of this one like the Nun was," said Alan as if he had read her mind. "When an Inner Being is caught in another world, she can't be fully in this one. Even though in this world Loretta deserves to sit at the table, she can't see it. Part of her is still living in the other world."

"Does this mean we can go to another world within this one to deal with it?" Babla loved these worlds within worlds and was ready to help.

Alan nodded yes.

Eternal Friend asked Loretta to take them to this other world where she didn't deserve anything. She agreed. This time, Rabia, Babla, Alan, Amazon Woman, and Eternal Friend accompanied her.

They left the room and descended a winding staircase. The further down they went, the narrower it became; and the stairs made of solid stone soon became steps of dirt. Babla wrinkled her nose in disgust at the musty air, full of mildew and sweat.

The staircase ended in front of a heavy old door. Alan helped Loretta crack it open enough to enter a darkened room. In this place, which looked more like a barn than a room, Loretta disappeared into the womb of a pregnant black woman, very young and very pretty. She was one of many black Beings with dark curly hair and shiny black eyes. They all wore rags and crowded together with barely space to move. A painful hush was in the air.

Knowing that she couldn't be seen, Babla watched with curiosity. She heard the door crash open and saw three white men come in with whips in their hands. They were calling the black Beings "lazy" and all sorts of mean things and cracking the whips at random. In a frenzy, the black Beings fled from the barn.

Amid the chaos, Babla felt like she might faint. The scene put her in utter shock.

"This is a world where white Beings are pretending that black Beings are unworthy and don't have the same rights," said Alan, trying to explain. "They are taking the black Beings as slaves and doing terrible things to break their spirit and make them obey. The spirit of the black Beings, fortunately, can never be broken. Even though they have been beaten up and punished, they've kept the spark in their eyes, which is the sign of their spirit."

Babla and the others witnessed the black Beings working in the fields day and night. They were given very little food and rest and were whipped.

Meanwhile, the pregnant woman had given birth to Loretta, a precious little baby. Loretta was abused and beaten by the white Beings from day one, put in the fields as soon as she could walk, and sentenced to a life of hard work, terrible food, little rest, and constant humiliation.

"No wonder she doesn't believe she deserves anything," Babla said to Alan. He nodded in agreement.

After looking at Loretta's world, they went back up the stairs to the room of Inner Beings. However, Loretta stayed at the entrance, refusing to come in and sit down. Her head drooped in shame.

Eternal Friend looked at Maya and Alan and nodded. These two then got up and opened a door on one side of the room. To Babla's surprise, out came a bathtub full of steaming bubbles. It was round and big enough to hold at least three Beings.

Maya took Loretta's hand and led her to the tub. She helped her take off her rags and slip into the water. Loretta was in such a stupor that she put up no resistance. Maya also got in and started to wash Loretta's exhausted, skinny body with love and care.

Alan, sitting nearby, did his part by combing Loretta's hair with his fingers. He massaged her face while talking to her in a gentle voice. "Those times are over," he said. "The world we just visited is a different world with different standards than the one we live in now. In this world, as one of Rabia's Inner Beings, you have equal rights. Your place is at the table with the rest of us. You are here to teach us patience, endurance, tolerance, gratitude, and the ability to wait without losing hope—the exact opposite of Eric's world. We can't assist him in his transformation without your help."

Babla eyed the bubbly water. She would do anything to be in it. Alan sent her an encouraging wink and beckoned. The next moment, she was in the tub, splashing and playing with the bubbles.

Even Loretta couldn't resist a smile. She breathed a deep sigh and her whole body relaxed. Maybe Alan was right and she did deserve more in this world now. She carefully looked around as if seeing the room for the first time. Then she really noticed the Inner Beings and the Guides. They all looked so beautiful.

Maya and Alan exchanged a knowing glance. It was working. Maya left the water and brought forth a simple dress in a vibrant peach color. Loretta, having dried herself with a luxurious towel, put on the beautiful dress.

As she moved toward the table to sit down, everyone clapped with delight—except for Eric. A dreadful feeling in his chest told him he was next in line for this so-called transformation. He was sure nothing was going to work for him, yet he couldn't deny how wonderful Loretta looked.

Eternal Friend informed the gathering that Loretta was beginning to let go of the other world to be fully present in this one. As a result, Rabia could utilize all of Loretta's qualities to dissolve duality and come into greater balance. He suggested that Maya and Black Panther stay with Loretta, who needed more time to completely let go. Everyone agreed.

Black Panther stretched out around Loretta's feet and Maya held her hand. With that, Alan, true to form, reached out and took Babla on his lap.

ERIC: Letting Go of Hopelessness

After a break, the Inner Beings came back to the room with the round table. To Babla's surprise, two men she hadn't met before were sitting at the table. Rabia asked them to introduce themselves.

The man on her left side stood up and said, "I'm Slimy Joe. I don't care about money or clothes or any material possessions. I live one day at a time and sleep on the streets."

This tall, thin man had pale blue eyes, worn out clothes, and an old gray hat atop dirty hair. Next, the other stranger to Rabia's right stood up.

"Wow!" whispered Babla to Alan. "These two are totally opposite from each other." Alan nodded in agreement.

The man was short and stout and wore an elegant dark brown suit, a white silk shirt, and a tie. He was as bald as a stone. "I am Mr. Money," he bragged. "I care a lot about money and worldly possessions. In fact, that's what I live for. I am very rich and greedy. I know that money can buy everything. In fact, I use my money to manipulate other Beings so I can get what I want. This is the only life I've got, and I want to squeeze every bit of juice out of it before I die."

Eternal Friend thanked them for coming and asked them to sit down. "Just be with us for a while," he said. "Right now we are exploring the attitudes of all the Inner Beings who are influencing Rabia in her relationships with men. After we are through with this subject, we will move on to money issues. We have done great so far. The Nun and the Slut are cooperating, Inner Judge has become modern, and Loretta feels more deserving. Soon, Rabia will be able to have a fulfilling relationship with an outer mate."

Looking at her beloved Inner Guide, Babla felt that something was strange. Eternal Friend was not talking and acting the way he usually behaved. As an Inner Guide of the highest order, he didn't care whether Rabia ever had a relationship with an outer mate or not. He was here to assist in Rabia's journey toward Oneness, her innermost Truth and Essence. It didn't matter to Eternal Friend whether this happened with or without an outer mate. He was up to something.

Alan, reading her thoughts, smiled. "He's trying to coax Eric to come out," he whispered.

In the next moment, Babla knew that Eternal Friend had succeeded. Eric, his feet on the table, grinned in his most sarcastic way. "I thought you were more intelligent than this, Eternal Friend. All these so-called transformations look great, but they're not going to work. They are just kid's play.

"The truth is that relationships are hogwash. Maybe they work for others, but not for Rabia. The whole relationship thing is an illusion, anyway. If the world listened to me, everyone would be either on mountain tops or on islands, living alone, keeping a sheep for milk, a few chickens for eggs, and a small garden for vegetables. Interacting with other Beings brings misery. Living alone and tending to our survival needs is the most happiness we can ever expect in this world. Sitting here is just a waste of time," smirked Eric the Cynic.

Babla noticed that the more he talked, the duller his eyes became and the heavier the air in the room. The Inner Beings were slumped over the table, as if an unbearable burden were weighing on their shoulders. Babla felt utterly depressed, cold, and lonely. Even the Slut had stopped combing the Nun's hair and was staring into space.

"Don't believe his words," Alan cautioned softly into Babla's ear. "This is not the truth. He is an excellent hypnotist, that's all."

These words shook Babla out of her depression. Alan was right; in reality, she wasn't feeling cold or lonely at all. In the company of Rabia and all her Inner Guides, she felt very loved, connected, and safe. And yet listening to Eric, she had somehow lost touch with her true self.

"How unusual," whispered Babla.

"Not really," Alan replied. "Remember, before White Swan came to you, you felt miserable and lonely? Even then, we all were there for you, but you couldn't see us or connect with us. You were not aware of your own feelings— you were feeling Eric's feelings. His feelings were so strong that you couldn't feel anything else. But now, his influence is not as strong. That's because you feel safe and connected."

"If I could feel only my own feelings, what would they be?" Babla wanted to know.

Alan was ready with an answer. "As the Inner Child in your most transformed state, you would be a Magical Child—spontaneous, playful, curious, beautiful, naturally spiritual, intelligent, intuitive, and in touch with your Essence. You are already much closer to this than you were before you met White Swan."

Babla let out an excited giggle. She knew Alan was right. "What is Rabia's role in all this?"

Alan smiled. "As the Adult Self, she adds her awareness and presence to your special qualities," he said. "She gives direction. She's like a bridge between you and us, the Inner Guides. Without her help, it would be almost impossible for us to get through to you when you feel lonely and disconnected. To create her life, Rabia combines our wisdom and knowing of the bigger picture, her own presence and awareness, your unique qualities, and the transformed qualities of the Inner Beings."

"Wow!" Babla exclaimed. "What a beautiful life!"

Then, she became aware of the others. She realized that after Eric's last words, nobody had spoken. There was a heavy awkwardness in the room.

Eric looked surprised. Whatever response he had expected, this definitely wasn't part of it. At last he baited, "Well, isn't anybody going to argue with me? I'm sure at least half of you don't believe what I just said."

No response was offered. Eric started picking at his clothes. His face even began to turn green.

"How do you feel?" Eternal Friend asked.

"Lonely. Lonely and cut off."

"Poor Eric," Babla thought. "Here he is, his head hanging, drowning in his self-created loneliness and misery."

At an eye-signal from Eternal Friend, all the Inner Guides and Inner Beings got up and encircled Eric. They lifted him up off his chair and laid him down on the floor, putting their hands on him, holding him, touching him with love and tenderness.

This was more than the Cynic could handle. When teardrops started to fall, he tried to stop them. But, so many teardrops waited to roll down his cheeks that they came out anyway. Soon he was lying in a pool of his own sorrow.

Babla found the sight of this very touching. After a long time of being held and embraced, Eric calmed down.

"What a big shift for Eric," Eternal Friend said with compassion. "He needs time now to rest and integrate. This was a wonderful start. For his full transformation to take place, however, Babla must have some experiences she hasn't had yet.

I suggest that one or two of the Inner Beings stay with Eric now and care for him."

Rabia suggested Miriam. Maya suggested Loretta.

When asked, Miriam said, "I feel so useless. I'm tired of waiting for Rabia to have an outer man in her life so I can give him all my love and take care of him. To be fully happy, I must give to an outer man. An Inner Being is not the same. But, I guess, while I'm waiting, it would be okay. I have nothing else to do anyway."

Babla saw Alan and Eternal Friend trying not to laugh out loud. Quickly, Maya jumped in and said how very generous of Miriam to accept.

Loretta also agreed to spend time with Eric, even though she wasn't quite sure what she could do. But she knew that Maya and Black Panther were with her, which made her feel more at ease. It was going to take her some time to get used to being deserving.

The Inner Beings and Inner Guides said good-bye to each other. Because Babla was leaving, they decided to meet again after she returned from her long journeys.

"This is like one happy family," Babla confided in Alan.

"Yes. You could call it your Inner Family."

FIREBALL: *Rage Comes out of the Cage*

One day, as Babla was exploring the forest, she heard a sound. She couldn't figure out what it was, and there was no trail leading in its direction. Just as she decided to forget about it and move on, she heard Amazon Woman's voice: "Babla, go find out what that sound is about."

Suddenly, Babla felt sick to her stomach. "Oh no," she thought. "I'm in deep trouble." She could see no opening, everything was covered with thick foliage. Hearing a rustle, she turned to see Black Panther. Her green-eyed Animal Guide was moving slowly and gracefully, his black fur shining as he came closer and closer.

"Hi, Babla," he greeted. "I'm happy to see you again. Let me go first and open up a trail for you. You can follow right behind me."

Babla sighed with relief. "Great! I'm so glad you're here; thanks for your help."

As he passed her, she put her arms around his neck. She could feel his powerful energy, so alive and alert, and yet so deep and present.

Babla bravely followed Black Panther until she heard the sound again. It was much louder now.

"Please don't leave me Black Panther," she pleaded. "I'm so scared!"
"I'm with you, Babla, don't worry," the panther reassured her.

A moment later, they came to a small clearing. In the middle of it, Babla saw a metal cage holding a little two-year-old girl with red curly hair and a freckled face. The cage was too small for her even to stand up straight. Babla realized that the sound she had heard was this little girl's voice. She screamed, "No! Let me out! I hate you! I hate this whole world! I hate everybody! Let me out! I hate it! I'm furious!"

Panic stricken, Babla wondered how anybody could be so loud. It wasn't nice! Spying them, the little girl glared at Babla with fiery blue eyes. "I'm Fireball, and I'm furious!" she yelled. "Who are you?"

"I . . . I . . . I'm Babla." Babla felt her legs weaken.

"Since you're here, you might as well let me out," Fireball almost demanded. The intensity from her eyes hit Babla like a dart.

"Oh no, no," Babla hurriedly found an excuse. "I can't do that. My Guides say it's okay to love and be with others, but it's not okay to rescue them. Everybody needs to learn their own lessons. I can't let you out; you need to help yourself."

Black Panther sat next to the cage, alert to what was happening. He fixed his gaze at a distance. Following his eyes, the two little girls saw Amazon Woman walking toward them.

"Wow!" yelled Fireball. "I can tell you're not afraid of me and my anger. I like that!"

Amazon Woman smiled at Fireball, then turned to Babla. "Babla, Fireball is one of your Inner Beings. Unlike the Outer Beings, it's always important to help the inner ones."

Babla sat next to Black Panther, disappointed. "I'd rather help the Outer Beings, they're so much nicer," she complained. She didn't like this little girl at all! "Why does Rabia have to have Inner Beings like this? Wouldn't it be much easier without them?" she thought.

The Amazon knelt next to Babla, stroking her hair. "I know," she said. "Looking out is easier than looking in. Yet, as long as some of the Inner Beings are locked up and not integrated, Rabia's inner world can't be fully balanced and whole. Thus, any happiness she finds will be only temporary."

"Oh well, I guess we need to let her out. What if she beats me up? Or causes some trouble in Rabia's outer life? I don't feel safe around her. Even if we let her out, couldn't we keep her mouth shut and her hands tied? She said such nasty things before you came." Babla felt defeated.

Amazon Woman turned to Fireball. "If Babla lets you out, will you beat her up?"

"I might," came the reply, "because she's the one who put me here in the first place!" Her eyes sparkled with half anger, half mischief.

The Amazon was laughing now. "I'm glad to see that you haven't lost your free spirit, Fireball." She then began explaining to Babla, "A long time ago, you had to make a decision to put Fireball in a cage and forget all about her existence. This was an appropriate decision then because, in your family, you had to be a 'good girl' to survive. Having Fireball around and active wouldn't have been safe. But now things are different. Fireball's fiery energy is critical to your well-being."

Amazon Woman was quiet for a minute while she crouched down near the wild little girl. "She's been in this cage for a long time, so she may be disoriented for a time. But that's normal. I'll keep her with me and teach her how to enjoy her beautiful energy without hurting others. She's an intelligent one. She'll learn fast."

"So, I have to open the cage door?" asked Babla tentatively. She wasn't enthusiastic about this, yet she totally trusted Amazon Woman.

"That's right," her Guide answered. "The key is hanging around your neck."

"Oh, that's what this key is for!" thought Babla. She had been wondering all along about the mysterious key. Carefully, she approached the cage, her big blue eyes glued on the little girl inside. "Do you bite?" she asked.

Fireball opened her mouth and pretended to roar, showing her teeth. Her eyes were so lit up and alive that Babla was mesmerized.

Babla walked toward the cage door, fumbling to get the key off her neck and into the keyhole. Her heart pounded as she slowly turned the key until it made a click. Then, she ran to hide behind Black Panther.

"You did great, Babla," praised Amazon Woman. Firmly but gently she opened the rusty, creaky cage door. At last, Fireball crawled out with a dazzled look on her face. She pinched herself to make sure this wasn't just a dream. Then she started shaking her body, jumping up and down, rolling on the forest ground, laughing, growling, howling, yelling.

"She sure has a lot of energy," thought Babla. "She is kind of cute, too, with her freckles and red hair. Maybe some day, after she calms down a bit, we can become friends."

Black Panther stretched gracefully and got up. "It's time for us to go on, Babla," he said. "Amazon Woman will take care of Fireball for the time being."

Babla said good-bye and followed her Animal Guide back to the forest path. She felt a profound sense of relief, as if letting Fireball out of the cage had relaxed a deep tension within her.

They stopped at a fork in the trail. Black Panther explained that the path with the ancient, gnarled trees would lead Babla into still other worlds. She needed to go on by herself; Black Panther would be waiting for her right there.

After saying good-bye, Babla walked toward the unknown, full of both anticipation and wonder.

GREEDY RICH MAN: Misusing Power

Babla followed the signs. She found a big tree with a trunk-door opening to large stone steps winding down to another door. This door was made of old wood, almost falling apart. She could hear different sounds from behind the door—people shouting, machines squeaking, rolling noises, grumbling sounds, all kinds of sounds. She opened the door and found herself in a factory. Many people were working on huge machines, and others were watching, telling them what to do.

All at once, everyone stopped talking; the air turned prickly with fear. Through a side door a fat, bald man had entered. He wore a brown three-piece suit and a tie, and he chortled with glee. But something about his smirk made Babla shudder.

"He looks just like Mr. Money in my world," she thought. She heard Alan whisper, "That's right."

The fat man pretended to be sweet and sincere, but his eyes were cold as steel. He said how much he appreciated these people working so hard for him, giving so much of themselves. He knew they all needed a raise, but times were tough. If he gave them more money, he would have to close down the factory. He would understand, he said, if people wanted to leave. Then he thanked them again with lots of flowery words and left.

The thick silence could have been cut into pieces. After a while, the workers started mumbling to themselves, then to each other. Because Babla was invisible in this world, she could walk freely among the people and listen to their talk. What she heard was disgusting.

The fat man, the Boss, was obviously rich and greedy. For seven years, he had not given anyone a raise. He owned five factories around this area and lots of land. Most of the available jobs were in his factories. Anybody who left this job would have to move to another town to find a new one. It was a hopeless situation if they didn't want to move away. They hung their heads and continued to work the machines.

Babla was outraged. How could one man take advantage of all these people? No wonder she hadn't liked Mr. Money when he had appeared at the table. She heard Alan's voice telling her to go to the rich man's office.

Babla left the factory room and went to find the office. The rich man was sitting in his chair, alone, looking gloomy and deep in thought. With Alan's guidance, Babla was able to read his thoughts, which took her to his childhood.

The factory had belonged to his father, a mild mannered man who was generous with his workers. When the rich man was 15, several workers had conspired against his father, killing him and his wife, the rich man's mother. His uncle, who was his father's opposite in character, took over the factory and taught the rich man how to run it.

His blood had been boiling with desire for revenge since he was 15, when he had vowed to make the lives of his father's murderers as miserable as possible. Now he was doing just that. Yet, Babla could see that he was miserable, too.

Quietly, she left the factory and returned to where Black Panther was waiting. Alan had joined him. Babla had a deeper understanding now and wasn't as disgusted with the rich man as she had been before. "I still don't like how he is treating these people, though," she told Alan.

Alan agreed. "Yes. He is misusing his power."

TWO PRIESTESSES: Uniting Earth and Sky

The next world for Babla to visit was far away. Alan and Black Panther brought her to a stream in the forest where a boat awaited. Babla jumped aboard and waved good-bye. The boat seemed to know where to go, so she closed her eyes and relaxed, feeling soothed by the gentle rocking on the water.

After a long time, she arrived in a beautiful, lush land dotted with olive and fruit trees, swaying palms, colorful flowers, and birds of all sizes singing their songs.

Babla got out of the boat, smelling the fresh, salty air. On the rocky shore, she climbed up to a white temple, simply built yet decorated with ornate columns on all sides. Walking up long steps, she reached the top just as a woman came out of the temple. She had long, wavy reddish blond hair and swirled her wide flowing skirts. Her greenish brown eyes cast a warm glow as she kissed the two large snakes coiled around her arms. Flute music floated from nowhere, and the woman moved with the sound. The snakes also undulated to the music.

"She is doing a snakedance," Babla heard Alan whisper in her ear. "She is the Snake Priestess, also called Snakedancer."

Babla felt Rabia's presence very close. Watching the Snakedancer through the Adult Self's awareness was spellbinding.

Babla's mouth and eyes opened wide to see the Priestess dance. The snakes seemed to be one endless extension of the woman, dancing in total harmony. Babla realized that Snakedancer was completely connected to the earth. It was hard to tell where her feet ended and the ground began. She was nourished by the earth and she graced the earth in return. The veils of separation lifted, and the Priestess became the earth. It was awesome, yet simple. Babla felt deeply affected.

About this time, a white puffy cloud drifted toward Babla, landing right in front of her. She got on it and the cloud began sailing to yet another world, a world too far to travel by foot.

Babla leaned against the cloud and relaxed, using this opportunity to integrate what she had just experienced. Watching Snakedancer had opened up a profound yearning, a yearning she hadn't known even existed.

When the cloud began to descend, Babla opened her eyes to see a very different scene: they were landing in a garden surrounding another temple, one made out of classic gray stone. It was huge and magnificent. Women in long dresses were working outside, despite the cold, windy weather.

The temple door opened and a tall woman emerged. She had pitch black hair, straight and pulled to the back, and cold, light blue eyes. She wore a long blue robe and in the middle of her forehead was another eye, a third eye. It was looking around, but it wasn't always looking in the same direction as the right and left eyes. Her body was very straight, to the point of being stiff.

"What a contrast to Snakedancer," thought Babla. Watching how the others interacted with the woman made Babla decide that she must be an important person. "She is the head Priestess," sounded Alan's voice in her ear.

Babla followed this Priestess into her room. She saw her kneel on the floor with arms outstretched, then lean back, her face turned to the sky. After a while she started to sway gently. A pure white light from somewhere above came right into her middle eye. With a groan, the Priestess collapsed to the ground and was very still.

Slowly, she returned to a sitting position and rang a bell. The door opened and people started coming in, asking all kinds of questions. For hours, she calmly listened to each person, giving each the answers needed. After everyone left, she lay down on her back and closed her eyes.

Babla left the room and went back to where the white cloud was waiting. She realized how expanded and spacy she felt, unable to find her feet. She was ready to return to her world.

After a long journey on the cloud and in the boat, Babla was back by the forest stream where Alan and Black Panther were sitting. They listened as Babla told them about the differences in the two Priestesses.

Alan mentioned that in Babla's world, Rabia needed to integrate both of these energies, so she could unite with the earth and the sky—and become a whole Being. "Tantrika is the ideal integration," he said. "The more she expresses herself in Rabia's outer life, the more Rabia will experience the Mystery of Oneness."

Wide eyed, Babla told Alan that Tantrika was turning out to be more important than she had imagined. Alan took Babla in his arms and laughed out loud. Black Panther rolled on the ground, making funny, happy noises. Watching with amusement, Babla wondered if panthers could laugh.

MIRIAM: Giving Love

Back at the round table with the Inner Beings and Inner Guides, Babla noticed some changes in Tantrika. Her energy seemed to be fuller and softer, more radiant and glowing, yet also very clear and direct.

Tantrika came over to give Babla a long hug. She said, "Thank you for making the journey to the worlds within worlds, Babla. Now that you have seen both Priestesses, I can directly integrate both their Essences—a spirituality that is well grounded in earth, and a spirituality that reaches out to touch the sky. The first is sensual, warm, and joyful and the second is clear, precise, and serene. Through me, Rabia will have access to both in daily life. Babla, this is so exciting."

Babla decided she liked Tantrika very much. Then she looked at Mr. Money and Slimy Joe, sitting across from each other; they also seemed to have changed. Slimy Joe got up and explained that his reason for being part of Rabia's inner world was to keep Mr. Money in check.

"It's necessary for Rabia not to be greedy in this world," he said. "It is crucial for her not to misuse power the way Mr. Money did in his world. As long as money is not important for Rabia, Mr. Money won't have any power over her. And, I'm making sure that money will never become very important to her."

"Boy," thought Babla, "for all his dirty clothes and slimy, careless look, he sure has a strong voice and very set opinions." She wondered how these two Beings, so opposite to each other, could ever come closer. There had been progress with other Beings, but this situation appeared hopeless. Her heart sank in despair.

All of a sudden, Babla understood: This hopelessness was not her own feeling, it was Eric's. As the Inner Child, she wasn't feeling hopeless at all; she was excited and curious. It was the Cynic's mindset she had taken on. With that insight, the hopelessness lifted and was gone.

Hearing a commotion at the door, Babla turned just as it burst open. Fireball shot in, with Amazon Woman calmly following. Fireball jumped onto the table, put her little hands on her tiny hips and spouted, "Here I am, like it or not; and I will be included." Babla could see Eternal Friend, eyes sparkling, swallowing a laugh.

More than a few eyebrows raised as this flashy-eyed little girl barged in. Amazon Woman explained how Babla had found Fireball in the forest and liberated her from the cage. "Just like the Slut and the Nun, or Mr. Money and Slimy Joe, Babla and Fireball can learn from each other. They need to work and play together, creating a balance of the opposites in Rabia's outer life."

Babla and Fireball looked at each other, checking each other out. Then, as little girls do, they started to giggle. The spontaneity and innocence of their laughter spread to the others, and soon all the Inner Beings, Inner Guides, and the Adult Self had joined in.

Rabia remembered Contented Sage's words. Relaxation is the key to living a life without fear, and laughter definitely is very relaxing. She marveled at these two cute little girls and felt her love for them. She didn't know how it would happen, yet she knew that somehow Babla and Fireball would one day be good playmates. Rabia leaned back in her chair, satisfied. Then, she saw that Miriam looked uncomfortable; getting more tense by the moment. A slight smile sat upon her lips as if it were painted there. Rabia leaned over to catch her attention. "Hi, Miriam, what is happening with you?"

"Oh," said Miriam, taking a breath, "nothing. I'm just waiting till all this is over so that you can find a man for yourself. Then everything will be okay."

"What exactly will be okay?" Eternal Friend interrupted. Even the most lost, confused Inner Being seemed to trust him.

"Oh," replied Miriam, unable to meet his gaze, "then I'll have someone I can give my love to. The only way I can be happy is when I am giving. Otherwise, I feel like I don't exist."

Babla and Fireball were aghast. How could she not exist? Here she was sitting at the table, not giving anything to anybody, yet she definitely was present.

"You could give to Babla and Fireball," said Alan turning toward Miriam. "They need a lot of love and attention."

"Oh no!" Miriam was curt. "That wouldn't do. I need to give to an outer man, not Inner Beings. Only this can make me totally happy. An outer man is way more important than any Inner Being could ever be." The Inner Beings were astonished.

"Thanks a lot!" Fireball retorted, fuming like a little bull.

Babla sat down, disappointed. Wasn't this ever going to end? As if it weren't enough that Slimy Joe and Mr. Money didn't like each other, and that she had to make friends with this angry little redhead. And now, Miriam was talking such nonsense.

"I don't know about you, Miriam," Babla sulked, "but no outer man Rabia has ever spent time with makes me feel as safe, as taken care of, loved, and appreciated as do Alan and Eternal Friend. No matter whether Rabia spends time with outer men or not, I feel very safe here and satisfied with my life. I don't need her to be with an outer man. And if she is, that's fine, too."

"But," countered Miriam, "to be really happy, I need a man outside of Rabia. I mean, that's the real giving. I just have so much love in my heart. I'm the happiest when Rabia spends time with a man so that I can give and give and give. It is like an endless pool of love that is in me."

"Oh great!" Fireball raised an angry voice. "Here I am rejected all my life and starving for love, and there you are refusing to give it to me. Thanks a lot. It was nice meeting you!" She turned her back on Miriam and started stomping on the table, strange sounds coming out of her mouth. Fireball was having her first temper tantrum in a long, long time.

Miriam sat speechless, looking foolish and confused.

All of a sudden, Babla smelled a freshness in the air. When she looked up, she saw the golden-white light of Higher Self come into view. Soon she could see the white robe and white hair and the faceless face. She took a deep breath and relaxed. She knew that now everything would be okay.

Higher Self sat down at the head of the table next to Eternal Friend and started talking to Miriam about love. "Remember the time you spent with White Swan? What you felt coming from White Swan was Love—unconditional Love. Unconditional Love doesn't have an object that it needs to go to, it is simply there. It comes out of every pore of your being and goes out to whomever is open to receive it. It is not directed to any Being in particular. It is a glow that emanates from you, and whosoever is close to you will feel it and be nurtured."

As if to let these words sink in, Higher Self paused. Babla felt a warm breeze momentarily ripple against her skin, and the wisdom continued.

"Conditional love is directed to a specific Being, like an outer man. If there is no outer man, you will have to stuff it and wait, which puts your life on hold. For example, an outer man might not want your love, or not all of it, which may leave you disappointed. The happiness you seek cannot be found through conditional love."

"But then what shall I do with all this love in my heart?" Miriam asked desperately.

"The seed of all Love is unconditional," came the answer. "Whether it expresses itself conditionally or unconditionally depends on what you believe in, on your attitude about life. Simply feel the Love that is inside you and don't worry about where to give it. Just lean back and let yourself feel."

At a signal from Higher Self, Maya knelt beside Miriam and started caressing her chest in a circular motion. Miriam relaxed in her chair and closed her eyes, her breathing deeper. Watching carefully, Babla noticed a shift in Miriam's energy; a subtle, warm glow spiraled out, first from her chest and then from her whole body. This golden glow became stronger and stronger as Maya continued her touch on Miriam's chest.

"Okay," said Higher Self. "Now, any of the Inner Beings who feel drawn to this energy, move closer to Miriam." Immediately Loretta and Fireball stood up and walked toward Miriam. After some hesitation, Mr. Money and Slimy Joe also moved closer. They all stood close enough to feel the warmth, closing their eyes and letting it touch their hearts. There was utter silence in the room.

"This is so wonderful," Rabia thought. "All of my Inner Beings, Inner Guides, and my Higher Self are working together—with me and for me. No wonder I am so deeply satisfied in my outer life." She felt grateful for the Mystery of Life.

After a long time, Miriam opened her eyes and was delighted to see her golden glow of Love nurturing four of the Inner Beings. She looked at Higher Self. "It is hard to believe," she said, her face wide open, "but I feel content."

Higher Self nodded slowly. "Yes. Giving from a place of unconditional Love always fulfills the giver."

They all could see how nurturing this was to the receivers as well. Higher Self suggested that Maya stay with Miriam awhile and assist her process of learning about Love. Loretta, Fireball, Mr. Money, and Slimy Joe were to stay close to get the Love they needed. Everyone agreed. Smiling with eternal grace, Higher Self shifted back to being the Light that it really was and disappeared. Babla noticed, though, that the fresh fragrance in the air remained.

WORLDS WITHIN WORLDS: *Delving Into the Depths*

It was time for Babla to explore more of the worlds within hers. Black Panther and Alan took her to the opening of a big black tunnel. Seeing Babla's wide eyes, Alan reassured her it was safe to go through. They would wait there for her until she returned. Trusting her Guides, Babla gathered enough courage to walk in. It was dark inside, but her eyes adjusted and she could see well enough.

When she came out the other end, she was in a small town with cobblestone streets. Women with long dresses, hats, and little umbrellas were milling around. Babla wondered why they had their umbrellas up; it was such a beautiful day. She walked aimlessly until she came upon a crowd in a large square. Some were selling fruit and vegetables, grains, and tools. Others were buying things, talking to each other, laughing and arguing. "This looks like a marketplace," she thought.

A boy, about ten years old with shoulder-length blond hair, caught her attention. Even through his dirty white shirt, Babla could see how skinny he was. He quietly walked toward a cluster of people and mingled with them. Looking to his right and left, the boy took money bags from two men in the heat of an argument. He stuffed the bags into his shirt and left as quietly as he had arrived.

Babla followed him, knowing that in this world she was invisible. The boy went to the wharf and met a small group of men standing in front of a huge ship. Another man came out of a bar, smelling heavily of alcohol. Clearly, he was the boss. He listened to the boy, grinning and nodding his head. All of them boarded the ship, which immediately left the dock. After it was under way, an unusual flag ascended the mast, waving a bold skull and crossbones.

As she watched from the shore, Babla heard Alan's voice in her ear: "This is a pirate ship. The boy has left home to become a pirate. He is a good-hearted boy, yet has chosen a wrong path in life. This will lead him to do many wrong things, like killing other Beings."

Babla stood there, thinking of the boy. Just then, a trap door opened in the stones, and she was compelled to take the steps down into another tunnel. This time, she was less frightened. Rabia certainly would be proud of her courage.

Before long, she found herself in the countryside under some trees on a large lawn. Quietly sitting in a wooden chair was a little girl seven or eight years old. When Babla went closer, she gasped in horror. The girl's face, arms, and hands were severely distorted. She could make some sounds and move her arms in slow motion—and that was it. Babla realized that the girl had to be totally taken care of.

Next to her was a tall, thin woman in a full-length black dress with a white collar. Her hair was dark and pulled all the way to the back. She was treating the girl with compassion and care, which Babla found heartwarming.

The only thing that seemed alive about the girl was her eyes. Through these eyes, Babla saw her Essence. "She has accepted her situation. She knows she is different, yet has been able to make peace with it. She is in complete surrender," Alan whispered.

Babla could see in those eyes how much the girl appreciated the woman and the deep Love she had for her care giver. They seemed to communicate beyond spoken words, in a much deeper way.

Another trap door opened and Babla was back in the tunnel. This time she came out at a very noisy place. Everyone wore layers of clothes from head to toe. Just their hands and a bit of their faces were showing. Babla found this strange, especially because the weather was so hot. Crouched on the street, leaning against the wall of a building, was a one-eyed beggar, hands outstretched to receive money from the people passing by.

As Babla approached, he looked at her and smiled; it was obvious that he could see her. He leaned over and whispered, "Don't look at the form, look at the Essence." Then he went about his business as if she weren't there.

Babla was taken aback. "I thought I was invisible in this other world," she said to herself, knowing Alan was listening.

"Mostly," came his answer, "except to this beggar. Normally, veils separate all these worlds within worlds. However, the beggar knows how to penetrate the veils. That's why he can see you."

Babla thought of Mother Hen and how she had seen Babla's Inner Guides even though they were invisible to most Outer Beings. Tears of gratitude welled up in her eyes and rolled down. Her little heart was about to burst with the rush of Love she felt. She realized that Mother Hen was in touch with the Essence of things more than their form.

The trap door popped open again, and Babla went through the tunnel. She was getting used to walking in darkness. She found herself in a huge house with exquisite hand-carved wood. Some sounds were coming from one room. When she peeked through the half-open door, she saw five neatly dressed children at a table on which there were books stacked high. At the head was a stern woman in a long, dark dress, who spoke harshly in a high-pitched voice. Seeing the anger and hatred in her eyes was painful for Babla.

"Alan," she called in her mind, "I want to leave this place. I don't like this woman at all. Her eyes are like ice."

"I know," came his answer, "but you need to stay awhile. Your fear of this woman is related to why you were also afraid of Fireball and locked her up. Simply looking at the woman will shift something in you."

Babla looked and looked, but couldn't see anything except hatred. This was so frustrating!

"Look through the hatred," Alan's voice sounded in her ear. Babla looked through the hatred in the cold eyes. Shortly thereafter, she felt an ocean of sadness. Looking through the sadness, she saw overwhelming fear and panic. Out of curiosity, Babla continued to look into the woman's eyes, now through the panic. After the longest time, she felt herself go through something like a curtain into an explosion of color—all colors of the rainbow were dancing in front of her eyes. When she looked through the colors, she saw a clear lake—totally calm, totally silent.

"Wow! There's no need to be afraid of her anger, is there?"

"No need, Babla," came Alan's loving reply. "Now you know the Truth. You never need to be wary of anger again—in the inner world, or in the outer world."

Babla felt that this moment was the beginning of her real friendship with Fireball.

Right in front of Babla, the trap door reappeared, and she went sliding into the tunnel. This tunnel was the longest yet. When Babla emerged, all she could see was earth and rock. There were no houses, nothing. As she examined her surroundings, she saw a cave. Out lumbered a hairy Being, draped with an animal skin and quite bent over. Babla wasn't sure what kind of a Being it was, but it was dragging another Being of its own kind, pulling it by its hair. She shuddered at the sight of this.

Hearing the sound of running water, Babla continued to walk and soon arrived at the sea. The trap door opened again, so she went into the tunnel, coming out at the sandy bottom of the water. She saw a jellyfish, opening . . . and closing . . . opening . . . and closing . . . .

"Isn't life just like this?" Babla thought. "Opening . . . and closing . . . ." She could feel Alan's consent.

The sand opened and she went through a passage to still another sea and found a sea star, just lying there. Babla detected no movement whatsoever, yet she felt a vibrant, intense aliveness all around the creature. It felt as if it were moving, even though it appeared motionless. Alan whispered, "Deeper than movement there is silence—where all movement originates, the beginning and end of all things. The seed of action is buried in the silence."

A tunnel formed in the sand and Babla entered, coming out at the beginning where Alan and Black Panther awaited. Babla was excited and full of news about her explorations.

However, she needed to explore one more world. "This world," Alan said, "is not within your world, but next to it. Slimy Joe has thrown a key that belongs to Rabia into that world. It will unlock her ability to receive money. You need to find this key and bring it back."

Babla didn't know the difference between all these worlds, yet it didn't seem to matter. Alan lifted his hand and a veil formed to the left of Babla. She stepped through it into the kitchen of a house. A woman was cooking while a little girl and boy sat at the kitchen table, playing together. They were about five years old and dressed alike. "They look like twins," thought Babla.

She approached them and said, "I'm sorry, I don't mean to disturb your game, but I've come from another world and need to find a key. Do you have it?" She knew that the woman couldn't see her, but wasn't sure about the children.

The twins looked at her giggling; then the boy took out a golden key from his pocket and handed it to Babla. She thanked them and left, wondering why children can see beyond the veils while most grownups cannot.

Back in her own world, she gave the key to Alan, who hugged her lovingly. "You did great, Babla. We'll take this to our next meeting and give it to Eternal Friend."

GOLDEN QUEEN: Enjoying Abundance

Back in the meeting room with all the Inner Beings, Inner Guides, and Rabia, Alan gave the golden key to Eternal Friend. Slimy Joe was obviously not pleased.

Mr. Money turned to Slimy Joe. "I understand your concern about my past behavior," he said. "But, I don't have to repeat the mistakes I made in the other world. Just like you aren't going around stealing money or pirating any longer."

Aha! Babla connected the world where she saw the pirate boy to her own; it was the world of Slimy Joe. Slimy Joe was nodding his head.

"I don't want to make the same mistakes," Mr. Money went on, "so maybe we can find one of the Inner Guides to help us."

Everyone looked at Eternal Friend, who merely pointed to the door. In the silence of anticipation, Babla heard the door creak open, inch by inch. "Whoever is here is definitely not in a hurry," she thought.

When the door was finally open, a woman stood at the entrance. She was dressed in a golden gown decked with glitter and white lace, her golden hair pinned up, except for soft curls that fell about her neck.

"Dignity and elegance," Babla thought, "dignity and elegance."

Slowly she came in and seated herself next to Rabia. "I am Golden Queen," she announced with a firm, yet liquid voice. "I am the missing Inner Guide. Mr. Money and Slimy Joe need my presence in order to avoid the mistakes of their past worlds. I am glad to be here." Her smile was as filled with light as was everything else about her.

Babla couldn't resist the temptation any longer. She walked over to Golden Queen to touch her dress. Then she realized that Fireball had come from the opposite side of the table to do the same. Golden Queen took both little girls on her lap. Babla felt her heart open up to Fireball. Reaching over, she gently touched Fireball's cheek. Fireball turned and stuck out her tongue, at which Babla leaned over and kissed it. Fireball was speechless in spite of bright blue eyes that danced mischievously. She took Babla's hand and they both settled down on Golden Queen's lap.

After Golden Queen was introduced to everyone, Eternal Friend presented her with the golden key. She took it and guided all of them down dark steps to a door. It was locked. The key fit, the door opened, and they entered. Babla thought she was dreaming: The room was brimming from wall to ceiling with gold and jewels. Soon, all of them were climbing up the golden mountain, laughing and throwing gold at each other. It was such fun!

"There is nothing wrong or bad about gold or money," said Golden Queen. "It is the attachment to money that creates misery. If we think our happiness depends on how rich we are, we will never feel happy. Happiness is an inner state of being. We can enjoy having money without being slaves to it. Likewise, if our joy is real, the presence or absence of money will not affect our contentment in life."

Both Mr. Money and Slimy Joe agreed to spend some time with Golden Queen, learning a more balanced view of money—neither being attached to nor rejecting it, but simply enjoying the energy and beauty of gold.

The three of them stayed in the golden room after the others left. Babla and Fireball looked at each other, giggling; they liked the sparkles of the gold.

MS. ROMANTIC: Opening to Intimacy

Back in the room with the round table, everybody took their places. Babla was curious—what was to happen next? Rabia began to speak. She said how grateful she was to everyone for creating this beautiful Inner Family, in which living had become a fun, joyful, meaningful process. The Beings at the table were holding hands, their faces open and smiling.

In the silence, a sigh came from above. Looking up, they saw Ms. Romantic lying on her cloud, glancing down in a trance-like state.

"You've handled everyone else's problems," she mocked in her dreamy voice. "Maybe now you can find my Knight in Shining Armor, so I can find happiness, too."

"Ms. Romantic," Alan said casually, "tell us exactly what you need to be happy."

"I told you already," her reply drifted down from the cloud. "I need my Knight in Shining Armor. He will come on a white horse, rescue me from this cloud, and live with me happily ever after. My dream will have come true."

"She must be joking," Babla thought, sitting on Alan's lap.

"No. She really means it," Alan replied.

Babla could see Fireball, who was holding Miriam's hand, start to make faces. "It's boring to live happily ever after," Fireball voiced her opinion.

Ms. Romantic's soft face came out of the cloud, her eyes blinking with surprise. "Boring?" she asked. "Why?"

"Because," answered Fireball, "happily ever after is not real. And anything not real soon becomes boring; it feels empty and numb."

"Fireball," Eternal Friend broke in, "tell us what is real."

"Look at nature," said Fireball. "What you see there is real. Trees grow and bend with storms, birds make nests in them, they go away and other birds come, they die and others are born. Things are happening constantly in nature.

Like in the sea, waves come and go—all the time. Change is what is real; anything that is 'forever' is stuck. I love change; it's exciting."

"All change in nature is grounded in earth," Amazon Woman added. "Because of the solid, supportive earth, everything else can flow and shift and change."

"Hm." Fireball looked directly at the Amazon, an intense spark in her eyes. "I'd never thought of the earth. Yet, what you're saying feels right."

Babla was in awe of the wisdom coming from Fireball. "So behind all her anger," she thought, "is an intense, focused, fiery energy that makes things move." She was delighted. Then she realized that it was Rabia's awareness coming through Fireball.

"Exactly," Alan whispered to her. "The more you have felt safe and taken care of, the more you have been able to see reality through Rabia's eyes. Something similar is happening to Fireball. The more her anger is acknowledged by all of us, the more it turns into enthusiasm. Now she can see the world more clearly, adding her unique Essence Energy to Rabia's life."

"What is Essence Energy?" Babla asked.

"Each Being has this powerful energy in his or her Center," Alan replied. "The Inner Beings who are not aligned with the Adult Self pull some of this energy away from the Adult's Core, leaving less energy for the person.

"When Fireball wasn't allowed her anger, the enthusiasm that is usually behind all anger wasn't accessible to Rabia. A big part of Rabia's fire energy became tied up in Fireball, and so it wasn't expressed in Rabia's outer life. Now, all this energy that Fireball has been sitting on can be used in creative and beautiful ways."

Babla felt warm and safe. She was glad to be in the room with the round table in the company of the Inner Beings and Inner Guides.

"But doesn't the earth move, too?" Eric asked.

"Yes," Amazon Woman explained. "But much more slowly than the rest of nature. This way it can be a steady foundation for all change."

"Right at the center of change is stillness," added Eternal Friend. "This is where all movement comes from. The silence nurtures everything."

"That means all change and movement come from a still Center, yet are supported by a slow-moving earth," Fireball summed it up. "I like this!"

Babla did, too.

"What about my Knight in Shining Armor?" Ms. Romantic asked, troubled. "I need my Knight!"

Looking up at the cloud, Babla wondered what it was that kept Ms. Romantic separate from the rest of them. Without knowing why, she thought of Contented Sage. "Our attitudes and beliefs about life, about ourselves, and about others create a kind of dream around us," he used to say. "This dream then comes in between us and the reality of the moment, whatever that may be. It all depends on the strength of the dream. If it is very strong, we can't see through to what is real. Thus, we miss out on life."

Upon first hearing these words, Babla had felt confused and couldn't understand what they meant. Now, her eyes lit up with insight: Ms. Romantic's dream was made out of the belief that true happiness can be attained only by being rescued by a Knight in Shining Armor. There is no other way. This dream creation seemed to be so strong that she wasn't able to see the reality of the situation, which was . . .

What was the reality of this situation, anyway?

Babla looked around. She saw the Inner Guides, Inner Beings, and Rabia sitting at a big table. She saw their clothes, their faces, their hands. She could see parts of the room, and there was a lot of space in it. She felt Alan's chest against her back. She heard his breathing. She noticed a freshness in the air and a sweet taste in her mouth. Babla felt content. There was nothing else she needed right now. She also realized how being in reality helped her relax.

"You have come a long way, Babla," said Alan. "Remember your life before you met White Swan?"

Babla did. "I was so miserable then. My needs were not being met. I was lost and terribly lonely."

Babla stopped and sat upright. "You mean," she turned to Alan, "that it was not reality, and I was just lost in a dream of being lonely and miserable?"

Alan nodded.

"Well," said Babla, looking up at the cloud, "if I could get out of my dream, I'm sure Ms. Romantic can get out of hers. But how?"

"Trust in the Mystery of Life."

Babla leaned back and relaxed, pondering Alan's wise words. She didn't know what to do, so she didn't do anything.

Miriam tossed a smile up at Ms. Romantic. "You and I are alike in some ways," she told her. "We both believe we need an outer man to find true happiness. And yet, look at me. Just feeling my Love and shining it out, I'm very satisfied. On top of it, when I see what it does to the Inner Beings who receive it, I feel grateful."

Ms. Romantic was nodding her head, not knowing what to say.

Eternal Friend took the floor. "Life is generous. It always offers more than one option for true happiness, depending on what our real desires are. For example, do you want a Knight in Shining Armor, or do you want to be happy?"

"Oh!" replied Ms. Romantic, nearly falling off her cloud. "You mean they don't just automatically go together?"

"That's exactly what I mean." The glow of Love surrounded him now, and it seemed to be getting stronger. Next, it started circling Ms. Romantic's cloud.

Ms. Romantic was so dumbfounded she didn't notice the Love. "Then, what I really want is to be happy. But I can't be without a man!" she objected, with a hint of alarm.

"I agree," said Eternal Friend. "You need a man, at least for now. Not necessarily an outer man, though. Let's start with an inner man."

Babla was confused. "Does Eternal Friend really believe she needs a man, Alan?"

"No, but until Ms. Romantic comes down from her cloud and sits at the table, she won't feel the Love and support available to her here. Because she's still lost in her dream, he is taking it one step at a time."

The door burst open and a young man barged in. He wore only a loin cloth over his reddish brown skin. His long, jet black hair was held by a narrow band around his forehead. His legs were strong and his body muscular. With black eyes ablaze, he came closer to the table and introduced himself.

"I'm Zak," he said. "I am the Inner Knight." Calling up to the cloud, he pronounced, "I've come to rescue you, Ms. Romantic, so we can live happily ever after."

With that, he pulled down the cloud, took her into his arms, and brought her to the table.

"Oh, my Knight," gushed Ms. Romantic, practically melting. "You have come at last!" Her cheeks were rosy pink, her eyes dazed. Zak sat down with Ms. Romantic across his lap, beaming. They gazed deeply into each other's eyes, the way lovers do.

Babla, watching intently, caught a glimpse of Fireball looking ready to throw up. Babla shook her head. Ms. Romantic and Fireball surely were like night and day.

Ms. Romantic was surprised when she saw the table and all the Beings sitting there. Glancing from one to the other, she demanded, "Who are you?" Rabia was the first to introduce herself, the Inner Beings were next, then the Inner Guides. By proxy, Eternal Friend also introduced Golden Queen, Mr. Money, and Slimy Joe, who were still in the golden room.

Then there was silence.

Amazon Woman was the first to speak. "Ms. Romantic, we need you here. You are an important part of Rabia. Because you were up in your cloud, disconnected from the rest of us, Eric's doubts about relationships got out of hand. His idea that relationships don't work became too dominant in Rabia's outer life. Therefore, she could not have a balanced relationship. All of us together will enable her to relate to men in a way that is healthy and joyful."

Ms. Romantic wanted to know her role in all this. "You're an important mirror to Eric because you believe that relationships do work," offered Amazon Woman. "When Rabia is relating to an outer man and you are not around, Eric starts questioning one thing, then another, and another. Soon the whole relationship is shrouded in doubt. This affects Rabia so she can't see clearly. When you are with us, however, we can balance Eric's pessimism with your hope and optimism."

Tantrika took over. "You are important in Rabia's life when she is relating to a man. That's why it's good for you to spend time now with Zak, rather than looking for an outer knight. If you are wishing that someone will rescue you, and Miriam wants a man to give love to, you two might draw in a relationship that is not good for Rabia."

"That's an understatement," retorted Fireball.

Ms. Romantic digested this information while they waited patiently. "I see," she said at last. "As long as Rabia is not relating to an outer man, you want me to be here and have a relationship with Zak. But when she is relating to one, you want me to accompany Eric so that his doubts won't cloud Rabia's sense of reality."

"You've got it," Amazon Woman said smiling. She went over and gave Ms. Romantic a big hug. "I am delighted to have you join the Inner Family," she added.

Eternal Friend told everyone that their time of transformation under the tutelage of the Alchemist was over. Supported by her Adult Self, her Inner Guides, and all the Inner Beings, Babla needed to travel about in the world, putting these teachings into practice while relating to Outer Beings.

As they held hands around the table, Babla felt grateful for all she had learned and was ready for her next adventure. The sweet sensation of Love was palpable in the room.

III.
the healing journey

outer beings, inner guides

OTTER: *The Dance of Us*

Out in the world, one day Babla came to a seashore. Soft smooth sand was everywhere. Playful waves were rushing to the shore, then falling back out to sea. It was such a restful place that Babla decided to stop for a while.

She sat down on the warm sand, giggling as she watched the waves rush in and out. It seemed as if they were in a hurry to get somewhere, and yet there was nowhere to go. Between each coming in and going out was a stillpoint, in which time stopped and everything expanded. All this was so fascinating.

As she was looking at the sea, a smooth, gray head popped up, then went back down. Babla decided to look more closely. That really was a head in there, coming toward her. It came as close as it could to Babla without leaving the water.

"Hello little girl," said the head. "It's nice to have some company here."

"My name is Babla. Who are you?"

"I'm Otter."

"Are you a boy or a girl?" Babla wanted to know.

"A male," he said smiling, as the sun's rays played on his shiny head. Something about him was very appealing.

"It sure must be nice to be in the water and swim," said Babla longingly. "I wish I was in there, too."

"Come in and I'll show you how to dance in water. It is an art. You have to trust that the water is carrying you; you have to let go into the sea; then you have to imagine you and I are one. It's not you here and me there; it's 'us,' a new Being created by you and me becoming one.

"If you dance only your dance and I dance mine, we can never dance together. To dance together, the 'us' has to dance our dance. When you and I become one, there is only one dance."

"Sounds good to me." Babla took off her clothes and walked in. When she reached the otter, he took her by the hand and started whirling her around. They were going deep into the sea now, twisting and turning, deeper and deeper. Babla couldn't figure out where her body ended and Otter's began.

"All right," said Otter. "As I start melting into you, you start melting into me. Trust the water—it holds you, it cradles you."

Their energy merged into each other until they became one. Suddenly, everything changed. Instead of twisting and turning together, they were dancing! The new Being called "us" was dancing its dance.

Time stopped. It could have been for one moment or an eternity. Then, suddenly, they found themselves back on the shore.

"I must return to the sea," said Otter. "I'll come back tomorrow and we'll dance some more."

Babla stayed by the seashore for some time. Every day Otter came to teach her more about the dance of "us." Babla was very happy. She soon started feeling more spacious inside, as if her heart had more room.

She learned to trust the sea; it was her friend and ally. She could lie on her back and let the water carry her, feeling the ripples on her skin.

Some days Otter came and they just played in the water. They giggled and laughed, splashing water into each other's faces. Then without warning, right in the middle of their frolic, the stillpoint would arrive. Time would stop, everything would expand, and the dance of "us" would begin.

For Babla, these were days, weeks, months of rejuvenation, of deep healing, of laughter and tears of joy. Then, one day, she knew it was time to continue her healing journey. Saying good-bye to Otter, she left the sea, happy to have learned the dance of "us."

LION WOMAN AND DEER LADY: The Beauty of Friendship

One day Babla came upon a valley. The big blue sky stretched above her with no beginning and no end. Lots of sun, beautiful rolling hills—everything seemed to be round, soft, and spacious here.

Ahead was a dark wooden house with a red roof and lots of windows. Flowers of every type and color were all around. Amazed, Babla's big eyes examined the flowers. She knew they were alive; they seemed to be dancing, or maybe they were singing. Were they trying to talk to her?

Out of nowhere came a roar. Babla wasn't quite sure whether she should be scared or not. She was searching for what had made the sound when the door of the house opened and a huge lion appeared.

Babla's little heart made a jump. "Oh my, I hope this lion had his lunch already. Otherwise, this will be the end of my journey." Her mind was telling her to run for her life, and yet she couldn't stop staring. The golden mane, the majestic body—so proud, so powerful, so strong. And, there was something else . . . .

The lion took a few steps toward Babla. She could see the light in his golden-green eyes. The whole sky seemed hidden in them. In contrast to his fierce image, the lion's eyes were laughing; in fact, they were giggling with amusement. Babla had never heard of lions with eyes like this.

Despite her impulse to run away, she couldn't stop herself from asking; "What kind of a lion are you?"

Right in front of Babla, the lion started changing his shape. Within seconds, she could see a woman emerging. The less visible the lion, the more solid the woman became until there was no lion left. She was magnificent, standing there with her silver hair and a long golden dress the same color as the lion's mane. Her eyes were also the same—an electric golden-green.

Stunned, all Babla could do was go into the vastness of these incredibly wise eyes. In their depth, she absorbed knowledge about the ancient earth, mysteries long forgotten, the masculine in the feminine, and the feminine in the masculine.

Babla spiraled down, down into the woman's eyes. At the very bottom was silence—penetrating, fully alive, fully present.

In a flash, the glorious eyes became the clear blue sky and Babla, a white seagull. She was soaring free, flying in ecstasy with no past and no future, the present the only place to be.

Babla gradually landed, only to realize that she was still looking into the eyes of a woman who, moments ago, had been a lion.

"I am Lion Woman. Welcome to my home," she smiled graciously.

"I am Babla, and I'm here because I need to learn things from you. At least that's what my Guides said. There's someone in this valley who will be my teacher. I hope it's you." At that moment, Amazon Woman, her Guide, whispered yes in her ear.

Babla asked why Lion Woman had come in the form of a male lion instead of a female.

"Because I'm here to teach Oneness beyond duality. The male is in the female, and the female is in the male," she answered.

They went into the house to make tea and prepare something to eat. Lion Woman said, "You must know, Babla, that growth is never in only one direction. As you learn from me, I also will learn from you."

Babla, who was listening and watching, realized that Lion Woman was making tea for three. She asked who else might be coming.

"There is a friend I want you to meet. It will be helpful for both of you to get acquainted."

They carried the brimming tray out to the lawn and were setting up for tea when Babla heard a faint crinkle of leaves. She looked up to spy a doe at the edge of the trees where the meadow ended. Babla was touched by her grace, her long elegant neck and big brown eyes as soft as velvet. A large round drum was hanging from her back.

With careful steps, the deer came closer. She watched Babla cautiously, her soft gaze focused now, penetrating Babla's very Essence.

Then she stopped, as if she had found what she was looking for and had made her decision. Babla could see her shifting from a grown-up deer into a youngster, then into a fawn and back again into her original size. Babla turned questioning eyes to Lion Woman.

"This is Deer Lady. She is still in a transition state. She hasn't yet come to her full maturity. That's why she keeps changing her form. Once she finds her wholeness, she will be called Deer Woman and will be able to change back and forth between a woman and a doe whenever she wants to. Then, she'll play the drum for us."

Deer Lady sat down on the grass, and all three had a wonderful meal together.

THE VULTURES: Facing Fear and Judgment

Babla stayed with Lion Woman in the beautiful, sunny valley and Deer Lady came and went as she pleased. In time, Babla realized the deep bond between these two Beings; many times they wouldn't even talk, yet the way they blended with each other was great to watch.

They were all having a picnic in the garden one day when Babla heard a frightful screeching in the air. She looked up to see two big birds flying toward them.

"Oh, no," Deer Lady sounded an alarm. "Not the Vultures again!"

Lion Woman became very quiet inside and out. The Vultures, flying in tandem, swept closer and closer. Then, with a fierce battle cry, they dove for Lion Woman. They were on her now, poking at her, going for blood.

To Babla's surprise, Lion Woman went totally limp; she seemed to have sucked all her life back into herself, not fighting back in any way.

Deer Lady got up and caught the birds' attention with a peculiar motion of her head. Interrupted, they just looked at her and flew away. But, stopping in mid-air, they started picking at each other while making awful noises so loud Babla had to cover her ears.

Then, unexpectedly, one of the Vultures dove for Deer Lady, aiming at her heart. She quickly turned aside to receive the attack in a less vulnerable area of her body. Fighting the Vulture in return, she took the bird by surprise and it retreated. After it had joined the other Vulture, both disappeared in the sky.

Babla had so many questions, she didn't know where to begin, so she remained silent. Lion Woman was back to life now from her place of inner retreat, but the golden-green eyes that usually reflected such depth and ecstasy were covered by a film of sadness.

"Years ago," she explained, "I befriended these Vultures, and they were good friends at first. After some time, though, they started attacking me. It is hard to understand because they don't always do it. That is, sometimes when they come, they are very nice and we have tea together. And, only one of the Vultures attacks Deer Lady. For some reason, the other never joins in; it just watches. They are strange birds."

"Yes," agreed Deer Lady, "very strange, indeed."

"Why didn't you fight back?" asked Babla, looking at Lion Woman.

"If I would become a lion and attack," she replied, "it would be their end. And that's not what I want. I still remember the good times we've had, and I don't want to harm them.

"In their own way, they've been helpful to me and a lot of other Beings. And, because one of the Vultures attacks her, Deer Lady is learning how to stand up for herself, which makes her stronger on her journey to become Deer

Woman. Life works in mysterious ways," concluded Lion Woman, her eyes now more wise than sad.

"Still," protested Babla, "growing by being attacked doesn't make much sense to me. I'd rather learn in a supportive way."

Lion Woman's golden-green eyes had regained their sparkle, and intense joy was shining through. "One would wish," she replied, "that we all could learn our lessons easily. However, it doesn't always happen that way. Sometimes we may benefit from a little friction, some sort of challenge."

Deer Lady and Babla looked at each other. They both were wishing it weren't that way, yet both knew Lion Woman was right.

"If that's the case," said Babla, "then it seems best to go toward the challenges and welcome them."

"That's a good idea," Deer Lady agreed. "It feels like this is exactly what I need to be doing with the Vultures: standing straight, fully facing them instead of ignoring them or running away." Lion Woman was nodding her head.

"What about you, Lion Woman?" asked Babla. "How are you growing through all of this?"

There was a moment of silence as Lion Woman went inside herself. Then, in front of Babla and Deer Lady, she started transforming into a lion again. moments later, Lion stood in front of them, his golden mane glowing in the sun, emanating power from every cell of his body. It was breathtaking. Slowly and deliberately he opened his mouth to emit an earth-shattering roar—one of rage, desperation, and frustration.

Absolute silence came over the valley. Even the birds had stopped singing. Then Lion started changing back into the Woman, her golden-green eyes aglow. Gazing into these eyes, Babla marveled at their power. Yet, it was a different kind of power than the lion's. What was it?

At that moment, Lion Woman started talking. "I believe my lesson is to stay in my Love, no matter what they do." Now Babla understood the power in those golden-green eyes.

It was time for Babla to leave Lion Woman and Deer Lady and continue her journey. The friends gave each other warm good-bye hugs, knowing that some day they would meet again.

On her way back to the forest, Babla wondered whether she also had some lessons to learn, some growing to do through the Vultures. She certainly hoped not. Just in case, though, she wanted to be prepared. She invited her Guides.

Amazon Woman appeared, her black hair tossing freely about her shoulders as she came closer. "You will be tested by them," she said. "If you pass the tests, they won't attack you. As a first step, just watch. Whenever you spot them, near or far, simply look at them with curiosity and interest, no judgment. I'll be with you." She gave Babla a hug that was loving, strong, and reassuring at the same time. Then she disappeared.

Forewarned, Babla went on her way. After a few days she reached the beginning of the forest. There were already some scattered trees nearby and on one of them sat two birds. "I wonder...." Her suspicions were confirmed when she recognized the Vultures. They were perched high on a branch, motionless.

Remembering Amazon Woman's suggestions, Babla observed with curiosity. "These birds have a singular intention," thought Babla. "Once they know what they want, they simply go for it."

Something about their focused, directed energy was very appealing to her. "If only," she sighed, "they wouldn't attack and hurt other Beings."

"It's hard to say whether that would be good or bad," argued Amazon Woman, who had reappeared at the sight of the Vultures. "We don't know each Being's unique growth process. The most important thing for you right now is to stay with your own unfolding, your own lessons; and for that, just observe them without judgment."

Babla was very close to the birds. As she passed by, she stopped and turned her gaze toward them. "Hi, I'm Babla."

"Hi," answered the Vultures. "It's nice to meet you."

Babla simply looked at their feathers, their beaks, their talons, their piercing eyes. "Have a good day, Vultures," she said with a smile, starting to walk again.

"You too, Babla," they replied. "See you soon."

"See you soon," repeated Babla to herself. "I guess I'm not done with them yet." She knew, though, she had passed the first test.

FUZZY BROWN BEAR: The Joy of Self-Acceptance

One day while Babla was walking in the forest, not quite knowing what to do with herself after she had left the Vultures, she came upon a bear. This was a stocky brown animal with bright green eyes. Even though the bear was much bigger and stronger than Babla, for some unknown reason she felt no fear.

"Hi, Bear," she said. "My name is Babla. I'm looking for something to do."

"Hi," replied the friendly bear. "I'm Fuzzy Brown Bear. You can call me Kiwi if you like. I'm looking for some help."

"Oh," said Babla, excited. "Maybe I can help you. That would give me something to do."

The bear sat on the ground and broke into tears. "I want to be a he-bear. My life would be so much better if I were a he-bear. I'm so unhappy. Can you do something about that?"

Babla considered her predicament. "I don't see anything wrong with being a she-bear. You're so wonderfully fuzzy and cuddly. I'm glad you're a she-bear."

"Oh dear," sighed Kiwi, "I wish I could believe you. You're just trying to be kind. But, if I were a male, I'd be much stronger and faster, and the forest creatures would give me more respect. I'd be much happier that way. Life is not fair. There are so many he-bears around; why can't I be one, too?"

Babla wasn't quite sure what to do, when she heard Alan's whisper, "Introduce Kiwi to her Inner Mate."

"Well," Babla began, "you can see that I'm a she-person, and there's also a he-person inside of me. It seems like everyone who is a she outside has a he inside, and everyone who is a he outside has a she inside. That way, everyone has both."

Kiwi stopped crying and peered up at Babla, blinking with curiosity. "Please continue," she said, intrigued. "I want to know more about this."

Babla told Kiwi about Alan. She told the story of how they had met and how knowing her Inner Mate had changed her life.

"You mean I can have a he-bear inside, too?" she asked, full of interest.

Babla nodded. "Sometimes," she said, "it's hard to believe Alan is inside of me. I can see him so clearly that I'm sure he's on the outside. But I'm the only one who can see him. That's why I know he's not really outside of me."

They decided to try it out. Kiwi closed her eyes and Babla asked her inner he-bear to show himself so that Kiwi would know he was here.

Golden light started coming out of Kiwi's heart and belly. Faint at first, it grew more and more dense, then began taking a form. When the light was fully shaped, a big brown fuzzy he-bear stood before them.

"But you can't be her Inner Mate!" objected Babla. "I can see you, too."

The he-bear smiled. "Yes, I am Kiwi's Inner Mate. And, eyes like yours can see the invisible. Just like Mother Hen's; remember how she could see your Inner Guides?"

"That's true," said Babla, scratching her curly blond head. "I hadn't thought of that."

Kiwi had opened her eyes and was examining the he-bear with a quizzical look. He took a few steps forward, plopped down in front of her, and took her paws into his.

"Hi, Kiwi," he said, gently. "I'm your Inner Mate, and my name is Zoran. I am very strong and will protect you from any possible danger. I have a big heart with a lot of love in it for you. I want to hold you in my arms and love you in every way you want to be loved.

"From now on, you can enjoy being a she-bear. Because I am a part of you, you are also a he-bear. You and I together make up a whole bear."

Soft tears of happiness were rolling down Kiwi's fuzzy cheeks, and her green eyes danced with delight. When Babla got up to leave, she heard Kiwi repeating softly, "My dream has come true, my dream has come true." She knew she would meet Kiwi again, next time as a whole and very satisfied bear.

HUMANGUS: Power of Wisdom

Walking in the forest, Babla stopped short when confronted by a pair of shoes—each one as tall as herself. Before she could move, a giant hand came down from the sky and scooped her up. Higher and higher she went, the air hissing all around. Her big blue eyes grew even bigger when the hand stopped moving and she found herself looking into an enormous face.

"Who are you?" she blurted. As the huge mouth opened, she could see white teeth and a big pink cave behind them. "What if he swallows me?" She shook at the thought. Then she heard rumbling sounds and realized these were words.

"I am Humangus the Giant, Humangus the Giant. And, if you don't do as I say, I will eat you, dress and all," the voice was saying.

Horrified, Babla, dared to peek down the huge body of a giant man. Catching her breath, she gradually became aware of his fire red hair and the beard that reached down to his ankles.

"Oh my," she gulped in a wave of panic. "What shall I do?" Not being able to get in touch with any of her Guides, Babla realized this must be a lesson of the highest order, so she called on the Higher Self, closing her eyes and trying to imagine a golden light at the top of her head as best she could.

She heard a quiet voice saying: "Open your heart, Babla."

Babla opened her eyes, and putting her hands on her heart, she shouted, "I love you, Giant!" She hoped her voice was loud enough for him to hear.

Surprised sea-colored eyes stared back. Slowly, a teardrop, as big as Babla herself, formed in the Giant's left eye. With a whoosh, it rushed down his body. The moment it touched his heart, Babla heard another sound, as if a door were opening.

Following the sound, Babla saw that the door to the Giant's heart had opened, and a very sad little boy stood slumped at the threshold. He sat down, head bent, looking lonely and forlorn. Humangus was speechless and so was Babla. "I would do anything to help this little boy," she thought. "What can I do to make him smile?"

"Be careful, Babla," Amazon Woman cautioned. "It's not your responsibility to make this boy happy. Only Humangus himself can do that. All you need to do is be truthful to yourself."

Babla closed her eyes and felt her heart to find Truth. A song burst out of her heartspace and she started singing. Quietly at first, then louder and louder she sang:

> *I love you, whether you know it or not,*
> *I love you, whether I show it or not.*
> *There are so many things I haven't said inside my heart,*
> *Perhaps now it's a good time to start.*[1]

---

[1] This is a Sufi Dance song I learned from Aneeta Makena

As she sang, tears gushed down the little boy's cheeks. Soon, his whole body was shaking with their power while he cried and cried for what seemed like an eternity. Babla kept singing her Heartsong, and the little boy's crying went deeper and deeper. The tears were now coming all the way from his belly.

And then his tears stopped as abruptly as they had started. As the boy looked up, Babla could see his pink cheeks and misty sea-colored eyes, bright and shining. There was even a faint smile on his lips. "Maybe that's a smile of relief," thought Babla, "or perhaps he is happy not to be hiding anymore."

They heard the Giant muttering, "I didn't know you were still in there. I locked you up so long ago, I was sure you were dead by now." His voice was soft now, almost nostalgic.

Babla asked, "Why did you lock him up?"

"Because I had to. I couldn't be a scary giant if people knew he was part of me."

"What are you going to do now?" asked Babla.

"I don't know." Humangus pondered. "What do you do when you don't know what to do?"

"I ask my Guides for assistance."

"Guides," repeated the Giant thoughtfully. "I wonder if I have any Guides."

"Everybody does," replied Babla enthusiastically. "All you need to do is really want to get in touch with them and invite them."

She heard the firm, loving voice of the Amazon. "Be careful, Babla. This is as far as you can go. Anything beyond this point he has to accomplish himself." Babla became quiet and sat down in the Giant's palm.

Humangus turned to the little boy. "How do you feel about asking our Guides for help?"

The little boy gazed at the Giant with hope in his eyes. It was clear that he didn't want to be locked up any longer. Humangus reached over with his empty hand and picked him up, so that the boy could lean against his fingers. Next, the Giant opened his mouth wide and bellowed, "If I have Guides, I need you now!"

There was absolute silence in the forest, and then they heard footsteps. Anticipation was in the air as the footsteps came closer and closer. Then, at last, they could see an old woman and an old man, holding hands and slowly progressing toward them. Both were dressed in long brown garments. The woman had gray wavy hair and was holding a large silk pouch in one hand. The man had a white beard and pure white hair, and was carrying a simple walking stick.

Seeing them approach, Humangus started to laugh. "You can't be my Guides. You're too old," he claimed.

Showing no sign of response, the couple continued walking until they were very close to the Giant. Then, both lifted their heads and looked straight at him, their eyes blue and clear as the sky.

Humangus was drawn into another world—one of wisdom, compassion, and inner joy. He took a deep breath and sat down, still holding Babla in one hand and the little boy in the other. Tipping his head, he examined the couple more closely. In spite of their frail, old bodies, he noticed a golden glow emanating from them.

"I see," he sighed in surrender.

"I'm glad," replied the old woman.

"Ask your question," said the old man. And so, the Giant asked what to do with the little boy.

The woman said, "He needs a mother."

The man said, "And you need a mate."

Humangus was confused. "How will I ever find a mother for him and a mate for myself? Every woman on earth is afraid of me!" he burst out.

The old man began telling the Giant about one woman who wasn't afraid of him. "This woman is deeply embedded within you. She is your Inner Mate. She has been dormant all these years, but when she awakens, she will be the perfect mate for you and the perfect mother for the little boy. Once you've found her, your life will change and you will be deeply content."

Humangus was intrigued but not convinced. "That sounds good, but what will I do if I'm content? Nobody will be afraid of me anymore. How can I protect the forest if nobody respects me?"

It was the woman's turn to speak. "You have been using only fear and anger to do your job. Now you will learn to protect through wisdom. The power of anger is not real, it is based on fear. The power of wisdom is strong, deeply rooted yet soft."

"But you must be willing to let us teach you," added the old man. His quiet yet powerful manner was very touching.

Babla's little heart was beating so fast she was sure everyone could hear. Just as she opened her mouth, she heard Alan's gentle voice. "Shhh, Babla," he advised. "Be still and watch. This is a decision Humangus has to make by himself. All you can do is keep your heart open to him."

Babla became very still and touched her heart, and it opened like a beautiful, blue-violet iris. Deep inside the flower, she could hear her Heartsong, and her cheeks became pink with gratitude and joy.

During this time Humangus had been silent, sitting with his eyes shut. Now he opened them and saw the little boy in his palm, nestled against his fingers. A teardrop, as big as the boy himself, started forming in the Giant's right eye and went tumbling down his body. When it touched his heart, a second door opened, and when the tear reached the Giant's belly, yet another door cracked open.

Humangus felt movement in his body. From the second door of his heart, the top part of an embryo emerged, and from the door in his belly, the bottom part of an embryo came out; then, both slid all the way down to his feet.

The old woman picked up the top part of the embryo and the man, the bottom part. Very gently they brought them closer together. Just before joining the parts, they stopped, closed their eyes, and aligned their breathing.

Then the man asked Humangus, "Do we have your permission? Remember, this will change your life."

The Giant, trying not to show his eagerness, replied with a simple nod.

One last slight move and the embryo was whole. The little boy took a deep breath, all of his muscles relaxing. His eyes filled with relief and gratitude.

As the old man offered his walking stick to the Giant to hold, the huge hand beneath Babla started gently to move. Soon she found herself sitting next to the little boy.

Now, the old woman went to work. Out of her silk pouch she took a large shell and held it over the embryo on the ground. Even Babla could hear the sound of the ocean coming from inside the shell. This rhythm gave breath to the small form. Although it was breathing now, it seemed barely alive.

Next, the woman retrieved two handfuls of earth from her pouch and covered the embryo. Starting to grow, the embryo became a fetus, a newborn baby, a toddler, a small child, a teenager, a young woman, and at last a beautiful lady giant, with straight black hair all the way down to her ankles. And yet, her body showed no movement.

This time, the old woman took a feather from her pouch. While she was holding it over the giant woman, the feather became a white bird—a beautiful, huge bird flying slowly and gracefully. The white bird entered the woman's body, and Babla could see a subtle change, as if life was in her, as if she now had Spirit.

The old woman nodded with satisfaction. She reached into her pouch one last time and removed a small wooden stick. The moment it was out of the pouch, the stick burst into fire. She handed it to the old man, and he, turning to Humangus, lit the walking stick the Giant was holding.

The old man said, "This is as far as we can guide you. The last step you must take by yourself."

Slowly, Humangus bent over and touched the flames of the stick to the woman giant's soles—first one, then the other—dowsing the fire when he was finished.

Immediately, her eyes opened and she sat up. She reached over and cradled the little boy, holding him close to her chest. "Rest now, little one. I'll always be with you." With a smile, she brought her lips close to Babla's ear and whispered, "Thank you for your Heartsong."

Babla blushed. All this time she had thought no one was listening to her sing.

Then, the newly-born giant turned to Humangus and announced in a clear, loving voice, "I am your Inner Mate."

Babla heard the sweet rumbling sound of two giant hearts meeting, then merging into one. She knew that Humangus was on his way to learning how to protect the forest through the power of wisdom.

When it was time for Babla to leave, she joyfully said good-bye to everybody and continued on her journey.

THE WITCH IN THE CAVE: *Fear in the Heart*

One day, Babla's path led her outside the forest. The further she walked away from the trees, the more stones she encountered. Soon she was surrounded by rocks and mountains. Because she was getting tired and hungry, she began searching for a place to spend the night.

At dusk, Babla came to the opening of what looked like a cave. Hesitating only a moment, she decided to stay for the night. Babla entered through its small opening, and was surprised to find the cave quite large inside. More surprising, however, was the sight of a fire burning deep within the cavern.

On the one hand, Babla was tempted by the warmth of the fire; on the other, perhaps the fire was attended by a not-so-friendly Being. She heard Alan's whisper in her ear. "This is part of your journey."

Babla moved toward the flames. At the very corner of the cave, huddled in blankets, was a wrinkled woman. She had wild, curly hair and the clearest of blue eyes. Something in these eyes reminded Babla of a trapped animal. This woman could have been anywhere from 30 to 100 years old.

"Hi, my name is Babla. I'd like to spend the night here, if it's okay with you."

"I'm the Witch in the Cave," the woman offered, grinning.

Babla was alarmed. "I hope you're not going to cast a spell on me," she said in a high little voice.

"I'm a wise witch. I won't do you any harm. Besides, I'm in such fear that I couldn't do anything anyway."

"What are you afraid of?" asked Babla, perplexed.

"My heart is closed," answered the Witch most sadly. "As long as I'm afraid, my heart will stay closed. But as long as my heart is closed, the fear won't go away. So, I don't know where to start. The earth told me that I needed to wait for somebody to come to my rescue. It has to be somebody with a very pure heart though, as pure as a child's."

With a jolt, the Witch sat upright in her corner and stared at Babla. "Maybe you are the one."

"I should ask my Guides," replied Babla. "But I'm hungry and tired now. Could we talk more tomorrow?"

The Witch got up and fixed some food for them both, then she gave Babla a blanket to sleep in. All night long, Babla dreamt of deep blue waters, of waves playing with rocks, of a land that touched these waters, of birds flying over this sacred land, and of Beings sitting in a circle crying, laughing, and being silent together.

In the morning when Babla woke up, the Witch was preparing tea. When she heard Babla's dream, tears of joy rolled down her wrinkled face.

"You are the one!" she screeched. "You are the one!" She took the little girl by the hand and led her to a dark part of the cave. Touching the wall as if looking for something, the Witch moved her hand in a circle on the stone. The wall moved to the left, creating a window to look out of.

What they saw was exactly what Babla had seen in her dream.

Now it was the Witch's turn to explain: "When I open my heart and am not afraid anymore, this cave will disappear and I will live on the land which touches the sacred waters. I am the Creator of Sacred Spaces. Many people will come to sit on this sacred land; we will heal each other through our love, through laughter, and through tears. But I must first heal my heart and my fear. Will you help me?"

Babla was willing. "I would like to," she said. "But I have to check with my Inner Guides to see if it's okay."

When they sat down to drink their tea, Babla called on her Guides, and they came. This time, rather than whispering into her ear, as they usually did when Babla was with other Beings, they arrived in person. Alan, Amazon Woman, Black Panther, and Maya all came and sat down.

"This is the first of many circles for you, Wise Witch," Maya began. "Babla will be a catalyst so you can open your heart and melt away the fear. At some point, you will also need to spend time with Lion Woman and Humangus the Giant. Stay on your journey until you find them.

"Even though it will look like you are learning from them, do not let the outer form of things cloud the deeper truth," Maya informed her. "You have a lot to teach them.

"You also have things to teach Babla and the others even while they are helping you. All Beings will learn something just by spending time with you; no words are necessary. Always remember this. A Being called Wondering Magician will be an important part of your healing journey. Open your heart to him fully, and the stars will shower upon you."

Soon the Inner Guides got up to leave. Alan said they would give Babla further instructions as needed to assist the Witch's opening.

When the Guides were gone, Babla and the Witch bubbled with questions. "I wonder," said the Witch, "who Wondering Magician is."

"Me, too," replied Babla. "I've never heard of anybody with that name. How do you suppose he looks like?"

They knew that when the time was right, they would meet him. In the meantime, Babla decided to leave the cave and continue her journey. The Witch would go to find Lion Woman and Humangus, then they would meet back at the cave.

THE WITCH'S JOURNEY: *Finding Courage*

After Babla had gone, the Witch prepared for her journey. Even though she was still afraid, she no longer felt paralyzed. She would make it to Lion Woman somehow. The meeting with Babla and her Guides had provided just enough courage for her to leave the cave.

The Witch packed her bundle and left. She hadn't been out of the cave in so long that she had to walk very slowly at first, to take everything in. She walked through the rocky land, amazed that her fear was bearable.

Her thoughts were disrupted by a whimpering sound. Where was it coming from? She looked around but couldn't see anything, so she waited and listened. The sound was coming from behind a huge rock to her right. When she walked behind the rock, she saw a small animal huddled on the ground.

The Witch had discovered a white and brown spotted dog with long ears and very soft fur. She examined the dog, looking for a wound, but she found nothing wrong. At last she asked, "Why are you whimpering, if you're not hurt?"

"I'm not hurt. I'm paralyzed with fear. I'm so afraid, I can't move," the dog replied, weakly.

"Oh, great!" thought the Witch. "This is exactly what I need. As if my own fear weren't enough, here I meet a panicked dog." She sat down next to the dog and started stroking her fur—slowly, gently, deeply, lovingly. In a short while, the dog began to relax.

"My name is M. I'm a very loyal dog once I get over my fear. I can help you in many ways if you let me come with you."

The Witch considered this for some time and decided that a dog might prove useful. "The afraid Witch with her afraid dog," she said out loud. As funny as it sounded, it was right.

"Come on, M," she motioned to the dog. "Let's go. We have several long days of travel ahead of us." M didn't seem to mind this at all. She was wagging her tail, happy to follow the Witch. The Witch had to admit that she felt less afraid with the company of M.

They came to the forest. Right at the edge, between the rock land and the trees, was a big stone outcropping. On a ledge near the top was a Mermaid, sitting very still. She had long black hair; a shapely, sensuous body; a beautiful, dreamy face; and a fishtail instead of feet. To find a Mermaid here, without any water around, was most strange. As the Witch drew closer, she could see that the Mermaid was indeed very sad.

"Hi," she said looking up. "I'm the afraid Witch on my way to becoming the Wise Witch, and this is my afraid dog, M. I'm surprised to see you on this dry land, Mermaid."

The Mermaid sighed, tears rolling down her cheeks. "Oh, yes," she cried, looking down from her rock. "I've lost my ocean. I don't belong here. I feel like I'm dying. Where is my ocean? Can you help me find it?"

To see this stunning Mermaid without her ocean was so heartbreaking that the Witch knew she must help. "Maybe you can get on my back," she offered. "I can carry you awhile, rest when I need to, then carry you awhile longer. I'm sure we'll come across the ocean on the way to Lion Woman."

"Oh, no!" wailed the Mermaid. "Any ocean won't do. It has to be my ocean, and I've lost it."

"Well, where is your ocean?" asked the Witch, not quite understanding.

"Far, far away. I'll never find it again. Oh, poor me!" The Mermaid was so totally into her sadness that she seemed to have forgotten the presence of the Witch.

So the Witch left her there, wailing on the rock. As she continued on her own journey into the forest she gave a sigh. "If somebody doesn't want to be helped, there's nothing we can do, is there?" she remarked to M, who yipped in agreement.

The forest was much different than the rocky land. All the colors, the smells, the sounds of it were compelling. The Witch decided to have some lunch in this lovely place. While she was resting on the forest floor enjoying her meal, she heard a rustle. She looked up to see three little fairies right in front of her, giggling. A brown-haired one stood in between her two blond-haired companions. They were looking at the Witch with curiosity and amusement.

All three gathered around and began petting M, who seemed to be in heaven. They wanted to know where the Witch was going. In response, she told them her story, after which the brown-haired fairy turned so the Witch could see that both of her wings had been damaged. She could fly no more.

"Oh Witch, will you please repair my wings?" she begged, her blue eyes alight with hope.

"I'm not sure I can," admitted the Witch. "I'm not in my full wisdom, yet. Let me go visit Lion Woman first. On my way back, I'll meet you here again and we'll see what I can do."

The little fairy was overjoyed at the possibility of flying again. She promised she would wait for the Witch to return.

The Witch and M continued through the forest until they came to a lookout above a lush valley. From Babla's description, the Witch knew that Lion Woman's home had to be nearby. The Witch started trembling half with fear, half with excitement. Going down into the valley, she soon saw the house.

And then she heard the roar—a huge and terrible roar. She shook with panic now, hugging herself. She felt M around her legs and kneeled to hold the dog . . . or was the dog holding her?

After a few minutes of sitting cuddled on the ground, the Witch felt more calm. She remembered Babla's words about the lion, that he was also a woman and that Lion Woman wouldn't harm her in any way.

With some trepidation, she got up to investigate further. Then, suddenly she stopped, her mouth dropping open. A magnificent lion with a golden mane had just walked out of the trees next to the house. He was looking at her with a silent intensity the Witch had never seen before.

The animal was so splendid that the Witch forgot her fear. The sun rays shone like a halo around his mane, making him look like a creature from another world. He approached the Witch, stopping when he saw the terror in her eyes.

"Hi," said the Witch, pale and trembling. "I am the afraid Witch. Babla's Guides sent me here . . . for you to help me become a Wise Witch."

Hearing these words made Lion's golden-green eyes twinkle. Right in front of the Witch, he started shifting into Lion Woman. "Babla!" exclaimed Lion Woman with delight. "She sent you here? You must be her friend, then. Welcome."

The Witch felt strong arms surround her in a big hug. Caught by surprise, she melted with relief into Lion Woman. After what seemed like an eternity, her panic began to disappear—it was as if the earth had opened and was sucking up the fear, leaving her a hundred pounds lighter.

With a loud sigh, Lion Woman let go of the Witch, took her hands, and looked deeply into her clear eyes. "That's better," she said, smiling luxuriously. "Now we can go in and have a cup of tea."

Over tea, the Witch told her story. After some silence, Lion Woman offered, "You may stay here with me if you wish. And your dog is welcome, too. I must admit you have a lot of courage to have traveled this far. Let's see what we can do."

Lion Woman's eyes smiled. She went over to a huge basket, searching among crayons, ribbons, feathers, and all kinds of other creative things.

In a wink, her face lit up. "Ah!" she said. "There it is." She took something out of the basket and handed it to the Witch. It was a pearl-colored silk thread. The Witch looked at the thread, then back at Lion Woman with questioning eyes.

"It's for the little fairy," grinned Lion Woman, "to repair her broken wings. This is a very special thread; and you need a special needle for it. As you continue your journey, I'm sure you'll come across the needle."

The Witch stayed with Lion Woman for a while—maybe a few days, maybe a few weeks, or maybe a few months. Time didn't seem to exist. Every day, she got huge hugs, and more of her fear was sucked into the earth. She began feeling light and bubbly, yet solidly grounded, too.

When it was time for her to leave, she felt relaxed and grateful. This had been a wonderful opportunity to learn and mature, but somewhere deep inside she knew the time would come when she could also share the wisdom. With M following behind, she departed with a sense of being full and empty at the same time.

LITTLE KNIGHT: True Identity

The Witch left the green valley to look for Humangus in the forest, following Babla's directions. On the way, she came to an intersection. She thought for sure she should go left, but she had an irresistible urge to go right, and right she went. The more she walked, the more she realized she was going into the desert, which definitely was not the place to find the giant.

Just as she'd made up her mind to turn around, M started barking loudly. This startled the Witch because her dog had been so well mannered. Before she could do or say anything, however, M took off, running wildly into the desert. Calling for M didn't help, so the Witch decided to follow.

She went deeper and deeper into the desert where she saw little else but hot sand and a few large rocks. She was so happy she was wearing a hat! From a distance, the Witch could see M panting by a large boulder. A figure sat on the sand, propped against the rock.

The closer she came, the clearer she could see it was a teenage boy dressed like a knight—with armor and all! How was he surviving in this heat? He didn't have his headpiece on, so she could see his curly red hair, fiery like the desert, and big hazel eyes. He looked tired and unhappy. Her dog, usually afraid of everything and everybody, was lying in his lap totally relaxed.

"Hi," she said tentatively. "I'm the afraid Witch on my way to becoming the Wise Witch. Who are you?"

"I am Little Knight," was his sullen answer. "I'm supposed to become the Knight of Fire when I grow up, but I'd rather be the Knight of Water." He stretched his arms out toward the desert. "Look!" he said in a dread-filled voice. "All this desert is mine, but it's all dead! Nothing is alive here. Just sand. Millions and millions and millions of grains of sand. I am so bored! I'd rather be in the water, playing with the waves. But here I am, stuck!" He glared at the Witch and added, "You don't look afraid at all!"

The Witch sat down next to him and thought about his words. He was right; since she had left Lion Woman, she had not really felt afraid.

"But I'm not quite the Wise Witch yet, either," she replied. "Maybe for now I should just call myself the Witch." This felt right. She leaned against the rock and surveyed her surroundings—lots of hot sand. "It's all dead," Little Knight had said. And that's what it surely looked like.

All of a sudden she felt herself sinking, as if she were falling through the sand, as if she were the sand itself, becoming the desert . . . Then, the truth hit her! The desert was breathing! It was alive! It was pulsating with life! Not only that, but she became aware of so much life in the desert, not visible at first sight. She felt overwhelmed by the realization of it.

And yet, Little Knight wasn't aware of any of this. The Witch paused, puzzled about what to do. "I wonder whether I'm supposed to help you or not. I wish I was already the Wise Witch. But as things are, I get so easily confused."

Little Knight's eyes sparked. "Let's pretend!" he perked up, suddenly more animated. "Let's pretend you are the Wise Witch! What would you do if you were?"

"Well, I'd create an oasis for you . . . with lots of water to play in," she replied with a smile.

Little Knight jumped up, took her hand, and started coaxing her to follow. Visibly excited, he took her to a place not far from the rock. In the middle of this desert was a tall stone wall, circular in shape. They went through an iron gate and the Witch realized it was an oasis . . . or had been. Dried up fountains were all around, as were stone huts, now empty. Skeletons of huge palm trees, which must have been gorgeous at one time, dotted the landscape.

"There was water here once," Little Knight reminisced. "Somehow, when I was very little, it just dried up and everybody left. I wanted to leave, too, but I couldn't because all this belongs to me."

"If only you could bring back the water," sympathized the Witch. "But how?"

She sat on the edge of a stone well, feeling helpless. Then she remembered Babla and her Inner Guides. "If I had Inner Guides, I wonder what they would tell me now?" she mused. She was startled out of her melancholy by a voice coming directly from her heart. "M is the key you are looking for," it said before all became still once again.

"Did you hear it?" she asked Little Knight, her eyes popping.

"Hear what?" he asked back, sounding sad. "All I ever hear is the dreadful silence."

Maybe the voice belonged to one of her Inner Guides. The Witch called M and kneeled down, stroking the dog. "M," she whispered, "go find water. I need your help to find water for Little Knight."

M became very still, as if listening to a faraway sound. Then she went to the very middle of the oasis and started digging. The Witch had never known her afraid dog to be so intent on anything. Seeing the dog dig, Little Knight went into one of the small huts and brought out two shovels. They both dug into the earth most of that day, trying to help. Each time one of them was ready to give up, they would look at M, gaining strength from the determined dog, who had not stopped digging for even one moment.

Finally, M began to bark and moved away from the big hole they had dug. The Witch realized that M wanted them to move away also. Just as she mentioned this to Little Knight, they heard a loud rumbling deep in the earth. Then water—lots of water—started spurting out of the hole. Soon, the center of the oasis had become a large pond, and Little Knight, his armor thrown to the sand, was happily rolling in the water.

By the end of the day, water was back in the well, and the fountains were overflowing. By the next morning, the palm trees were back to life, standing tall and swaying with the gentle breeze. Not knowing how to thank the Witch, Little Knight took her by the hand and they started to dance, the sound of water their only music. For the first time in a long while, the Witch found herself laughing out loud.

"You know," she said, admiring his playfulness, "as much as you love water, you really are the Knight of Fire. Used correctly, fire warms us. It is our inspiration and radiance. Spending time with you has certainly warmed my heart. You've brought laughter back into my life, and I thank you for that."

She could see Little Knight turning into the Knight of Fire before her very eyes. Now that he had his oasis, he could accept all the fire that truly belonged to him. She knew that in time he would experience more of the vitality in the desert.

Feeling the call of her own journey, the Witch prepared to leave. The Knight of Fire gave her a big hug, warm and loving, and thanked her for her wisdom. "You are already more the Wise Witch than you realize," he said with affection.

The Witch smiled, knowing he was right.

THE NEEDLE: *Mending the Heart*

The Witch left the desert and found her way into the forest, feeling lighter and happier. She noticed that the adventure with the Knight of Fire had opened her heart—at least one part of it. She wondered how many parts of her heart were still closed.

Lost in thought, she had ignored her surroundings and was dumbfounded when she bumped into something blocking the trail; it looked like a foot—the largest one she had ever seen. When she gazed further up and saw blue-green eyes looking intently through flaming red hair she realized she had just met Humangus.

"Hi, Giant," she said. "I am the Witch in the Cave. I've been searching for you. When Babla described you, I was sure she was joking, but now I see that she didn't exaggerate at all." The Witch was doing her best to keep a smile on her face even though her insides were shaking.

"Babla?" Humangus boomed with delight. "You are a friend of Babla? Then, welcome to my forest, my Giantdom." The earth trembled as he sat down and motioned the Witch to come closer. Then, he closed his eyes and became very still.

After a long time, he opened his eyes and said, "There's something you are looking for that I have, but I don't know what it is. All I can see is a broken wing. Does that mean anything to you?"

The Witch's blue eyes opened wide. "Yes," she exclaimed, taking out the silk thread. "I'm looking for a very special needle for this thread that Lion Woman gave me. It is to repair the broken wing of a little fairy. I promised I would return to help her."

"And so you shall," said Humangus with a smile. He reached into a special pocket and took out a pouch, handing it over to her. In it, the Witch found a silver needle. The thread fit perfectly through the small hole.

"I'm so glad that I'll be able to help the little fairy," she said with tears in her eyes. "Thank you, Humangus." Then she told him about her visit with Babla and added, "Her Inner Guides suggested I come see you for my healing, the healing of my heart."

Humangus nodded. He told her about his visit with Babla and Wondering Magician. They had made plans for everyone to meet at the Sacred Land. The Witch was thrilled.[2]

"That will be the best time for us to hold your heart," he added. "For matters of the heart one, needs to be surrounded by pure-hearted Beings. But, first, go find the little fairy."

He leaned over and carefully hugged the Witch. Then he got up and left, going on his way to the Sacred Land.

The Witch put the pouch with the silk thread and silver needle into her pocket and went in the other direction to find the little fairy. When she came to the place where the three fairies had appeared, she started singing, calling the little fairy with the broken wing. Nothing happened. She became very quiet and listened deeply.

[2] Even though Humangus had already met Wondering Magician and Babla, that story will be told later.

Somewhere in the distance she heard a sound. Slowly walking in that direction, she soon spied the little fairy sitting on a fallen log, crying. The Witch came closer and put her arms around her friend, who was inconsolable. "I'll never be able to fly again, ever!" sobbed the little fairy in despair.

"I am not so sure of that," the Witch replied. Taking the silk thread and silver needle out of her pocket, she told the story of her adventures. When the little fairy lifted her head, a glimmer of hope was in her eyes. She turned to show the Witch her broken wings.

Without hesitation, the Witch went to work. This was a delicate repair, demanding a lot of patience. With each stitch, something deep inside of the Witch was also being mended. When the Witch had finished, she put the needle and the remaining thread back into the pouch, knowing another part of her heart had just opened. She felt fuller inside, and the colors in the outer world seemed brighter. Satisfied, she took a deep breath.

The little fairy turned to the Witch, putting her little arms around her neck. "I love you," she said sincerely, radiant with new life. Then, in a flash, off she went to join her fairy friends and learn again how to fly.

The Witch sat there for a long time, quiet tears streaming down her cheeks. She felt deeply sad and joyful at the same time. She wondered how many parts of her heart had yet to open. With that thought, the Witch remembered the meeting with the others and set out for the Sacred Land.

CHENG LI AND WISE OWL: *Dragon Wisdom*

While the Witch was learning from Lion Woman and Humangus, Babla had continued her journey, wondering what was next. She didn't have to wonder very long.

Reentering the forest at dusk, she decided to stop for the night. She was searching for a place to rest when she heard a strange noise. Looking in it's direction, she saw two glowing yellow circles side by side. "Those must be the eyes of a Being. It is either very tall or sitting on a tree branch," Babla thought, trusting it was the latter.

"Come follow me," said a very low voice.

"Who are you?" asked Babla.

"I am Wise Owl," came the answer. "Follow me."

Babla did so, and eventually she could see the owl's wings, the feathers on its body, and the shape of its head.

They came to a clearing and Babla heard the sound of water. Then she saw it—a little stream bubbling happily, running at the back of a house. Babla had never seen a house like this one. It's green roof curved and spiraled, and dragons in all colors were carved onto the outer walls.

"This is the most colorful house I've ever seen," Babla thought, delighted with the fiery dragons.

As they approached the few stairs leading to the door, an old man with long gray hair and a long gray beard came out. He wore a long gray robe with very wide arms, and on his head was a gray hat. He came closer, and Babla saw small brown eyes that stretched out to the sides. There was something in them for which Babla could find no words.

"Hi, Babla," he said, taking her hands into his. "I am Cheng Li. I'm very pleased to have you here."

"How do you know my name?" Babla's eyes were wide with wonder.

"Because I am one of your Inner Guides. We know such things. She is one, too," he said, pointing toward the owl.

"What do I need more Guides for?" Babla wanted to know. "Don't I have enough?"

"We are different," answered Cheng Li. "Wise Owl and I are not here for your growth; we are here to assist you in helping others grow. We are Guides of intuition and wisdom—different kinds, of course. That's why you need both of us."

Babla was intrigued. "You mean you will help me with Wise Witch and the other Beings I'm supposed to meet?"

"Yes, that is right. But it's getting late now. Why don't you come in and sleep in my house tonight. We'll talk more tomorrow," he said kindly.

Babla gratefully accepted the invitation and went in. The inside of the house was like the outside—colorful paintings, carvings, and statues of dragons were everywhere.

In the morning, Babla woke up to sounds from the kitchen; Cheng Li was preparing breakfast. She found the kitchen, and at the entrance, stopped in surprise at what she saw. Cheng Li's back was turned and Wise Owl was perched on his left shoulder, her feathers showing a mixture of brown, gray, and pearl white.

Babla blinked a few times to make sure she was awake. These two seemed like one Being, yet when she focused on Cheng Li alone, she saw him separate from the owl. And when she looked only at Wise Owl, she saw her as being different than Cheng Li. If she looked at both, however, they seemed to be one Being. How strange!

Cheng Li turned and greeted her. "I see that you have discovered our secret," he said, smiling. "I am the male part of wisdom and intuition; Wise Owl is the female part. This is true in your world of duality. In reality, there is no separation. You might say that Wise Owl and I are two sides of the same coin. Actually, there is only one coin, and only one side to it. Having said that, the Truth is there is no coin, only infinite energy that moves in different colors in and out of itself.

Listening to his words, Babla became aware of a deep stillness in them; they made her feel peaceful, as did the quiet expression in his eyes.

At breakfast, Babla asked why the owl was called "wise." She wanted to know the true meaning of wisdom.

Cheng Li answered, "True wisdom is to see beyond illusion, beyond deception, beyond the dream that surrounds most Beings. Wise Owl can see through the veils of their dream. When she assists you, you will also be able to see through others' dream of separation into their Essence.

"Then, you will know their purpose in this life, and can assist them in living it fully. Wise Owl will reveal the shadow to you, so that you can see the whole Truth."

Babla was moved. "I like this," she said. "But then, what is your job?" Cheng Li simply smiled.

Babla felt she was seeing him for the first time. She had been looking at him throughout their conversation, yet somehow this was different. She noticed all the little wrinkles on his pleasant yellowish-brown face. She saw his slanted eyes—what was he seeing through them? There was something even deeper in them than the peace.

Babla felt Rabia's presence strongly around her. By partially merging with Rabia, she could penetrate into the mystery that Cheng Li seemed to be.

He could be 60 or 200 years old. And, he was unassuming, matter of fact. Babla searched for the most fitting word—*humble*. Yes, there was something very humble about him. His hands looked ancient; they were strong in a delicate way with fine, long fingers. Cheng Li's whole presence, his whole being felt soothing, reassuring, and inspiring to Babla.

Babla came back to his eyes; looking into them was like falling into another world. There was a glimmer, a spark there that Babla had never seen before. They seemed textured somehow. The first layer was calm, still, and spacious. It reminded Babla of air.

The second layer looked red and hot; Babla could almost see flames dancing in Cheng Li's eyes.

The third layer felt cool, thick, and fluid. Babla felt it slowly wrap around her body. It was sensuous and relaxing at the same time, like lying on her back, floating in a quiet pool.

The fourth layer was again very different; it was dense and solid. Babla felt herself on the ground in a supportive way. "Earth!" she thought. "This reminds me of earth."

Then she met the fifth layer, and nothing was there! She was falling in a void for what seemed like an eternity until, in one instant, everything lit up. The light was so bright Babla had to cover her eyes.

When she looked again she saw Cheng Li sitting patiently at the table with Wise Owl still perched on his left shoulder. "Who are you really?" she asked.

"I come from one of the worlds within this one," he said looking intently at her. "In that world, I am known as Dragonkeeper. I once lived with the dragons and took care of their eggs. In return, they taught me their mysteries, so their wisdom won't be forgotten.

"Most of your Inner Guides and Inner Beings come from worlds within this one, Babla. The rest belong to this world. The more we go back and forth between these realms, the thinner the veils of separation become.

"You see, just like Wise Owl and I, all these worlds are part of the dream, the illusion of your world. In reality, there is only one world."

Babla was totally confused. "The other worlds looked very real to me when I was there," she said, rubbing her head.

"I know," replied Cheng Li. "When you look at me, you see me as distinct from Wise Owl. Our separation seems very real, but we are one Being. You have to go through the veil into our Essence, to experience our Oneness."

"If I looked at all of these worlds together at the same time, would the veils between them disappear, too?" Babla wondered.

"Exactly," replied Cheng Li. "The veils would disappear, and you would see one world which includes all of the others."

"Wow!" Babla was speechless.

"Yet as long as you perceive these veils, you have to pretend that all these worlds are separate and work with that," Cheng Li added. "One day, when you look at all the worlds within worlds, you won't be able to find any veils. You'll have no choice but to experience the one real world. Then you're done. Your journey will be over. You won't need to be separate from Rabia any longer. Rabia and you are like Wise Owl and I; in reality you are one Being."

Breakfast was over. Babla knew that it was time for her to continue her journey. She hugged Cheng Li, said good-bye, and stroked Wise Owl's feathers.

"Doesn't she ever speak?" Babla asked.

"She does, when necessary," came his answer. "She spoke to you in the forest, remember?" Yes, Babla remembered.

On her way out of the house, Cheng Li reminded Babla that she could count on him and the owl whenever she needed assistance with an Outer Being; they would be there for her, sitting on her left shoulder.

Babla left the house, filled—with a delicious breakfast, with the love of two remarkable Guides, and with Dragon Wisdom: All worlds are one world.

WONDERING MAGICIAN: Understanding Self-doubt

Back in the forest, Babla heard the sound of footsteps—very delicate and light. She decided to stop and wait; soon she could see a tall, lean man coming toward her. He wore a long, dark blue robe with twinkling stars, gold-rimmed glasses, and a Magician's hat, which was tipped to his left. When the hat was almost ready to fall off, a little hand would come out of his left temple and push it back up as a voice said, "Yes, you are!" When the hat was straight on his head, another hand came out of his right temple and pushed it to the left. A different voice said, "No, you're not!"

Babla couldn't believe her eyes, so she decided to ask this man about it. When he saw Babla, he smiled gently and stopped right in front of her. With his arms outstretched he said, "Well, hi there, little girl. How are you today?"

Babla couldn't wait to ask, so she replied, "I'm fine. My name is Babla. What's yours? And what is happening with your hat?"

"Oh, my hat." Even though the man was still smiling, Babla could see something else in his deep blue eyes. It wasn't quite sadness, or was it? Or maybe it was sadness mixed with—what?

She heard the voice of Wise Owl in her left ear: "Sadness mixed with settling for less."

"Yes!" thought Babla. "That's it."

The man looked directly at her and said, "I'm glad to meet you, Babla. I am Wondering Magician."

Delighted, Babla told him about the cave and the Witch, and that the Witch needed to spend time with him. "What are you wondering about?" she asked finally, fascinated with this Being.

The Magician gave a sigh and sat down by a big tree, and Babla sat next to him. "People call me that because I wonder whether I am a real Magician or not," he began, "the voice to my right says I'm not and keeps pushing away my hat to prove it; yet the voice to my left says I am and keeps pushing my hat back into place. This has been going on for a long time."

"Aren't you tired of living like this?" asked Babla.

"I am," he replied, "but I don't know what else to do." Then he added in a cheery voice, "Life goes on, and I feel good about my life in general. Certain things one has to accept as they are and make the best of it, I suppose," he said with a hint of resignation.

Babla remembered that her Guides had suggested she accept some things just the way they were . . . and say "yes" to the moment. Still, she wasn't quite sure whether this applied to Wondering Magician's situation.

She looked toward her left shoulder. "Don't believe him," she heard Cheng Li's voice say. "He's not satisfied with his life and he shouldn't be. His mission in life is much bigger than he realizes. Even though he has to do the work himself, you can point out the direction."

"Oh, my!" thought Babla. "What if I point out the wrong direction and mess things up?"

She felt the top of her head open, and golden light of the purest quality came in. "The Higher Self!" she thought, relieved. "Now I'm saved!" Higher Self showed Babla three images, then left.

Babla turned to Wondering Magician and said, "You need to go see Lion Woman first; then Humangus, the wise Giant; and then the Witch in the Cave. After that, you and I will talk again."

Wondering Magician was very grateful for these suggestions and gave her a big hug. As Babla kissed his soft cheek, she thought, "One day the Magician will be one of my best friends."

LOST & FOUND MAN: Who Am I?

The next day, while Babla was walking in the forest, she came to a clearing. In the middle of it stood a man, who had a drum in front of him, a big toolbox to his right, a bird in a cage to his left, and a walking stick behind him. He was busy gluing two pieces of wood together, while making some strange clicking sounds with his tongue.

Hearing Babla, he lifted his head and welcomed her with a smile. "Hi, little girl. Anything I can do for you? Anything you need to have fixed?"

Babla opened her mouth to answer and then stopped dead in her tracks: The right side of his face and body looked about 15 years old, but the left side looked 115! "Who are you?"

"I'm Lost & Found Man," he said. "The right side of me keeps asking 'Who am I?' and the left side knows the answer, but the two sides don't seem to be able to communicate. And, I don't know how to help them. Here, touch my right side."

Babla reached over and touched him. Immediately the Teenager grabbed her arms, his clear blue eyes intense. He asked, "Who am I? Who can help me find out? Where do I need to go? Can you help me? What am I doing here? What is life about?" He repeated the same questions over and over again.

Babla then touched his left arm and, amazingly, he stopped in mid-sentence. Now the Sage was looking at her, his blue eyes shining with deep wisdom. "I am," he said quietly, "and I am not. It is all the same. I am you and you are me, and even this is not true."

He took the walking stick in one hand and Babla's hand in the other. They walked through the forest, hardly speaking, yet their hearts were as one.

She heard Alan's voice in her ear: "You are the catalyst for Lost & Found Man, Babla. You need to find a way that appeals to both parts of him and show them how to heal this split."

"This looks like hard work," complained Babla to her Guide. "I don't have a clue where to even start."

Alan replied, "There's a split second of stillpoint when he is switching from one to the other. You need to catch that and touch both of his arms at the same time. But before you can do this, go back to Lion Woman and ask her for an eagle feather. Next, you must visit Humangus and ask him for a hawk feather. Bring them back here, then, with the eagle feather in your left hand and the hawk feather in your right, touch Lost & Found Man."

Babla was delighted that she was going to see Lion Woman and Humangus again. Explaining their next step to Lost & Found Man she left, grateful that there was a way to help this wonderful Being.

EAGLE FEATHER AND HAWK FEATHER:
Balancing Opposites

Babla wandered in the forest, not knowing how to find Lion Woman. Feeling frustrated, she stopped to think. She felt the wind in her hair, she heard the leaves rustling in the wind, she saw all shades of green and brown around her, she felt her feet on the ground.

Taking a deep breath, she said out loud, "Forest, I need your help." From the deep silence of the forest, she heard footsteps—very slow, quiet, careful footsteps. Babla looked in that direction, curious about to whom they belonged.

A deer came out of the trees, moving gracefully toward her. As it did so, it changed back and forth between a grown-up deer, a young deer, and a doe. "Deer Lady!" Babla called out, running to meet her. "I can't tell you how glad I am to see you. I think I'm lost."

"You asked for help, so here I am," said Deer Lady with the softest expression in her brown eyes.

Babla explained, "I need to go back to the valley, find Lion Woman, and get an eagle feather from her. Can you show me the way?"

"I can take you there on my back if you want." Babla was glad to be riding on Deer Lady's back. She also hoped to get to know her better during their journey.

When Babla got tired, she rode on Deer Lady. Otherwise, they walked together. Surprisingly, Deer Lady never seemed to get tired. Sometimes they traveled in silence, the only sounds being their own footsteps. It was comforting for Babla to walk quietly with her deer friend; a bonding was occurring between them, a connecting that words alone could not accomplish.

At other times they talked, sharing with each other what needed to be said.

Then they arrived in the lush valley. Ahead, they could see Lion Woman's house. As they climbed up the stairs, the door opened and a woman's form appeared. Lion Woman was smiling her big smile, her golden-green eyes flashing with the pleasure of seeing Deer Lady and Babla.

She gave them both a long hug, and all three stood in the doorway, merged in the ocean of Love. After what seemed an eternity, they separated and entered the house to have tea, as was Lion Woman's custom.

When Lion Woman heard the reason for their visit, she got up and motioned them to follow. She went out to her backyard and started making some strange sounds. After a while, she lifted her arm and pointed toward the sky.

Babla and Deer Lady looked up and saw a tiny black dot coming closer. Soon the dot became a bird, and a moment later a huge eagle was gliding elegantly to the ground.

Lion Woman greeted Eagle with great respect. Then she asked if Eagle would be willing to give up one of her feathers for Lost & Found Man. The bird made a deliberate sound and turned her side to Lion Woman.

"She has agreed," translated Lion Woman. "She wants me to pick one for you." Firmly but gently, Lion Woman pulled out a long feather, giving a big sigh as she did.

Eagle slowly turned to Babla and looked directly into her eyes. Her presence was awesome. Then she turned again and gazed at Deer Lady. Stillness filled the air. When she turned to Lion Woman, there seemed to be almost no separation between them. While they were looking at each other in deep silence, Babla thought they must be very old friends.

"Thank you," Lion Woman broke the silence. Eagle nodded her head and took off, gracefully spreading her wings. Soon she was again a tiny black dot in the vast sky, with one feather still on earth.

As Lion Woman handed the feather to Babla, she said lovingly, "The eagle talks to us about freedom of the skies. She brings us illumination, teaches us about Spirit, and is our connection to the Divine. The eagle shows us what is beyond our sight; she reminds us of the bigger picture. This feather is a reminder that we can live on earth and stay connected to the sky, that we can bring the freedom of the skies down to earth. Such is a balanced, joyful life, lived from the depths of our hearts. This is what you need to tell Lost & Found Man."

Back in the house, they went right to bed because Babla had a long journey ahead of her the next day. She was going to find Humangus the Giant and ask for a hawk feather.

The next morning, Babla looked out the window and saw a tall, skinny man in a long, dark blue robe. He had on a magician's hat, which seemed to be sliding from one side to the other.

"Wondering Magician!" she pointed, calling Lion Woman to the window. "He's come to see you." Babla decided to stay with them and see if she could assist him in any way.

When Wondering Magician reached the stairs, Babla opened the door. The surprise and pleasure on his face were wonderful to see.

"Babla! Now I know I'm in the right place. It's so nice to see you again."

After a long hug, Babla led him to the table where Lion Woman and Deer Lady were having breakfast. A fourth plate and cup were already set out. Looking at them, Wondering Magician asked in an almost disbelieving voice, "Is this for me?"

"Come, have breakfast with us," invited Lion Woman. He sat down on the edge of the chair, looking most uncomfortable. Lion Woman asked about his travels, pouring him some tea. The more he told them about his life and all the places he had been, however, the more he relaxed into his chair.

After a while, he looked at the others and said, "I feel so welcome here, so at home. I don't remember feeling this way ever before."

Lion Woman caught his eyes and wouldn't let go. Babla reached over and held his hand, and Deer Lady came to his back, giving him support and gentle love.

Wondering Magician dove deeper and deeper into Lion Woman's eyes. Babla could see the changes in his whole body. Lion Woman opened her mouth and said very slowly, "I welcome you, Magician."

Two silent tear drops rolled out of his eyes. "There is no doubt, then?" he asked.

"No," replied Lion Woman. "There is no doubt."

Wondering Magician took a deep breath, the deepest breath Babla had seen him take. He looked different. She couldn't figure out what it was, but decided to ask later because now something beyond words was happening.

Looking at Wondering Magician and Babla, Lion Woman said, "I know both of you need to see Humangus. Why don't you go together? I think spending time with each other would benefit you both."

The Magician and Babla looked at each other and smiled. It was a great idea. They said good-bye to Lion Woman and Deer Lady and left the house in the valley, walking toward the forest.

On the way, Babla asked what had happened when he was looking into Lion Woman's eyes.

"Oh my!" he replied, wiping his forehead. "Ask me what didn't happen. I've never felt loved and supported like that before. It felt like she was coming right into me and there was no hiding from her. She looked into every corner of my being. Then she called me a magician. I've never felt so deeply validated. She went to my very Core, my Essence, and called me a magician. How can I doubt it any longer?"

"So then you won't settle for less any more?" Babla wanted to know.

"I hope not," was his answer. "There are still some things I need to learn, though. The voice that says I'm not a magician is not as loud now, but it's still there. Tell me what's happening with my hat. It feels strange up there."

When Babla looked up, she saw that the "yes" hand on the left side was much larger now, and the "no" hand on the right side was smaller. When the "yes" hand put his hat back in place, it stayed there for a while before the "no" hand could push it away. Wondering Magician was very pleased with this and so was Babla. Her friend seemed more self-assured now, his eyes reflecting deeper satisfaction and less sadness.

Wondering Magician knew a lot about nature, birds, animals, the sky, and the waters. During their time walking through the forest, Babla learned a lot. The most important thing she came to see was his love of nature and the Beings who lived there.

"You're so good with animals and birds," she observed. "The 'no' voice doesn't seem to be there at all then. Why is it so strong when it comes to you?"

"That's a very good question," replied the Magician. "My mother said that I was born with my magician's hat. Everybody was congratulating her for having a magician child when the Lost Magician of the village put a curse on me. Lost Magician had also been born with his magician's hat, and he was to become the village magician when he grew up. But sometime in his teens, he lost his hat and never found it for the rest of his life.

"A magician can't do magic without his hat, so this was the end of it for him. He grew up a bitter man, always teased by the villagers. When I was born, he was very old. Nobody ever suspected he could do me any harm. I guess he was jealous.

"The 'no' voice is actually his voice telling me I'm not a magician. But over the years, I started believing it myself. It's hard not to believe a strong and convincing voice when you're hearing it every day inside and outside of your head."

Babla was thoughtful. "Maybe Humangus can help you lift this curse."

"I sure hope so. Since my visit with Lion Woman, I know that nothing is impossible."

All of a sudden, they heard a loud rumbling and found themselves up in the air. Before they knew it, they were in the Giant's palm, peering into huge sea-colored eyes. "Oh great!" cheered Babla. "We don't need to look for him any more. He's found us."

"Hi, Babla," said Humangus in his strong giant voice. "I'm very glad to see you again. Who is your friend?"

Babla introduced Wondering Magician. Then both of them explained why they were looking for him.

"A curse and a hawk feather," Humangus summed up. "Let's deal with the hawk feather first." He closed his eyes and turned his head slightly toward his left shoulder. Babla could almost see his Guides, the old man and old woman, sitting there talking to him.

After a time of listening, Humangus said thoughtfully, "Hawk is a bird of prey. He has very keen eyes. He flies very high and sees everything there is to see, every little detail. And yet, because he flies so high in the sky, he also sees the big picture. My Guides tell me that Hawk has a bold heart and is the messenger of Truth. He cuts through the illusion, through unconsciousness. Hawk's cry is a wake-up call to greater awareness.

"Eagle brings us expanded awareness, and Hawk brings focused awareness. They teach us how to see the big picture while paying attention to detail."

He put two fingers into his mouth and whistled, looking up at the sky. Out of nowhere, a dark brown hawk appeared high in the air, flying toward them.

He landed on the Giant's right shoulder, looking intently at Babla and Wondering Magician.

"This bird is a handful," said the Magician nodding his head knowingly. He was right.

Humangus greeted Hawk respectfully and asked for a feather for Lost & Found Man. The bird, staring into Babla's eyes, gave a piercing cry and turned his left side to Babla.

"He wants you to pull a feather from this side," explained Humangus. "This is the first time he has let anyone except me touch him." The Giant was obviously surprised.

The hand that was holding Wondering Magician and Babla moved closer to the bird. Babla reached over and put her tiny hands on the Hawk's feathers. They were soft and strong, with a wild quality about them. The silence of this fierce bird vibrated with potency.

Babla asked Cheng Li to help her find the right feather for Lost & Found Man. As she was going over the feathers, her hands stopped when she heard her Guide whisper "yes" in her ear. She pulled the feather out and smoothed the affected area.

Hawk turned toward Babla and met her eyes. Behind the fierceness there something very soft and delicate. Then, with another shrill cry, he took off and disappeared as suddenly as he had appeared.

"He really likes you," said the Giant. "It's not easy to be accepted as a friend by a hawk. He must have seen your pure heart." Humangus was smiling.

Babla remembered her first unintentional visit and realized the Giant had changed quite a bit since finding his Guides and his Inner Mate, and now that he accepted the little boy. He was softer, more available, and wiser, too, even though his presence was as strong as ever. She smiled back, feeling very warm in her heart and remembering her Heartsong. She loved this fiery giant. And, as odd as it seemed, she knew he was her friend.

Humangus turned his attention to Wondering Magician. "So, Lost Magician put a curse on you," he said. "I'm sure something can be done about it. A curse is a powerful thing. I can do a lot, but I can't lift all of it by myself. We need others with a pure heart, and we need a very special place—a sacred place to lift the curse."

"I know a special place," chimed in Babla without thinking. "It's the place of the Witch I met in a cave. Once she is not so afraid anymore, she is going to live in her sacred place. Could we do it there?"

"That sounds good," replied Humangus. "The Witch must have a pure heart if she has a sacred place. And Lost & Found Man must have a pure heart if Eagle and Hawk have given him feathers. Now we must find other Beings with pure hearts."

"Kiwi has a pure heart," added Babla.

"I'm sure we'll meet others along the way before we get to the Witch's Cave," said Humangus optimistically.

Wondering Magician was so thrilled he was jumping up and down. "Maybe I won't have to live with this curse for the rest of my life after all," he said. "Even if we can't lift it fully, I'll still have met wonderful Beings with pure hearts. That's a lot."

Babla smiled. Her magician friend had such a pure heart himself. She felt strong affection for him. Through the corner of her eye, she saw that Humangus was smiling. He seemed determined to assist Wondering Magician in lifting the curse.

After explaining how to get to the Witch's Cave, Babla left to find Lost & Found Man because now she had both of the feathers. Wondering Magician and Humangus decided to take different routes, looking for other Beings with pure hearts on the way to the cave.

WONDERING MAGICIAN AND THE WITCH:
Words With Meaning

After leaving Babla and Humangus, Wondering Magician went deeper into the forest toward the Witch's Cave. He wasn't sure what to make of what had just happened. Babla seemed to have a lot of energy and enthusiasm, and the Giant was something else.

"Let me tell you," he said out loud to himself. "Your life will never be the same."

It was lunch time, or so he was told by his stomach. He decided to sit on a fallen tree trunk and eat a bite. While he was enjoying his food, he heard footsteps—two different kinds. He became all ears and listened; one set of steps belonged to a two-legged Being, the other to a four-legged one.

He waited in silence until a wrinkled woman with fuzzy hair and a dog came out of the trees. His hat told him they were not dangerous. So Wondering Magician put down his food and got up. Opening his arms wide, he said in a cheery voice, "Hi, I am Wondering Magician. Would the two of you care to join me for lunch?" He couldn't stop looking into the woman's clear blue eyes.

"Wondering Magician!" she beamed. "Oh, great! I am the Witch in the Cave, and I'm supposed to find you and spend some time with you."

Then she saw his hat and stopped in utter amazement. The Magician told the Witch his story, and the Witch told hers. The more they talked, the more there was to say. Maybe they talked for minutes, maybe for hours, maybe for days, maybe for weeks—nobody knows.

Time went away and they entered another world—the World of Words with Meaning. There, each word uttered created certain colors of the rainbow around it. These colors connected with trees, birds, flowers, rocks, clouds, Beings, shifting and changing the reality of the moment.

One of the reasons the Witch had not left her cave for so long was that she couldn't bear to hear words without meaning. They made her feel empty and depleted, so she had decided not to use words any more. Now she realized that some Beings, like the Magician, knew how to access the World of Words with Meaning.

"Lion Woman, Babla, and Humangus must know about this, too," she thought. Every word that came out of the Magician's mouth seemed to create a change in her heart. She guessed that the same was true for him.

Time came back, and there they were, sitting in the forest having lunch. They decided to journey together for a while because both were going to the Witch's Cave.

For Wondering Magician, the most mysterious thing was that around the Witch his hat stayed on his head; the right hand, which usually pushed it away, didn't seem to interfere.

When he commented about this, she replied, "Well, maybe it's because I *know* you are a magician. I have no doubt about it. Could it be that my knowing strengthens the left hand and weakens the right hand?"

"I guess anything is possible," answered the Magician. "It's just that it never happened so strongly before."

The Witch looked him directly in the eye. "Maybe you have never opened your heart like this to anyone else," she said in a quiet voice.

"Maybe," came his soft reply from a very deep place inside. They both knew this was true. They got up and walked for a long time in silence, marveling at the Mystery of Life.

Halfway through the forest, Wondering Magician decided to take a detour to look at some birds he had never seen before. They would meet at the cave. Before he left, time went away again, and they were once again in the other world of Words with Meaning. This time, they couldn't even tell who was talking and who was listening; both seemed to be talking and listening at the same time, yet every word was crystal clear. Words tumbled out of their mouths, rolling around as they wrapped themselves in colors, touching everything around, then tumbled into their ears, echoing all the way down into their bellies.

When time came back and they found themselves in the forest, both felt deeply satisfied, relaxed, and full of life. The Witch understood that words with meaning, spoken from the heart, could nourish one's Soul.

When the Witch was again walking by herself, followed by M, she thought, "Now that I know it's possible, I will surround myself with Beings who know how to enter the World of Words with Meaning."

RETURN OF THE VULTURES:
Love, Fear, Anger, and Avoidance

Babla was tired. She decided to rest because it was still a long way to the forest where Lost & Found Man lived. Making sure the eagle feather and the hawk feather were safe, she leaned against a rock, and closed her eyes.

She was startled by an insistent voice in her ear saying, "Wake up, Babla, wake up!" It was Amazon Woman. Babla realized she had fallen asleep. She looked around and saw two birds in the sky, coming closer very fast. "Oh, no!" she yelled in frustration. "The Vultures. What timing!"

"When you are strong and centered, they cannot touch you," said the Amazon. "That's why they waited until you were tired. They are expecting a feast now."

"Oh well," replied Babla. "What am I supposed to do?"

She felt a tingling on her left shoulder and felt Wise Owl's presence. "One thing Vultures cannot touch or destroy is pure Love," the Owl explained. "Stay tired, yet surround all of what you are feeling right now with pure Love."

"Remember your Heartsong, Babla," added Amazon Woman.

Babla started singing parts of the song: "I love you whether you know it or not. I love you whether I show it or not." The more she repeated these words, the more she felt a greenish-pink film come out of her heart and surround her. This was fun!

The Vultures arrived. They dove for Babla, then stopped in mid-air. They tried again, but couldn't seem to come close enough to attack. As if she hadn't noticed their intention, Babla began talking to them, asking them about their journeys. They landed on the ground and began to visit as if everything were wonderful. Then they said good-bye and left.

As soon as they were gone, a fuming Fireball appeared, followed by Amazon Woman, as calm and strong as ever. Fireball was very angry with Babla for not having been honest with the Vultures; rather than tell them that she didn't like them at all and didn't want to have anything to do with them, she had pretended everything was okay.

Babla was confused. All she knew was that she was afraid of the Vultures, and she would do anything to avoid being attacked.

Fireball, on the other hand, wanted to attack the Vultures and scratch their eyes out. Both girls felt stuck and frustrated, not knowing what would have been the right thing to do.

With questioning eyes, they looked at Amazon Woman. She sat down between them and took their hands. "There is no one right way of doing things," she said. "Each situation demands a unique response. In this case, attacking them would not have been a wise choice because they are stronger than you, both of you.

"A wise choice with Beings who like to attack is to gain their respect. Then attacking is totally out of the question for them. This is the outer work. The inner work has to do with the lessons these two birds of prey are bringing to you."

Both Babla and Fireball firmly believed that the Vultures couldn't possibly teach any lessons because they were such obnoxious Beings. Amazon Woman just smiled.

RETURN TO LOST & FOUND MAN: Duality Versus Unity

At last Babla reached the clearing in the forest where Lost & Found Man was living. He was busy drumming. As Babla drew near, her eyes caught movement at the edge of the forest. She looked closer and saw a mare grazing. She was a beautiful horse, her mane full and dark brown, her shiny coat a lighter shade of brown.

Seeing Babla, Lost & Found Man came over and gave her a big hug. He was excited to see Babla because he knew what it meant.

"I didn't know you had a horse," said Babla, admiring the mare. "Do you know how to ride?"

"Yes, I do. But, she won't let me ride until I heal. In the past, I would start switching from one part of myself to the other while riding, which totally confused her. The Teenager rides dangerously. He is wild and reckless, whereas the Sage is peaceful and silent, going slowly and enjoying every moment. Going back and forth like that drove the mare crazy, so I stopped riding her. I'd really like to ride her again, though."

"I hope you'll be able to," said Babla. "It could be such fun. She looks alert."

It was time to use the feathers. Babla called on Alan for help. "I'm here," whispered Alan in her ear. "The time is right. Afterwards, he needs to be alone. Ask him to join you for the Healing Circle in the Witch's Cave. He has a very pure heart, and it will be good for him to be there for his complete integration."

Babla was happy to hear these words. The idea of Lost & Found Man joining the Healing Circle of pure-hearted Beings sounded wonderful to her; she really liked this Teenager/Sage man.

She took out the feathers and approached Lost & Found Man. The eagle feather in her left hand, the hawk feather in her right, she touched his right arm. The Teenager started jumping up and down, looking at Babla with unseeing eyes, asking nonstop, "Who am I? What is life about?"

Babla lifted the eagle feather and touched his left arm. Before he could switch to the old Sage, she touched both arms with the feathers.

There was a pause, and Lost & Found Man froze. His eyes were wide open, with no expression. Babla watched the gradual transformation with amazement.

It started with his face; the clear line in the middle, which had separated the young and the old, became fuzzy. Just like two rivers running into each other, the young face and the old face started merging. The same slow process happened with the rest of his body.

The outer integration was complete. In front of Babla, a very handsome young man was standing, his long brown hair playing in the wind and his clear blue eyes looking at her with appreciation. He took Babla's hands into his. "I need a new name," he said in a strong, deep voice.

"Yes," replied Babla. "That is true. Come to the Healing Circle. Humangus, the wise Giant, will give you a name."

They agreed to meet at the Witch's Cave. Feeling another Being's presence, they looked up. The beautiful brown mare had come very close and was looking at them. If a horse could smile, she was smiling. She reached over and started nibbling at his hair and ear. He put his arms around her neck and rested his new face in her mane. She whinnied.

"Wow!" he looked up in surprise. "She wants me to ride her."

"Have fun," said Babla, satisfied. "I'll see you soon."

"I'll be there," was his response. "Thank you for everything."

ORACLE: *Abiding in Truth*

After leaving Lost & Found Man, Babla continued toward the Witch's Cave. She was looking forward to seeing her friend. She knew that Humangus, Wondering Magician, and Lost & Found Man would soon be there for the Healing Circle. Humangus had said they needed Beings with pure hearts to help the Magician lift the curse and give Lost & Found Man a new name.

Babla decided to look for a few more Beings with pure hearts. She consulted her Guides.

"Go find Kiwi," came the answer. Babla was delighted; she started jumping up and down, hugging all the trees she passed, singing out loud, "Kiwi, Kiwi, I'm coming. Where are you?" She simply let her song lead her feet deeper and deeper into the forest, trusting.

She heard other feet, strong and steady, coming toward her. Soon her bear friend, Kiwi, was standing right in front of her. They hugged for a long time, Babla comforted by Kiwi's soft and fuzzy fur. When Babla told Kiwi what she was up to and why she was looking for her, soft tears of joy appeared in Kiwi's eyes.

"Oh, Babla," she said. "I'm so glad for your invitation. And I definitely would like to meet other Beings with pure hearts. I will arrange everything and meet you there." Babla left feeling great; she loved her fuzzy friend.

Walking happily she thought, "Who else can I find?" She didn't have to wait long. Right as she passed some bushes, she saw a lion cub lying on its back, looking dead. She leaned over and saw blood oozing out of its chest and belly. "Poor Baby," said Babla, reaching out to touch the wound.

To her surprise, the baby lion became a huge black panther and sprang at her. If Amazon Woman had not reached out and lifted Babla above Panther's head, who knows—this might have been the end of Babla's story.

But Amazon Woman did reach out and lifted Babla up in the air, and Panther encountered Black Panther, Babla's animal Guide. Suddenly, there were two huge black cats, facing each other with blazing green eyes. Panther was very angry and ready to kill, but Black Panther, calm and peaceful, remained present and ready to act if necessary.

The silence grew thicker by the moment. Then Panther reverted back to a lion cub and collapsed onto the forest ground.

"I'm too wounded and in too much pain to attack," she said in a frustrated, female voice.

Amazon Woman put Babla back on the ground. The group moved closer to the baby lion. "I have no desire to harm you, little lion," said Babla. "If it is okay with my Guides, I would love to help you, if I can."

"Your Guides?" Lion Cub opened her eyes and lifted her head. When she saw Amazon Woman and Black Panther, she put her head back down and mumbled, "They look pretty real to me!"

Babla was very surprised; her Inner Guides did not usually show themselves to outer Beings, but there were a few exceptions. She decided that this must be a special occasion. "I am Babla," she said. "What is your name?"

"They call me Oracle," came the answer. "Don't ask me why, because I don't know. Everyone keeps asking and it gets frustrating sometimes. I don't even know what the word means."

"I don't either," said Babla. "Maybe I can ask one of my Inner Guides." She turned around to ask the Amazon and saw to her surprise that Eternal Friend and Alan had joined them. This was amazing!

"An oracle," Eternal Friend said in his soft yet firm voice, "is a Being who knows the Truth. No one can lie to an oracle. Some oracles see the Truth, some feel the Truth, and some hear or smell the Truth. The life purpose of an oracle is to be the Truth and to help other Beings who are lost."

"Very impressive!" replied Lion Cub, sounding bored. "I'm supposed to be this Oracle of Truth, yet here I am, in so much pain that I don't know whether I'll live to see tomorrow."

"What happened?" Babla asked.

"A huge bird of prey attacked me and tried to take out my heart and guts," answered the baby lion, trying to stay calm, but Babla could see teardrops ready to roll down her little cheeks.

Babla looked up and saw Eternal Friend nodding. Gently she reached out and put her hands close to the wound on the baby lion's belly. Huge teardrops came out of the lion's eyes, rolling down, down, all the way to her belly. Each teardrop that touched the wound mysteriously disappeared into the earth, leaving the wound a little smaller, until there was only a tiny spiral going into Lion Cub's belly.

Alan told them that the tiny spiral couldn't be healed right now, so Babla moved her hands from the cub's belly to her chest, as close to the wound as she could get. This time, heart-shaped teardrops started rolling down the baby lion's cheeks. As they touched her heart, this wound also started shrinking, becoming a small spiral.

Alan stopped Babla and explained that this was all they could do for the little lion's heart wound right now.

Amazon Woman stepped forward and said, "There is another wound, an invisible one, exactly between your belly and your heart, Lion Cub. Babla needs to touch you there, and then I will lift her up and out of the way, because only Black Panther can help you heal the third wound."

Black Panther came close, as present as he always was and totally relaxed. Babla leaned over and touched Lion Cub's tummy. Once more, the raging black panther sprang toward her, ready to kill. Just in time, Amazon Woman lifted Babla away, leaving the panther to face Black Panther.

"You again!" roared Panther in dismay. "I can't kill you! You are too centered to be killed. Give me the little girl. I would love to rip her apart."

"I didn't do anything bad to you!" Babla declared from Amazon Woman's shoulder where she was sitting.

"I don't care," he ranted. "My sole excitement comes from ripping things apart. If I can't do that, I'll die in desperation."

Black Panther's calm yet strong voice caught his attention. "I'm a black panther, too," he said, "but I don't need to rip things apart for excitement. I haven't done that for ages and I'm still alive."

Panther was puzzled, not knowing what to say. He hadn't realized that there was any other choice.

Looking down from the Amazon's shoulder, Babla saw Alan on the ground, drawing some funny lines. "This is Inner Guide language," Amazon Woman informed her. "He's trying to call one of Lion Cub's Inner Guides."

Out of nowhere they heard a voice. "I am Daniel. I am Daniel. Let me in." The black panther was in rage, trying to claw the bodiless voice. Then he collapsed and Lion Cub reappeared. She sat up and announced that she was too hurt to be angry, and that she needed help. If this voice that called himself Daniel wanted to help her, she was going to let him in.

Babla gave a big sigh. She knew how important her Inner Guides had been and still were for her, and she hoped Lion Cub would find some strong and loving ones also.

Daniel's voice came closer and closer. He explained that for the time being, he had to stay a formless voice, but in time he would take a form.

Babla had never seen a voice touch a body, but it did. Daniel's voice was very close now, and when it touched the baby lion's tummy, out sprang the black panther again, roaring in rage.

"Panther, what are you hiding behind?" Daniel asked. The black panther stopped in mid-air. "You don't want to know," he said in a very quiet voice, his anger gone.

"Yes, I do," Daniel insisted. "As long as you don't show us what you are hiding behind, Lion Cub can't heal."

Panther dug his claws into the earth. Then he rolled himself into a tight ball. In the penetrating silence, all that was audible was his breathing—in and out, in and out, in and out.

Then Babla saw the tight black ball start to move and stretch very slowly. Why, it seemed almost seductive.

"Scratch 'almost,'" Alan whispered into her ear. In wonder, Babla watched the black ball stretch itself into a tall skinny woman, dressed in a tight black dress, with long black hair. Only her intense green eyes reminded Babla of the black panther.

"I am Isabella," she announced licking her lips seductively while moving her hips in circles. "You wanted to meet me? Here I am."

"Yes," answered Daniel's voice. "You are the key to Lion Cub's healing and becoming an oracle. But, as long as you are hiding behind Panther, nothing can happen."

"Are you sure?" Isabella asked, confused, yet rebellious. "I was told that if I ever came out for longer than five minutes, Lion Cub would die. That's why I've been hiding. And how can I be connected to the 'Knower of Truth' anyway? All I can do is think about men."

"I'm sure the Slut would love to meet you," said Babla, climbing down the Amazon's arm. Isabella was even more confused now. Babla sat down next to her and told her about the Nun, the Slut, and Tantrika. This opened up a whole new world for Isabella. "I feel so lonely hiding behind Panther," she admitted.

"Hi, Isabella," sounded a voice right behind them. Lifting her head, Babla saw a smiling Tantrika in a flowing orange, purple, and white dress. She sat down next to Isabella and took her hand.

"Your sexual energy is the seed for Oracle's ability to know the Truth," Tantrika explained. "The key is to allow yourself to think of men as much as you want, and simply observe it. After a short time you'll feel a gap between two thoughts; the seed of Truth is in that gap.

"The more you allow yourself to think of men, the wider the gap will become, and you can slide in and get the seed. If you don't allow yourself to think of men, you'll never find the seed, and Lion Cub won't be able to heal."

"If this is all I have to do, I'm sure I can manage," said Isabella, with a sigh of relief. "What will happen if I get the seed out?"

"When you get the seed," Tantrika continued, "it still has to go through Panther on its way to Lion Cub's heart."

Babla scrunched her face. She didn't like this panther, he really scared her. She couldn't imagine how a tiny seed would survive Panther's rage.

Seeing movement, Babla looked up and saw Maya arriving with two other women, who also had the Inner Guide glow. Babla guessed these must be some of Lion Cub's Guides.

Then she saw two golden-white shimmery orbs in the sky. One of them she recognized as her Higher Self, the other she guessed to be Lion Cub's. This surely was turning out to be a very special occasion!

Maya introduced the two women as Amanda and Miranda—the light one and the dark one. They all gathered around Isabella and touched her arms.

"As your Inner Guides," Amanda said, "we are here to assist you in understanding the light and the dark aspects of life."

"You and Panther are the dark side of Lion Cub, and Lion Cub is the light side of you," Miranda added. "For you to transform into Oracle, you need to explore both the dark and the light. You need to live both in full acceptance, respecting the dark when you are exploring the light side of life, and respecting the light when you are exploring the dark side. Any Being who hasn't experienced both cannot be a true oracle."

Isabella took a deep breath. "Then there's a place for me in Lion Cub's life," she said, her green eyes shining with intensity.

"Yes," Daniel's voice came in. "Now that you are finding your place, I am also able to take form."

With this, his voice started taking shape. All the colors of the rainbow came around the voice, moving, dancing, and blending. Then the colors moved further and further away, forming a large egg-like, glowing cocoon around an empty space. Slowly, the empty space took the form of a handsome young man.

Isabella couldn't speak. When she found her voice, she asked, "Are you really as young as you look? Judging from the wisdom in your eyes, you could be 100 years old."

Daniel smiled. Babla knew this smile so well; it was Alan's wise smile, it was Eternal Friend's smile of total acceptance.

"As your Inner Guide, I am ageless," he replied. "We take the most appropriate form to assist you in the best possible way. For now, your part in Lion Cub's life is to think about men. Therefore, I'm to be your man. Only a man who sees you as the attractive, seductive woman you are can help you own your energy and live it in its totality. As an Inner Guide, I know how to receive you in your full womanhood. The moment you open yourself to me, the way a flower opens itself to the sun, you will find the seed of Truth deep within your womb."

Isabella was loving Daniel's attention. "A man just for me? Who wants to receive all of me? Wow!" she said, her seductive smile back on her lips and in her eyes. She walked to Daniel and started rubbing her body on his. Babla saw his eyes deepen in color and space. He was taking in Isabella's oozing, seductive energy, almost drawing it out of her.

Their bodies wrapped and entwined together, and a dance began. Babla realized that neither of them was "doing" the dance; it was simply happening— just the way her dance with Otter had happened. "Otter!" she smiled. He had taught her so many things, the most valuable being the Dance of "us." Now, Isabella and Daniel were dancing it. It felt so good to watch!

Babla felt the warm glow of her Higher Self all around her. When she looked up, she saw both Higher Selves observing the dance. Nodding, Lion Cub's Higher Self stepped forward and made a hand gesture, which made Lion Cub and the black panther appear, even though Isabella was still visible.

Leaving Isabella and Daniel to their dance, Higher Self turned to Lion Cub and Panther and said in a simple manner, "The first step has been taken. Now we can prepare for the second step, which is connected with you, Panther. As long as Lion Cub disappears when you appear, you won't know that you are a part of her. As long as you are alone in your rage, you are also stuck in it. The first step for you, Panther, is to look at Isabella and Lion Cub and realize that all three of you are parts of one Being—Oracle.

"The seed of Truth, soon to be Isabella's, will go through you to be initiated, because your panther energy (the potency and fire you carry within) is necessary for this initiation. If you are stuck in rage, however, the seed will burn. For you to go beyond your fury and feel the Essence of your pantherness, you need to connect with Lion Cub."

Babla had to give Panther credit because for all his ferocity, he was quick to understand. Within moments, the glow in his eyes had shifted from out-of-control rage to sheer vitality, and Babla had lost all her fear.

Panther moved ever so slowly toward Lion Cub. They sat, facing each other for a long time, with Amanda and Miranda on either side and Black Panther close by, just in case. Now that many of her wounds had healed and she was not in death pain anymore, Lion Cub looked soft, cute, and lovable to Babla. At the same time, Panther looked strong and intense.

One moment Panther was quietly gazing at Lion Cub and the next, he grabbed her, rolled over, and plopped her upon his chest. Lion Cub curled up, totally relaxed. They lay there for a long time, melting and merging into each other.

Then Isabella walked over and snuggled up to Lion Cub, her long black hair spreading onto Panther's chest and the ground. After some time in this deep connecting, Lion Cub's Higher Self nodded, and a silhouette of a woman appeared exactly where Panther, Lion Cub, and Isabella were lying. She had long black hair that was striking against a pearl-colored gown. She was barely visible and Babla had to look and look to see her at all.

"I am Oracle," she said in a way that reminded Babla of Lion Cub, Panther, and Isabella all in one. Her voice was soft, intense, and sensual, and her face was getting clearer. Her eyes were dark and light at the same time, penetrating deeply to see the Truth. As Oracle came into full view, Babla's mouth dropped open. Why, she had wings—two huge brown wings that reminded Babla of . . . what? Where had she seen these wings before? "Wise Owl!" Babla called out, remembering. "She has owl wings!"

Oracle smiled gracefully. "Yes," she said, "owl wings. You and I have the panther and the owl in common; that's why my birthing had to happen through you. I am very grateful to you, Babla, and to all your Guides." With that, Oracle disappeared.

Everyone looked at the Higher Selves. "When Lion Cub's healing is complete, Oracle will be able to stay," Lion Cub's Higher Self explained. "The next piece will happen at the Healing Circle; Humangus's presence is needed for that."

Babla was delighted. She wasn't quite sure whether Panther and Isabella had a pure heart; Lion Cub definitely had one, and Oracle certainly had Truth in her heart. What could be purer?

After telling the others how to find the Witch's Cave, Babla said good-bye and left. Since leaving the Alchemist's Exotic Land, she had not seen all of her Inner Guides and the Higher Self in one place. Feeling relaxed, nurtured, and fulfilled after her encounter with Oracle, Babla now sensed Rabia's presence close by. This made her feel very safe, as if she were wrapped in a soft warm blanket.

MOUNTAIN LION: Loss of the Heart

Babla walked along a path that was leading her out of the forest. She knew this wasn't the way to the Witch's Cave, yet somehow she felt the urge to continue. She stepped into a clearing surrounded by mountains of all sizes, from very high peaks to small hills, and decided to explore this place before going back to the forest.

Each mountain seemed to have a different color. In between them Babla saw green plants, trees, and flowers. Even though this was nature at its most pristine, the whole area looked well kept. She wondered whether any Being lived there.

Just as she asked herself the question, Babla saw a huge creature out of the corner of her eye. It stood atop a nearby mountain and was preparing to jump. The next thing she knew, she was on the ground, held down by this enormous Being. She shut her eyes tight and said in one breath, "Hi, I'm Babla. If you're going to eat me, please do so fast because I don't like pain very much."

There was a terrifying pause. Then, in a thick, rich voice, the Being replied, "I never eat anyone before I see their eyes."

Babla opened her eyes and looked straight into a pair of deep blue ones; in her journeys she had seen many beautiful eyes, but never like these.

"Hi," said the creature, towering above the little girl between his paws. "I am Mountain Lion. Welcome to my Kingdom." There was no desire to hurt or kill in his eyes.

Babla took a breath and tried to relax. "Why did you jump on me?"

"I didn't want you to run away," he explained. "If you had seen me coming slowly down the mountain, you would have surely gone running back into the forest. Besides, I like to greet my guests personally."

"This encounter is definitely very personal." Babla's slight smile showed he was winning her over, even though he was still on top of her, staring into her eyes.

"Well, I like physical contact," admitted Mountain Lion. "As the King of the Mountains, I don't get much if I don't look for it myself." They started rolling around; now she was on top of him, a moment later he was on top of her.

Then something shifted, and Babla thought of Otter. From "doing" the rolling, they had started "dancing" it. Rolling was happening by itself without either of them initiating it. Babla was fascinated.

All movement stopped. They stayed on the ground for a long time in total silence, breathing in and out, feeling, sensing, relaxing. Babla didn't know where her body ended and his started.

Eventually, they separated, and Mountain Lion offered Babla a tour of his Kingdom. He told her he didn't have just one place to call home. This whole area was his; and every day, he ate and slept in another spot.

Babla told him that she was on her way to the Witch's Cave to meet other pure-hearted Beings. She looked up and said, "What about you? You seem to have a pure heart, too. Would you like to join us?"

There was silence, and it smelled of sadness.

"Well," said Mountain Lion at last, "the truth is that I don't have a heart at all. My heart is in a box inside the highest mountain, which is called the Green Mountain of the Lionheart."

Babla wanted to see his heart. She jumped on Mountain Lion's back, and they ascended the Green Mountain. The very top looked like a cap, and it was. Mountain Lion took it off, and Babla saw a dark tunnel going into the earth. They went down, with Babla holding onto his tail because he could see so well in the dark.

In the cavern below, Babla could barely make out a large crystal box with a huge heart in it. The heart was pumping, only because it was hooked up to the life in the crystal.

"What happened?" asked Babla.

"I don't remember," Mountain Lion answered, sounding hopeless. "All I know is that this is my heart and that a long time ago it was in my chest. I really don't know what happened."

Babla examined the heart carefully. After sensing Alan's approval, she said, "I think your heart is very pure, in your chest or not. I would like for you to come and join the Healing Circle. And maybe Humangus, the Witch, or another Being there can help you."

Mountain Lion nodded. His eyes were even deeper now, partially because of sorrow, but also from gratitude. This was the first time that anyone had thought he had a pure heart.

Very carefully, Babla took the crystal box and placed it on Mountain Lion's back. They climbed up the tunnel to the top, then went down the mountain. The journey took a long time because of the crystal. When they reached the forest, Babla found some long leaves and vines and tied the heart to his back. Now he could travel by himself. This seemed very important to him. Looking lovingly into her eyes, he said good-bye and started his journey, knowing he must stay alert to protect his heart from possible predators.

Babla went further into the forest and sat down on a fallen log. "I don't understand," she said out loud. "Why couldn't he have just come with me? I'm going to the same place."

Alan appeared and sat next to her, putting his arm around her. "Because he is a male Being, and also a king. This is his initiation," he said in his warm voice. "Sometimes a male Being feels the urge to accomplish something all by himself; it is very satisfying. And a king needs to know he has enough strength to protect his Kingdom.

"This is a very important moment in Mountain Lion's life. He is about to transform the past and let his heart back into his chest. The path of the heart can be started only by oneself. When he reaches the Witch's Cave, Mountain Lion will be ready to receive help from other Beings. Remember, you had to start your journey alone, too."

Now she understood. Alan disappeared, and Babla continued on her way to the cave.

FROZEN MAN AND GAYLAND: Ice in the Heart

After several days of walking, Babla reached the end of the forest and came to the stony area surrounding the cave. She was excited because soon she would see her friend the Witch. She was also curious about what adventures the next days, weeks, and months would bring.

At the cave, Babla was greeted by a smiling Witch and M, wagging her tail. She was eager to share details about her journeys and hear the Witch's story. It was clear that the Witch had become wiser somehow. This warmed Babla's heart.

The next day while having tea, the Witch said to Babla, "There's still a place in my heart that I can't reach. It feels numb. I wonder what is in there?"

Babla wondered if they should consult the Guides. Just then, a sound at the cave's entrance signaled the presence of a Being. It was frozen from head to toe and staggered in slowly and stiffly. "Who are you?" asked the Witch in surprise.

"I am Frozen Man," came the brittle answer. "I need your help in melting this ice." At that very moment, the Witch felt ice in her heart, in the part that had been numb before.

They made a fire in the fireplace and Frozen Man stood in front of it. Nothing happened. Babla was puzzled. How could this be? If anything could melt ice, it was fire. "Maybe he needs another kind of fire," she said to the Witch, not knowing the full meaning of her statement.

"Another kind of fire," repeated the Witch thoughtfully. "Well," she said at last, "if outer fire doesn't work, maybe inner fire will."

They looked at each other and went to work. Babla knew about the inner fire in her Center, so she taught the Witch how to access it. They stood on either side of Frozen Man and imagined fire from both their Centers coming out and entering him. The ice started to melt and at least one layer of it dissolved. But Frozen Man was still covered with a thick layer. Babla whispered in his ear, "Frozen Man, what kind of fire will melt your ice?"

"The flame in the Witch's heart," he managed to say. They looked at each other, perplexed. They knew that the heart carries many things, yet they had never seen a flame there.

"I can't find any fire in my heart!" the Witch protested. "There is only ice."

"Maybe the ice in your heart is somehow connected to Frozen Man," suggested Babla, searching for a solution.

The Witch stared intently at Babla, her clear blue eyes a mix of uncertainty and a sense of loss. The two friends stayed there, looking into each other for a long time.

Then an inner door opened, and Babla heard White Swan: "Accept what is. Go with what is. Go totally into what is happening now. Be fully in it with awareness. Enjoy."

"Go with what is," Babla mimicked. "Go with what is." She started thinking out loud. "Imagine," she said half to herself, half to the Witch. "Imagine that we accept what is, that is, Frozen Man and your frozen heart. We've already accepted Frozen Man. Now we can accept your frozen heart by going totally into it."

"What's the difference between being in my frozen heart with or without awareness?" the Witch asked.

"Hm," said Babla, thoughtfully. "That's a good question."

They heard the fluttering of wings and Wise Owl took form on Babla's left shoulder, her yellow eyes shining with a deep, fiery, yet quiet wisdom. Wise Owl came right to the point.

"Awareness," she said, "means watching. You watch what is happening without needing to change it. Going into the frozen heart with awareness means you go in with no agenda, no expectation. You are simply there, and each step you take leads you to the next step without knowing beforehand what this will be. It is an unfolding.

"Without awareness you would have a preconceived idea of what you want to find or what you think should be different. If you want to find fire, for example, and all you see is ice, you will miss the beauty and the lessons of ice. If you fully accept the ice, it will reveal its truth to you."

In both Babla's and the Witch's eyes Wise Owl could see the thrill of her message mixed with anticipation and fear. She agreed to stay longer, in case they needed more assistance. The owl made an opening gesture with her wing and suddenly the Witch's frozen heart slid out of her chest and grew nearly to the size of the cave. Holding hands, Babla and the Witch took a step into the heart; it was cold and icy. They took a few more steps. All ice. Nothing was there but solid ice.

The Witch was ready to give up. "I don't know why we are here," she moaned.

"Let's try something," Babla suggested. "Remember what Wise Owl said? If we fully accept the ice, it will reveal its truth."

They closed their eyes, took a few breaths, and started saying, "Yes. Yes, ice. We fully accept you."

After a while of saying "yes," Babla asked the ice, "Will you reveal your truth to us?" Then they became very quiet and listened.

Out of the silence came a faint sound. Somebody was crying. Babla and the Witch began to walk toward the crying sound. Soon they realized the weeping was coming from the inside ice. The Owl brought two shovels, and the two friends dug into the ice. They dug a big hole and found a four- or five-year-old little girl with blue eyes, reddish blond curly hair, and a very sad face.

She looked up, startled. "Who are you?" she asked. "How did you find me here? I thought I was lost forever. Lost and lonely." She started crying again, putting her face into her little palms.

The Witch said thoughtfully, "Since this is my heart we're in, you must somehow be connected to me, little girl. Let's get you out of here."

Together with Babla, she helped the child out of the hole, out of her heart, and back into the cave. They realized that another layer of ice had melted from Frozen Man.

"I don't understand it," said the Witch with a smile, "but it seems we're on the right track," and Babla agreed.

Sitting in front of the fire, Babla asked the little girl her name.

"Gayland," she answered. Just like Frozen Man, Gayland couldn't seem to get warm from the flames, she shook and shivered uncontrollably, so the Witch took her onto her lap where the girl could lean against the Witch's chest and be held by her strong arms. Meanwhile, Babla began stroking the child's fuzzy hair.

It didn't take long for Gayland to feel the Love being poured into her. Her tears changed from the sad tears of a frozen, lost, and lonely little girl to the warm tears of the opening heart. Soft and tentative at first, not quite trusting, not quite sure whether it was safe to open, she was hesitant to receive the Love flowing from these two strangers. But as steady Love kept coming, her little heart kept opening.

Gayland was soon sensing that her heart had wings. At the same moment, the Witch felt intense heat rising in her heart. Flames sprang out so hot that the ice melted: solid one moment, gone the next.

"Ahhh!" came a distant sigh. Startled, the Witch looked up to see that Frozen Man was moving. He was even able to bend his arms and legs. He sat down, leaning against a wall. "Good work!" he said smiling. "You have found the flame in your heart."

However, one thin layer of ice still wrapped around his body. "This last layer needs the Giant's touch," said Wise Owl, answering Babla's questioning eyes. Then she suggested that the Witch rest, taking some time to be with Gayland.

Babla also needed to rest and get ready for the Healing Circle. Saying good-bye to them both, she left the cave, Wise Owl perched on her left shoulder. After a while, the Owl became invisible, yet Babla could feel her supporting presence.

On her way, she saw Wondering Magician walking toward the cave. She was pleased that the Magician and the Witch would spend time together before everyone else arrived. Then she remembered that a long time ago her Inner Guides had suggested exactly that.

THE WORLD OF SILENCE: *True Connection*

Cautiously, Wondering Magician entered the cave and glanced around, trying to be sensitive to his surroundings. He saw that the Witch had made it to the cave ahead of him and was resting, a small girl asleep in her arms. He immediately apologized for disturbing them and was about to leave when he heard the Witch calling. "Magician! Welcome. Will you come and sit with me awhile?"

Thankful for this invitation, he sat near the fire and listened to her story about Frozen Man. The Magician noticed a stiff man in a dark corner of the cave and was relieved that at least he could move. He seemed to be patiently waiting for the last layer of ice to melt away—when the time was right.

The Magician turned back toward the Witch—and time disappeared. Once again they entered the World of Words with Meaning. For a long time they talked, and each word seemed to nurture a forgotten part in them.

Then, a door they hadn't known about opened, and they entered yet another world—or did they?

The Magician's hands began shaking and he got up, pretending to be cheerful. He said, "It was so nice seeing you, Wise Witch. But now I must be on my way. I have other things to do. I'm sure you do, too. The little girl on your lap will probably soon need your attention." His hat slid to the left as he prepared to bolt.

Before the Witch could utter a word, the fire in her heart burst out. Flames surrounded the Magician, dancing and playing all around him. They wouldn't let him move. Then, out of nowhere, the Witch's hand reached over and took his hand, and they went beyond the words of meaning to the World of Silence.

Hand in hand, they found themselves in a jungle; everything was and green and utterly quiet. Wondering Magician, his hand still shaking, examined his surroundings. He was a Being who loved nature, yet this . . . this was different somehow. The silence was so deeply penetrating, so alive.

When they started walking through the Jungle of Silence, his hands stopped shaking. They were still now, one of them at his side, gently moving with each step he took; the other one holding the Witch's hand, feeling the warmth of her presence.

After a few attempts to push his hat to the left, the hand at his right temple gave up. It wasn't working! It was as if the Silence kept his hat on his head. In wonder, the Magician realized that he had never before felt his hat this solidly on his head.

Used to living in the World of Words with Meaning, he opened his mouth to express astonishment, but instead of sounds, colorful bubbles gushed out like a liquid rainbow. There was only silence—thick, pulsating, and ever-present.

Taking a deep breath, he relaxed into the World of Silence, letting it in. He felt a deliciously sweet nectar oozing into his heartspace, sweeping away all leftover bitterness. Blissfully, he looked at the Witch, who had been observing him. She smiled back and squeezed his hand.

The Silence was thicker now, pressing to be acknowledged. As they stepped into it, their movements slowed. Lifting even one foot took an eternity. Waves of Silence filtered through them; waves of Bliss followed. Here they were, the Witch and the Magician, moving in slow motion through Silence and Bliss—so mysterious, so alive, so expansive, so still.

Gayland stirred. The Witch and Wondering Magician looked at each other; they were sitting in the cave next to the fire, holding hands, the little girl on the Witch's lap. With her free hand, the Witch stroked Gayland's hair and face, feeling the Love in her heart for this little one, who was waking up to a new life.

The Magician also reached over with affection. When Gayland woke up from a peaceful sleep, she saw two pairs of blue eyes resting tenderly upon her. She knew then that her time of sadness and loneliness was over.

DEER WOMAN: Maturing

Babla wandered in the forest, not knowing exactly why she was there. Wise Owl had told her just to enjoy the forest and that things would unfold. Babla talked to the trees, the birds, and the plants; there was so much life here. She realized that she could enjoy life with or without an obvious purpose. In fact, every moment seemed to reveal something new. It was as if each moment was a bud, and if she enjoyed it, it would become the flower that it was meant to be. If she didn't enjoy the moment, however, the bud stayed closed, revealing nothing. She also found that every moment she enjoyed made it easier to enjoy the next one. And so, many flowers opened, revealing their beauty to Babla.

In awe, Babla felt the stillness behind each flower. She understood how beauty was born out of this immense silence.

One day while in the forest, Babla heard the light footsteps what seemed to be a cautious traveler. Curious, she waited as the sound came closer.

Out from behind a tree, a deer appeared. Seeing Babla, it stopped, then changed into a young doe, then a baby deer. "Deer Lady!" shouted Babla as she ran up to hug her.

Returning to her adult form, Deer Lady happily greeted her friend. They talked for a long time, exchanging stories.

Then, Deer Lady rested her big almond eyes on Babla. "I'm stuck. I know I'm on my way to becoming Deer Woman, yet I don't know what's next. It seems I've done everything I know to do, and I have come to where I am now. But I feel frustrated about how to proceed."

Babla felt deep compassion and could understand her friend's predicament, remembering times like this on her own journey. "Maybe you need to learn new tools," she suggested.

"It almost feels like I need someone to guide me," Deer Lady replied. "I know I have everything I need inside, but I don't know how to get there. I need help finding the key. All I feel is a deep yearning."

They sat, holding each other in stillness, enjoying the Love they were sharing. In her ear, Babla heard the faint voice of her Higher Self. "Tell her to follow the yearning. It is the key."

When she told this to Deer Lady, two teardrops, one from each eye, rolled down her cheeks. She looked at Babla, knowing that Higher Self was right.

"If I do follow the yearning," said Deer Lady after a while, "it will lead me out of the forest. I've tried to find other Beings who would come with me, but somehow it didn't work out. I'm not sure if I can make it alone outside of the forest."

"Maybe," said Babla, "you need to find some of your Inner Guides before you leave the forest."

She heard Higher Self's voice again, "Tell her to follow the yearning. It is all she needs to do."

When Babla repeated these words to Deer Lady, her friend nodded her head. "Yes," she said with a sigh. "I see that until I follow this yearning, nothing else will work. And it will lead me out of the forest, at least for a while."

It was time to say good-bye. They gave each other a long hug, feeling nurtured by their friendship. Babla continued her journey, not knowing what was next, while Deer Lady went through the forest, in quest of her deepest yearning.

Deer Lady wandered for a long time. She felt so alone, even though she was aware of the beauty all around her. She loved the forest, for it was her home. She loved everything about it: the fresh air; the lush foliage; the huge trees, each so unique; the birds of many different colors and sizes; and all the other Beings with whom she shared it.

The thought of leaving for some unknown place to follow her yearning was frightening. She felt ripples of resistance travel all through her body. What if she got lost? She couldn't imagine living without the forest. What was life like outside?

She felt herself getting smaller and smaller until she was a baby deer. She curled up on the forest ground and waited, frozen in panic. As little fawn, she couldn't take even one step out of her beloved forest. That was that. She felt such intense love for her home that huge teardrops, filled with this love, rolled down her cheeks into the ground, nourishing the earth.

Slowly, she felt her body shift into a young deer, and her panic disappeared. She felt stronger inside and sat up, looked around. She didn't see any reason to leave her forest. Why should she, anyway? Just because some little girl had said so? She was happy here, and she wasn't about to go anywhere.

She felt the flames of her inner fire rising, leaping to burn everything in sight. Deer Lady swiftly shifted into a grown-up deer and calmed down the fire; she definitely didn't want to harm the forest. She sat there, feeling so lost, so desperate.

What was her truth? Talking to Babla, she had felt very clearly that following her yearning was the right thing to do. Yet now, between the frozen panic of the baby and the raging fire of the young deer, she had lost all sense of direction. In utter desperation, she begged the ancient trees, "I need help. What is my truth?"

All sound stopped as the forest seemed to go to its very Core with her question. Then, from the depths, the Voice of the Forest spoke. "Follow your yearning."

Slowly, Deer Lady got up and started to walk, her yearning her only guide. She listened to the different sounds in the forest—birds singing, leaves rustling, rabbits running in the brush.

"Perhaps," she winced, "I'm hearing these sounds for the last time." Nevertheless, she resigned herself to being in the not-knowing, and it felt okay in a strange, unfamiliar way.

When she came to the edge of the forest, Deer Lady saw sand all around— hot, vast, flat desert. Walking into it, she felt so out of place, so lonely, that she almost turned back. But her yearning was stronger, guiding her feet. There was no stopping now.

With hesitant steps, she continued into the red-orange desert. If the yearning had brought her here, there must be a reason. Deer Lady stopped, her fear subsiding. She waited without a clue about what she was supposed to do.

Then she remembered the Voice of the Forest; maybe the desert also had a voice. She took a long breath and asked, "Voice of the Desert, will you guide me?"

From deep within the burning sand, the answer came. "You are here to heal the young deer. Her fire needs to become one with mine. Lie on me, lie in me, take me fully into you. I am the Desert; I am hot, yet never angry. Learn to celebrate your heat without needing to lash out.

"My gift is about containing the heat, about embracing it without doing anything. When the flames of the young deer merge into me, she will be no more, and you can leave."

Deer Lady nodded and gave herself to the sand. Lying still, she felt the heat enter her body. When she was filled with the warmth, she got up and dug a hole, nestled into it, and covered herself with sand. She knew the desert was entering her being.

After a long time buried in the desert, her very Core accepted the heat. She started shifting into the young deer, feeling the flames of her rage, her resistance to everything that was happening in the moment. The young one wanted to burn up the whole desert. The more she spread out her fire, however, the more the desert simply sucked them in and they disappeared.

At last, the young deer had no more flames left. All she could do was surrender and let the desert consume her. Gradually, as she relaxed, she dissolved. It was the adult deer who was now lying in the desert.

Deer Lady stayed there and rested. When she got up, she thanked the desert, her heart overflowing with gratitude. Turning inside, she asked her yearning to guide her.

Deer Lady's feet led her out of the desert to the ocean. She stood on the shore, looking out into blue-green water—vast, ever-moving, ever-flowing. "What now? What am I supposed to do now?" she thought, panic setting in.

She knew that if she went any further in this sea with its huge, powerful waves much taller than herself, she would drown. Remembering the Voices of the Desert and the Forest, she asked, "Ocean, do you also have a voice to guide me?"

"Yes," roared the liquid blue. "Lie on me, then lie in me. You will not drown. By taking me fully into you, you can heal the baby deer, her frozen panic, and her deep sadness."

Deer Lady gingerly took a few steps into the welcome coolness of the water. She edged in, then lifted her legs to let the water carry her.

Immediately she again became the baby deer, petrified. With her feet off the ground, there was no support. The ocean could do with her whatever it wanted; she was at its mercy. For a long time, the panicked little fawn floated, curled into a tight ball.

Then she heard a gentle voice—the Voice of the Ocean. "I am your support. I am not your enemy. Let me hold you. Let me carry you."

Deer baby opened her eyes; she was still alive. "Well, maybe the ocean is telling the truth."

Her body relaxed a little as she started to see that the waves really were carrying her. With their support, a more trusting Deer Lady became a grown-up deer once again. This was fun; she totally relaxed and let herself be taken by the waves. A broad smile came over her face; she felt fluid.

Then she remembered the second phase of this process and let herself sink into the ocean, all the way down. All was quiet here. She felt the support of the sand beneath her and the flow of the water all around her and became very still.

After a while, she felt herself shift into the baby deer again, feeling profound sadness. Out of nowhere, tears began rolling down her cheeks, merging with the ocean. There seemed to be no end to them.

After what seemed an eternity, and as suddenly as they had started, the tears stopped. The baby deer dissolved into the ocean, and Deer Lady was back to being an adult again. She stayed there, letting the water deeply enter her Core. "The Flow of Life," she thought, "this is the Flow of Life." And she was right.

Deer Lady came out of the water and saw that she was in a lush, beautiful valley with rocks and flowers everywhere. It looked somewhat familiar to her. So she walked around, enjoying the colors and the fragrance of her surroundings.

Then she remembered that she had a drum hanging on her back. On impulse, she started beating it. She was so deeply engulfed in the sound of the drum that she didn't notice she wasn't alone.

When she looked up, she saw a wooden house with many windows. At the top of the steps leading to the house was a gorgeous lion—so regal and full of himself. Realizing that Deer Lady had seen him, he started shifting into a woman—with a smile as bright as the sun, silver hair, laughing eyes, and open arms.

"Lion Woman!" smiled Deer Lady. "It is so nice to see you!"

Lion Woman gazed at her, with ancient wisdom in her eyes. "Welcome, Deer Woman," she said at last. "Welcome to my house."

IV.
the place beyond paradise

DOLPHIN AND EMANUELLA: *Unveiling the Longing*

After leaving her deer friend Babla spent more time in the forest, marveling at the beauty of life. One day Rabia appeared and said that it was again time to visit the Place Beyond Paradise. White Swan was calling them back. Babla was excited and wondered whether the same loving Beings might be there and how they would find the way. Rabia told her that White Swan had given directions and it was easy to find. Babla was grateful for an Adult Self like Rabia, so strong and resourceful, and trusted her totally. She knew that together they were capable of having a lot of fun.

After completing their preparations, they took off for the Place Beyond Paradise. They arrived at a place where a huge bird was waiting to fly them to their destination. Babla and Rabia climbed aboard the bird and enjoyed the spacious sky, relaxing into a new adventure.

Finally, after a long flight, they landed. The Place Beyond Paradise seemed even more beautiful than Babla had remembered. But this time, she also saw Beings who weren't very loving.

When she asked Rabia, her Adult replied, "Living here doesn't automatically make Beings loving. As Beings, we have a choice. If we choose Love inside, this place gives back Love. If we choose fear, then that's what we find instead. The Beings who aren't very loving have chosen fear."

Babla started looking into their eyes, and slowly she could understand what Rabia had meant. The Beings in fear had a dark ring in their eyes. Moreover, they didn't look at her directly or, if they did, they stared coldly.

The ones who had chosen Love, however, had a spark in their eyes as if they were laughing from the inside. They looked deep into Babla in a warm, soft way. Babla told Rabia she wanted to play only with the loving Beings and not with the others.

Rabia smiled, understanding. "I know," she said. "It's easier to be around loving Beings and feel accepted and nurtured. It is a good place to start. But you and I are strong enough now to explore being around others who have chosen fear. Can we feel loved and accepted from the inside, no matter what others think? Can our hearts stay warm and open, even if theirs may be closed and cold? The more we choose Love, the less our Love is dependent on how others around us feel."

"Then the fearful Beings could learn from us how to love!" offered Babla joyfully.

"That's very true," said Rabia with a smile. "Yet remember, little one, this must be their own choice. Even if they don't choose to learn from us, we still can radiate Love no matter what."

One of the most wonderful things that happened for Babla during her stay was the arrival of her beloved friend Butterfly. They were overjoyed to see each other again, to explore and to share their experiences. Butterfly's wings were almost totally healed from the Archer's wound. She was able to fly long distances now without any pain. In the Place Beyond Paradise, Babla and Butterfly had a wonderful time together.

One day, Rabia took Babla by the hand and introduced her to Dolphin. Slender and graceful, there was something different about her. Babla realized it had to do with her breath; she seemed to be breathing in a certain rhythm that relaxed and revitalized her. Dolphin appeared to be in motion and yet totally still simultaneously. How could this be?

"Dolphin," explained Rabia, "has the key to the next step in our journey of surrendering to Love. You'll be staying with her, and I will come get you when it is time."

After Rabia left, Dolphin took Babla to a deep and dark lake. Its surface looked calm, yet there was something unsettling about this quiet. Babla decided that she did not like this lake. It took her by total surprise when Dolphin asked her to dive into it. Seeing the shock in Babla's eyes, Dolphin smiled gently and said, "I will dive in with you. You won't be alone."

She gave Babla a little blue pill to swallow to be able to breathe in the water. Then they both dove in. It was cool and dark. Babla started to feel scared and alone. She was sure she was never going to make it out alive.

"What a way to die," she thought. Within her desperation, she heard Rabia's words in her ears, "You have a choice between Love or fear."

Babla realized she had been choosing fear and decided to choose Love. But how? "I need some help," she cried into the dark water. All of a sudden she remembered that Dolphin was diving next to her.

As she took a deep sigh, she heard Dolphin's voice. "Great, Babla. You chose Love."

"This can't be true," thought Babla. "It is impossible to talk under water."

"This is telepathy," replied Dolphin. "As long as you were choosing fear, I couldn't use telepathy. Fear separates you from all life around you. It makes you feel lonely and lost. When you choose Love, the separation simply disappears and you feel connected and supported. The moment you chose Love, you felt my presence, which had been here the whole time."

Babla was intrigued. She realized the darkness of the lake had a certain beauty. Dolphin nodded in agreement.

Suddenly tears were rolling from Babla's eyes. They came in large drops from a deep place inside of her. When they stopped, Babla felt the beauty of the blackness once more. Then, they started again, melting into the waters of the lake. With each cessation of the tears Babla felt the radiance of the dark lake expanding until it was all around her, vibrating.

At last Babla and Dolphin came to a cave. Babla was happy to have reached the bottom of the lake.

"This is not the bottom yet," corrected Dolphin. "We can't go on without stopping here, though."

As they glided into the cave, Babla saw a warrior, fully armored, standing in the middle. She couldn't see whether this was a male or a female warrior because metal armor was covering every inch of flesh.

"Who are you?" asked Babla. "What are you doing here?"

In a rigid, tense voice, the answer came: "I am Rabia's Inner Woman. I am very strong and independent. I don't need a man in my life. Rabia doesn't either. Men just create trouble. She is much better off without one. I am totally fulfilled and happy alone."

"Then why are you wearing this armor?" Dolphin asked softly. There was silence.

"I don't remember," finally replied Inner Woman. "It seems like I've always had it on."

Babla was curious. "Will you show yourself to us without the armor?"

"I can try," came the answer, "but I might need your help." With Babla and Dolphin's assistance the armor came off, and to Babla's total surprise out came a beautiful woman. She had wavy, shoulder-length black hair and flashing black eyes and was dressed like a gypsy. Sitting down on the cave's stone floor, she began to sob.

"What is your name?" Babla wanted to know.

"I am Emanuella. I feel a deep longing to merge with a man. I feel so empty in this cave alone. And yet I don't believe I'll ever find the right man. That's why I created the armor and started pretending not to need a man in my life. I'm afraid to let myself feel the desire and the despair. So when a man approaches, the armor automatically pushes him away, saying he could not possible be the right one for me. The more the armor pushes men away, however, the emptier I feel and the more desperate I become."

Babla was at a loss, but Dolphin wasn't. This slender, graceful Being moved toward Emanuella and sat next to her. Then, Babla saw something miraculous; it was as if Dolphin as Dolphin had disappeared, even though her body was there, and something else had entered.

Babla heard Rabia's voice in her ear: "She has chosen Love, she has allowed Love to enter her fully. She has become Love now."

Dolphin spoke to Emanuella. "Be empty," she said. "Allow yourself to be totally empty, and feel the longing to be filled, the longing to merge with the man, the waiting. As the Inner Woman, this is your nature. Be empty, waiting to be filled, without knowing whether it will happen or not, without expecting it, without giving up. As long as you are empty, celebrate the emptiness. If and when the man fills you, celebrate the fullness. Your misery comes when you think you shouldn't be empty, or when you believe it is not okay to want to be filled. Accept totally that you are empty and that you have a longing to merge with a man."

At this moment, Emanuella's whole being lit up, as did the entire cave. Looking up, all three of them saw White Swan. "It is totally empty," thought Babla, "and yet it is also totally full. How can this be?"

As if Babla's realization were enough, White Swan disappeared.

Emanuella was wailing now; deep, old tears were creating little puddles on the stone floor. Soon the puddles started to blend with each other, becoming a sea of tears. In utter surprise, Babla saw the stone floor of the cave crumble under the power of these tears. With a huge crack, the floor opened and the walls tumbled, leaving Babla, Dolphin, and Emanuella floating in the lake.

All three floated up to the surface of the lake. As they emerged, Dolphin said to Babla, "This is not the only time you will need to dive into the lake." It was fine with Babla because after this experience she wasn't afraid anymore.

MANUEL: Finding the Inner Man

The three of them rested on the shore for a short while. Then Dolphin said it was time for Emanuella to meet Rabia's Inner Man. She waved toward the sky, and a large white cloud drifted down to where they were. When the cloud landed, Dolphin told Babla and Emanuella that the Inner Man lived up in the clouds and this cloud would carry them there. Emanuella was shaking with fear and anticipation, but Babla was mostly curious.

After they were comfortable on the cloud, it lifted them up, drifting higher and higher in the sky for what seemed like forever. At last their cloud stopped right next to a gray cloud, on which a man was stretched out motionless, staring up at the sky.

"He looks like he's daydreaming," thought Babla when she saw that his face lacked any expression of emotion. This tall, thin man had pale blond hair and green eyes and was wearing gray clothes. Babla heard Dolphin say, "Hi", at which the man turned toward them, startled because he had not heard them.

"Hi" he responded tentatively.

"You are Rabia's Inner Man, are you not?" asked Dolphin.

"Yes . . . ," he almost stuttered. He was clearly uneasy.

Dolphin introduced him to everyone and told Emanuella's story. "It's time for you and Emanuella to meet each other and start interacting. As the Inner Woman, she needs your participation in her life. When you two fully meet and merge, her longing will dissolve, and Rabia will experience an ecstatic, silent fulfillment she has never known before."

The man, turning toward the sky again, started speaking. Babla couldn't figure out whether he was talking to himself, to the sky, or to them. "You know, I am so content here by myself," he said, "nobody to tell me what to do and how to do it; no woman needy and nagging, criticizing me all the time. Why would I want to interact with a woman?" His voice sounded dreamy and far away.

"You are a part of Rabia," Dolphin answered calmly. "As long as you and Emanuella are separate, Rabia can never be whole. I'm only suggesting that you look at Emanuella for a few minutes and tell me what happens."

"What is your name?" pitched in Babla, who couldn't contain her question any longer.

"Manuel." Inner Man slowly turned around to face them. Even though his face was as blank as before, Babla could see fear and bitterness in his eyes. His gaze wandered from Dolphin to Babla, then slowly to Emanuella. "I'm tired of women expecting things from me," he told her. "All I want is to be left alone."

Dolphin turned to Emanuella and said, "Simply look at him; feel your longing to be met, feel your emptiness, and fully accept it as your nature. You don't know whether Manuel will want to fill you or not. All you know to be your truth is that you are empty. As you dive into the emptiness, you will receive any necessary help along the way."

Just as Babla was wondering where this help might come from, she heard the soft flapping of wings. White Swan had landed on the white cloud and was looking at Emanuella with deep compassion. She couldn't hold back her tears—tears of longing, of needing, of feeling empty, of waiting.

Babla was so immersed in this experience that a jolt of the white cloud took her by surprise. She looked up and saw that Manuel had left his gray cloud and had jumped onto the white one.

"What happened, Manuel?" Dolphin asked.

"I don't know exactly. I just got mesmerized. I could see her need and her longing, yet she wasn't expecting me to fill it. This has never happened before."

Emanuella wasn't even aware of Manuel. All she could feel was the emptiness and her intense longing to fill it. The presence of White Swan was helping her to dive deeper and deeper into it.

Her tears stopped abruptly. She felt ecstasy coming out of the emptiness, spreading in and through her, surrounding her. Her despair had turned into bliss, full of beauty and silence.

Feeling someone at her left side, she turned and was shocked to see Manuel sitting there, very close by. He lifted his hand and gently touched her shoulder, his green eyes sparkling.

"When I saw you feel your longing and emptiness without expecting me to fill it, I realized that I wanted to fill it," he said to Emanuella, suddenly animated.

"I am the man who is meant to merge with you. Even though I'm still afraid, it's what I want to do."

Dolphin turned to Babla. "If we realize that we have a desire, admit it to ourselves, and simply be with it, feeling it to the fullest, something happens, something shifts and we are transformed. I can't explain how or why, I just know that it happens. And nobody knows what form it will take. This is one of the Mysteries of Life. "

"It sounds like fun," said Babla. "The less I'm afraid of life, the more I enjoy having things be unknown and unpredictable."

Manuel told them that he was ready to leave the clouds and go back with them. When Babla looked around, she realized that White Swan had disappeared.

All four made themselves comfortable on the white cloud as it started drifting down. After quite some time of floating, the cloud landed in a garden. This beautiful garden, a part of the Place Beyond Paradise, was full of flowers, huge trees and plants, waterfalls, and all kinds of birds. They found Rabia sitting there, watching a waterfall, happy to see them.

Dolphin explained that the next part of this process involved Rabia's body. Emanuella was to enter Rabia's left leg and Manuel, her right leg. Inside Rabia, they would walk hand in hand until they got used to each other. Only the Mystery of Life knew what would happen next.

FLUTE PLAYER: The World of Relationships

Babla was lying in the sun, enjoying the sound of a waterfall nearby, when she heard flute music. At first, she thought it might be the sound of the water, but gradually, she could tell it was really the music of a flute. Slow, steady, and strong, the melody enchanted Babla, who started wondering who was playing such magical tunes. As the music came closer, she opened her eyes and saw a young man walking toward her, playing a bamboo flute. His walk was as rhythmical as was his music.

He was tall and thin, with a long gray beard and fascinating green eyes. Even though everything about him and his music seemed to be slow and quiet, the intensity in his eyes reflected a different world that was strong, determined, and present.

"What an interesting Being!" Babla thought. Beyond anything else, she loved the way he played the flute.

Just then, he stopped playing and introduced himself. "Hi, I'm Flute Player." His eyes were looking directly at her.

Babla told him her name and said how much she liked his music. Flute Player sat down near her and started playing again. As the music swirled around her, Babla felt an unknown world inside her begin to open.

She lost all sense of time. She didn't know whether they had spent minutes, hours, days, weeks, or months sitting there beside the waterfall. Sinking deeper and deeper into her newfound inner world, she sensed a hardness melt within her, accompanied by a wave of despair.

"It is Eric's hopelessness," whispered Eternal Friend into her ear. "He's having a very difficult time right now. He spent a lot of time creating a wall between you and your inner world, hoping you'd never find this place. And here you are now, entering."

"Oh, poor Eric," sympathized Babla. "How can I help him? And why did he build this wall? What am I not supposed to know?" She was full of questions, wanting to know everything at once.

Eternal Friend smiled and suggested they ask Eric. Even though during their previous meetings the Cynic had mostly been in a foul mood, sarcastic, and hopeless about things, there was something about him Babla had always liked. Now, as she saw him approaching in his green tights, she felt the same affection. His cynical attitude toward life was foreign, yet compelling to Babla.

He sat next to them, looking at her and shaking his head slowly in disapproval. "Oh, Babla," he said. "When are you going to give up? You simply have to understand that certain things are not meant for you in this lifetime. One of them is going into that world inside."

"What is in there?" Babla asked.

"It is the World of Relationships. If you go inside, Rabia will be able to have a relationship with a man. And I know that they don't work. If you go in there, she will have a useless relationship and waste her time. And you'll end up getting hurt. It's you I'm trying to protect."

Babla's eyes were wide open, and she was feeling more confused with every passing moment. She felt herself falling into Eric's despair.

In the following silence, she again heard Flute Player's music. The pure, crisp tones brought her out of hopelessness and into the reality that she was sitting in a beautiful garden with a waterfall. She took a deep breath and, with the outbreath, felt herself sinking once more into the captivating new world inside. The door was open somehow, so she took a step in.

Suddenly, she heard loud cries behind her and the sound of feet running fast. She turned to see Fireball racing in her direction, yelling, "No! You can't go in! Not without me!" with Eternal Friend in close pursuit.

Babla was perplexed. Catching her breath, Fireball gasped, "Eric is right. You'll get hurt if you go in alone. I need to come with you for it to work."

"Eric doesn't believe relationships can work at all," Babla muttered in a shaky voice.

"Nonsense!" Fireball shot back. "If they aren't supposed to work, why would Existence have put this World inside of Rabia? It's there because we— all the Inner Beings—need to learn how to make relationships work for Rabia. We must never give up!"

Eternal Friend was nodding with a big smile. They felt a strong presence to the left and turning, saw Amazon Woman standing tall.

"Fireball is right," the Amazon said to Babla. "You two have to enter the World of Relationships together, hand in hand. To add to this, so that Rabia can have a healthy, adult relationship with a man, Emanuella and Manuel also need to enter right behind you, holding hands. If the relationship between the Inner Man and Inner Woman is not working, an outer relationship will not work either."

It was starting to make sense to Babla. Beyond it all, she felt safe. She heard the flute music again. It brought her back to the beauty of the moment, sitting in the garden, listening to Flute Player. She felt her little body relaxing; she was breathing softly and evenly.

When she sank once again into the inner world, Emanuella and Manuel were there, holding hands and grateful to be part of this adventure. Fireball was ready and couldn't wait.

Babla hesitated. "What about Eric?"

"Oh, that schmuck," snorted Fireball. "Just forget about him. He's no good."

"But I like him!" persisted Babla. "I don't want to leave him behind all by himself." This was her truth, and she was not about to give in.

From the corner of her eye, she could see Eternal Friend smiling. He turned to Eric and asked in his loving, yet no-nonsense way: "What if relationships *did* work, Eric?"

The Cynic looked at Eternal Friend for a long time before he answered. In this silence, they all heard the flute playing a well-known tune from the Place Beyond Paradise, about the beauty and wisdom of White Swan.

"I wonder what White Swan would say if it were here with us," Babla said.

To their surprise, they heard these words as the great bird appeared, "I would say that Eric is stuck in an old belief, which once served a purpose but is no longer Rabia's reality. Beyond that, I would say, just relax and surrender to Love and the Mystery of Life. Surrender to the beauty that is all around you, inside and out, while being fully aware of the old pattern Eric is acting out.

"In other words, if you ignore this old belief, it will live your life for you, and if you focus on it too much, you will think it is a big problem to be solved. Life is not a problem to be solved, it is a Mystery to be lived. Live it fully, ecstatically, and with awareness.

"And always remember, Babla, whenever you need me, I am here for you." As silently as it had appeared, White Swan disappeared.

Tears of joy welled up in Babla's eyes, as she experienced White Swan's immense beauty and touching words. Full of wonder, she observed Eric. Something was different about him. There was a softness and a sparkle in his brown eyes, which had been dull and listless until now. Even his sarcastic smile was more tender and sincere.

"Well," he said, looking at Eternal Friend, "I guess I'll need a new job. Here I am the eternal cynic, but if this way of protecting Babla and Rabia isn't appropriate any more, I'll need something else to do."

Feeling the presence of White Swan so deeply in her heart had opened up Babla's spontaneity. She climbed onto Eric's lap and said most adorably, "You can love and play with me."

Everyone burst out laughing. Soon Fireball joined in, and all three were wrestling on the ground.

"That's definitely one important job for you," they heard Eternal Friend say through their laughter. Without having to look, they knew that he was also laughing.

Eric raised his head to look at the Inner Guide. "What else?"

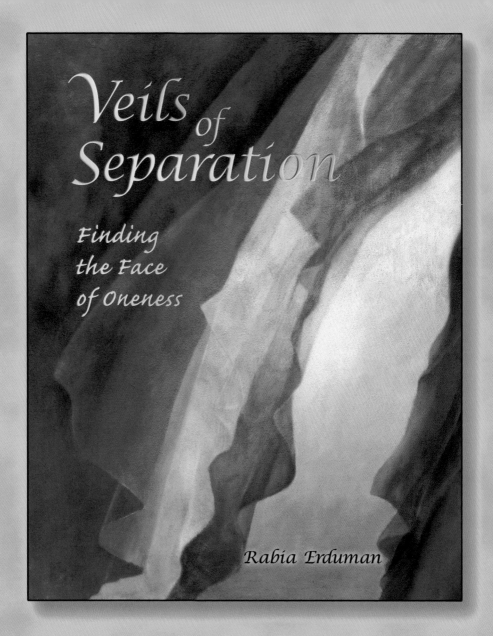

Veils of Separation

Finding the Face of Oneness

Rabia Erduman

*B*abla didn't know what to make of this all, yet
something had changed. Somehow her heart was
feeling lighter. "Surrender to Love, surrender to
Love," she repeated, touching the key around her
neck. "I wonder what it means..."

Rabia Erduman proudly announces the publication of

Veils of Separation

Finding the Face of Oneness

ISBN 0-9705260-9-1 • 240 pgs. • $18.00

Veils of Separation is an adventure story of the heart. As you wander with Babla on her search for clarity and understanding, you will shed light on your own journey as well. If you are drawn to discover your personal truth, this book will be an enchanting companion along the way." ~ Lynn Z. Foster, Ph.D., Psychologist

"Don't let the enchanting fairy tale format fool you! This is a book of supreme insight into the nature of our mind and the path of self-discovery and personal power." ~ Don Panec, Publisher, Treasure Bay Books

Two new guided imagery tapes by Rabia are also available:

- *Chakra Meditation*
- *Higher Self Meditation/Core Meditation*

Website: www.WuWeiWu.com • email: WuWeiWu@earthlink.net
Phone: (831) 642-2358

A bit more serious, Eternal Friend answered, "You have a very keen intellect, sharp and to the point. I'm sure Rabia will have lots of uses for it. If you can just doubt the right thing at the right time, you will be an important asset to her."

Eric grinned with confidence. "To doubt the right thing at the right time," he recited. "With all your help, I'm sure I can learn that."

Once more, Babla was brought back to the garden through the sound of the flute. The beautiful music went into her heart, as if her heart were dancing with it. For a long time she listened to Flute Player's different tunes—steady, fluid, solid melodies that warmed her all the way through.

Then there was silence. They sat together listening to the sound of silence until Flute Player got up, gave Babla a long hug, and went off quietly upon his journey.

V.
healing circle

HEALING CIRCLE:
The Beings of the Circle Meet Each Other

It was time for Babla and Rabia to leave the Place Beyond Paradise.

The big bird was right there to fly them back to the cave where they could rest while sharing their experiences with the Witch and Wondering Magician. They had a pleasant journey and were welcomed heartily by the others. Rabia disappeared because the Healing Circle would start soon and Babla needed to go through it by herself. Babla played with Gayland, talked with the Witch, and took walks with the Magician.

Sitting in the forest near the cave, Babla heard footsteps and spied Emanuella through the trees. With delight she jumped up and gave the Inner Woman a big hug. Emanuella was so beautiful to look at, yet deep in her eyes, Babla detected sorrow. Holding hands they sat down and Emanuella told Babla the reason for her visit.

"Babla, I need your help. In spending time with Manuel, I have realized that I'm missing a part of me. We love each other very much, and he is good to me, but something is not quite right. I have a strong feeling that I've left a part of me in the dark lake. Will you go and get it for me?"

Babla's heart quickened. Dolphin had foretold that she would go back into the lake, so she guessed this must be the reason. But, she felt growing apprehension. What if she got lost in there and never found her way back?

She heard the beloved voice of Alan in her ear. "You don't need to do this alone, Babla. When you go back to the Witch's Cave, Humangus will guide you into the lake. Remember, it's okay to ask for help."

Babla sighed with relief. It was wonderful to be reminded again and again that she wasn't alone. When she told Emanuella what Alan had said, the Inner

Woman's beautiful face lit up with hope. She gave Babla a long hug, then left to go back to Manuel.

Babla also got up and walked back to the cave. She loved Emanuella and wished to see the Inner Woman and the Inner Man happy and fulfilled.

One by one they arrived—all the Beings with pure hearts that either Babla or Humangus had invited to join the Healing Circle. Kiwi the Fuzzy Brown Bear came first and announced joyfully that she adored caves.

While they were having tea with honey and listening to Kiwi's adventures, the door inched open and in came Lost & Found Man with a drooping face. He had lost his horse. Somewhere in the forest, he had decided to take a nap and when he woke up, she was gone. They held him while he cried and mourned the loss of his companion. He was grateful to be with loving Beings.

Mountain Lion was next to enter the cave. Seeing Lost & Found Man in tears, he came around and supported his back. Lost & Found Man gratefully leaned against him, held by the others.

The door opened again and in rolled something that looked like a bunched up bird with gray feathers. Babla bravely walked toward it and introduced herself. "Hi, I'm Babla. This is a Healing Circle of Beings with pure hearts. Did Humangus the Giant send you here? Are you a bird?" She was full of questions.

A pair of light blue eyes peeked out of the dull gray rumpled feathers. They looked around and around, checking out everything in the cave. Then a faint voice trickled from the mass, "Yes, I am a bird. They call me Unloved Phoenix."

"You are a phoenix?" asked Mountain Lion taken aback. "I always wanted to meet a phoenix. But you sure don't look like one!"

"I know. This is the unloved side of me." She paused. Then, with a tiny glimmer in her eyes and a slight lilt to her voice, she asked, "Would you like to see my phoenix side?"

"Yes!" cried everyone without hesitation.

In the following silence, Unloved Phoenix closed her eyes and went inside. After a short while, Babla saw the gray feathers start to quiver. With supreme elegance and gracefulness, the feathers spread out to become two huge wings in all the colors of the rainbow, the tips touching the walls of the cave.

"Wow!" Babla gulped, her eyes big. "Look at this! The dull feathers on the outside were just hiding this color and light show on the inside!"

It truly was spectacular; with every tiniest move of the wings, the colors would shift and change, blending in and out of each other. Even more fascinating was a light, shining from inside the Phoenix, that made her feathers sparkle and glow.

"Where does this light come from?" asked Wondering Magician.

"This is the Divine Light I was born with," her answer came in a deep, strong voice. "This light is the Truth."

"Even your voice is so different!" Babla blurted, jumping up and down, too excited to sit still.

"The brilliance you carry inside, outside, and all around you is beyond words," commented Lost & Found Man.

Kiwi was also impressed. "If you stay like this, we won't need any other light," she added.

"Welcome to my cave," said the Witch, smiling. "I am thrilled to have you here."

Gradually the wings started to fold. They folded and bent and tucked until all that could be seen were dull gray feathers and two light blue eyes.

"What happened?" inquired Mountain Lion.

"I don't know," replied Unloved Phoenix. "I don't seem to have any control over when my wings open and close. When they are collapsed like this I feel pitiful and miserable, and I can't imagine that anyone could ever want to be with me and enjoy my company. I feel utterly unloved. All I want to do is die. Strangely enough, though, I feel accepted by all of you here. Maybe Humangus was right in suggesting that I come and join the Healing Circle. I'm tired of this going back and forth."

"I can understand that!" Wondering Magician pitched in. "I was tired of my extremes, too, before I started my journey. Rest assured, Unloved Phoenix, this too shall pass. You've come to the right place." Everyone nodded.

Due to a commotion outside, they opened the door to witness a huge pumpkin rolling down the hill. It rolled and rolled, coming to a halt right in front of the cave. Mountain Lion, physically the strongest, stood in front of everyone else to protect them if necessary.

Babla closed her eyes, then opened them, closed them again, and opened them again. This couldn't be true; even though the pumpkin had stopped, it was still moving somehow. It wasn't going anywhere, it was just moving in place in a funny way. What kind of a pumpkin was this?

"It's undulating!" chuckled Wondering Magician.

"An undulating pumpkin!" cackled the Witch.

"And look at all those doors and windows!" Babla pointed with amusement.

The lower half of the pumpkin was covered with doors, one next to the other; the upper half was filled with windows—two of them very close together, then a gap, then two very close again and a gap, all the way around.

"This looks like a house," Kiwi remarked. And it was.

A door opened and closed. The next door opened and closed. Then the third one opened and was filled with the egg-shaped face of a male Being. Hesitantly, he asked, "Is this the right door to come out of?" He looked frazzled and confused.

Lost & Found Man stepped forward. "Sure," he said. "Any door will get you out to the same place. Isn't the real question whether this is the right place you have come to?"

"Oh, no. Not at all," replied the man, emerging fully from the door. He wore an orange velvet robe, the same color as the pumpkin, and a round, flat, dark brown hat, tilted to one side. Scattered all around his hat and face were long twisted strands of hair. "The place is not important at all. I can mold myself to fit any place or Being I'm with. That's no problem at all. But it's not so easy to find the right window to look out from, and the right door to come out of. Because, you see, the first thing I encounter out of a door or a window is what I mold myself to. That's the real important moment. The rest is easy."

Babla wasn't quite sure whether he was talking to them or to himself. Either way, she couldn't make any sense of his words.

The man looked up, as if realizing for the first time that he wasn't alone. "By the way," he said sweetly, "I'm the Wizard in the Pumpkin. I live and travel in this undulating house and can't imagine myself without it. Although at times, it seems to take control and go wherever it wants, rather than following my directions. Like coming down the hill just now, it took over and started twisting and turning. I would have appreciated a more graceful landing.

"Anyway, I met Humangus the Giant one day, and we spent some time together. Nice chap. Before he left, he mentioned a Healing Circle and said he'd like to meet me there. So I figured why not? Is this the right place?"

"The right place and the right door," replied Lost & Found Man with a smile. "Come in, Wizard. Let me introduce you to the other Beings."

"What a strange Being," Babla thought to herself. She hoped he could be trusted. The Witch glanced at her, rolling her eyes.

"I wouldn't mind undulating in the pumpkin," the Witch whispered to Babla, unable to restrain her grin.

During the introductions in the cave, Babla had started to like this Wizard-Being. He had the most fascinating brown eyes. They were so tiny, she almost missed them until she sat close by. At first she was unimpressed. They were just regular brown eyes. But as she kept looking into them, something shifted, and a door opened to invite her into their depth. They welcomed Babla like two dark, smiling wells, and she sunk into their vastness. Once in a while, something akin to a star or a well-cut diamond would pop up and open, and the brownness of his eyes would momentarily lighten and disappear. Yet, something in his eyes told Babla there was more to understand.

"Untapped power," sounded Alan's voice in her ear. Babla shuddered.

"I hope he's not going to tap into it now," she thought. "It sounds dangerous, and besides, I wouldn't know what to do with it. I kind of like him sweet and scattered."

"He needs to find his substance," Alan whispered again. "That's why Humangus sent him here."

"Well," thought Babla, "I hope he knows how to handle this power when it starts coming through. Otherwise, I'll run." Alan almost giggled. Was he making fun of her?

The door opened gently and a light blue swan entered. Slowly, elegantly, she came close to the Beings and inquired whether this was the Healing Circle that Humangus had mentioned. Receiving a positive answer, she gave a sigh and settled down next to the fire to warm herself.

Blue Swan told her story. Since birth she had been scared of water. She had lost her family because of this fear, and wasn't able to make any swan friends because she couldn't swim. So far, nobody had been able to explain or help her with this issue.

Then one day while sitting on the shore of a lake, feeling a mixture of fear and sadness, staring longingly at a family of swans swimming in distance, she had met Humangus. "Maybe something can be done at the Circle," she ended her story in a weary voice.

The next Being to enter was an armadillo. It rolled in, tumbling to the far corner of the cave. "I don't know who any of you are, but you can't hurt me.

And don't try to come any closer! I'm going to wait here until Humangus the Giant arrives," a female voice announced.

Babla stepped forward. "I'm Babla. If Humangus sent you, you are most welcome, but we would like to know who you are and why you are here."

Still rolled up tightly, the crusty Being answered, "I am Armadillo, and I am tough. But my underside is very soft, which makes me vulnerable. As long as I stay rolled up in a ball like this, my outer armor protects me. I am invincible.

"It's a struggle to get around, though. If I could straighten out and use my feet to walk, it would be much easier. But then, my underside would be visible. My life's purpose has been to survive without getting hurt. But I'm also very unhappy.

"A little while ago, I was curled up like this, hiding in the forest. Humangus stumbled upon me and stayed with me, telling me about a different life that was possible—one much happier and more relaxed. The way to this happier life, he said, was through showing my vulnerability and softness. This caught my attention. I'm tired of hiding in the forest and being armored all the time. When Humangus invited me to the Healing Circle, I thought, if worse comes to worse, I can just roll up. So, here I am."

"Wow!" said Wondering Magician. "You are courageous. This is a big step." Everyone agreed.

Armadillo took a deep breath and nestled into her corner; she had finally realized that she was welcome.

The door opened again and in came an eel—upright and wearing a golden crown. Underneath his tail he had two little feet, which helped him walk. His shimmery skin looked wet and, unlike other eels, he had two tiny fins.

With blue eyes dancing mischievously, he smiled—if an eel can smile! "Hi," he said lightly. "I hope I'm at the right place. I'm Eelprince, Prince of the Eels. My father is the King. He sent me on a special mission to find the secret beyond all secrets. My family brought me to the forest and have gone back home. I see you are looking at my fins. All the royal eels have fins.

"I had no idea where to start and was wandering aimlessly. One day, when looking for a place to sleep, I found a huge shoe. It really made a comfortable bed. But then, in the morning, I discovered that the shoe had an owner. That's how I met Humangus. He suggested I find this cave and join the Healing Circle. Maybe with your help I'll get some clues about the elusive secret I'm to find." he concluded.

Imagining him in the Giant's shoe made everyone laugh, even Armadillo. "You sure are funny," said Wondering Magician. Eelprince smiled graciously.

"Interesting," thought Babla. She realized that behind his slippery skin and light-hearted chatter was something else.

"He has keen determination," whispered Alan.

"Yes, that's it!" she thought. "But, I definitely wouldn't want to be his enemy!"

At the sound of huge footsteps approaching, the Giant opened the door with a self-assured push. Stepping in, he looked around the cave at the fire in the fireplace and all the Beings. His eyes took in everything before he turned to Babla. "Who is the missing one?"

"Oracle. I mean, Oracle hasn't been born yet, so Isabella, along with Lion Cub and Panther." She was amazed that Humangus could tell that one Being was missing.

"He can see energy," Rabia whispered in her ear. "So can I."

"Wow! That's great!" Babla thought. She loved the fact that Rabia could do all these things. It made her feel safe.

The door swung open one last time. Isabella appeared in a tight black dress, holding Lion Cub in her arms. She came in, followed by Panther. Seductively, she walked toward the Circle, surveyed the group, and sat exactly opposite Humangus.

"I can see that this is the right place," she announced. "I want to go first."

"You will," replied the Giant, standing up. "But first, we have to deal with the cave. Where is the secret window?"

The Witch led them to it and, moving the stone, revealed an opening. Everyone took turns looking through it to the Sacred Land; even Armadillo took the risk. There was a sense of mystery and elation in the air.

Humangus invited them all to hold hands, wings, paws, and fins. They started creating a circular energy from right to left at first, then from left to right. After a while, this alternating caused a swirl of energy. All the Beings focused on this swirl.

"This is the creation of the Healing Circle," Babla thought.

"This is the creation of the Healing Circle," Humangus said. Then, very gently, he reached over and touched the wall next to the window, and the entire side of the cave crumbled.

One by one, they walked into the Sacred Land, drinking in the sight of the deep blue waters that lapped the rocks. A rumbling sound made Babla reel. Without warning, the rest of the cave had collapsed. "Wow!" everyone exclaimed. They grasped each other, watching the earth beneath what was left of the cave crack open like a giant mouth and swallow it all.

Grass began sprouting, and within minutes, one would never have guessed a cave had been on that spot.

Humangus led them to the middle of the Sacred Land and seated himself. He smiled in the direction of Isabella, his sea-colored eyes flashing with anticipation. "It's your turn."

BIRTHING OF ORACLE: *Back to Oneness*

Isabella told her story to the Circle—Oracle had appeared ever so faintly and then disappeared, because Lion Cub's healing wasn't yet complete.

Humangus looked at Isabella, Lion Cub, and Panther. "There is a part missing," he declared.

Before anyone could respond, Panther sprang toward the Giant. Babla could see he was ready to kill. Like lightning, Humangus was on his feet reaching out to catch Panther's neck mid-air.

"Look at this!" he half smiled, half gasped. "Our friend Panther doesn't seem to like the idea of a missing part. I wonder why."

Lion Cub sat up and suggested, "Maybe if the hidden part were found, Panther would lose his power."

"So you know about this other part?" Babla asked.

"Not really," Lion Cub answered. "But lately I've sensed something new around me, different from anyone else's energy. It's softer and sweeter. But then it disappears. I wish it would stay."

"It will," Humangus reassured her, still holding Panther. "First, we need to make sure Panther doesn't feel threatened by it."

"I can help you hold him," offered Kiwi.

"Me, too," added Mountain Lion.

"It seems like he has a reflex," Eelprince said thoughtfully. "It's like you push a button and Panther springs. I wonder what pushes the button?"

"And what reverses it?" Babla stressed. "I don't like this angry panther. I feel afraid of his energy."

"I'm not afraid of him because he can't hurt me," Armadillo chimed in. "Still, I don't like to be around this much rage."

"I love Panther's intensity," said Lost & Found Man. "But I don't see why it must turn to anger. Intensity can be expressed in beautiful ways, too." Everyone agreed.

The Wizard nodded his head, eyes closed and deep in thought. "Intensity," he repeated. "I've been thinking about intensity. When a potent energy is out of balance, what is needed to bring it into balance?" He looked around and saw that the Beings were waiting for him to continue. "Well," he said at last, "air. I think too much intensity needs to be aired out." They all gave a sigh of relief.

"We could put him into an air bubble and come back to it later," suggested the Witch. And that's what they did. The Magician, the Witch, and the Wizard put their magical powers together and created a huge sphere. Then Kiwi, Humangus, and Mountain Lion, combining their physical strength, put Panther inside it and sealed the opening.

Turning to Eelprince, Humangus came to the point. "Now we can explore your question. It is an important one."

Before anyone could do or say anything, Isabella jumped up and wrapped herself around Humangus. After the initial shock, Babla realized that this was a trick; Panther's anger and Isabella's sexuality were simply diversions to occupy the Circle so the missing part would never be found. Babla looked over at Lion Cub, whose wounds had opened up and were bleeding again.

At that moment, the Witch whispered in Babla's ear, confirming her suspicions. "This is just a trick to keep the hidden part away." Simultaneously, both arose and went to the Giant, wrapping themselves all around him, imitating Isabella.

Isabella moved away, indignant. "How dare you disturb my process!" she yelled—or tried to yell; only a weak voice leaked out. She was trying to get angry, but somehow it wasn't working. Frustrated, she sat down and glared. When she noticed Panther, she nearly gagged.

"I've got it!" Lost & Found Man blurted out. "Your energy is totally tied to Panther; without his rage you can't express your sexuality!" There was a much more relaxed atmosphere now, the sense of letting go that follows insight.

Babla went over to Lion Cub and held her gently. "What do you need to heal?" she asked.

"I need to find the missing part," Lion Cub whimpered, tears in her eyes. Seeing this, the Giant's eyes shone with understanding. Reaching over, he stroked Isabella's hair and said gently, "I see that Panther and you have been trying to distract us so we wouldn't find the hidden part. Please, tell me why."

Isabella bent her head. "Because," she confessed, "Panther and I are dark. We don't want to lose our power over Lion Cub, who is light. Also, if the missing part were found, Oracle's birthing would be near, and that would mean death to Panther and me."

"So that's the button!" Eelprince exclaimed, overjoyed to have found it. "As long as you are into sex and Panther is into rage, nothing will change." Isabella agreed.

"What about Lion Cub?" Babla asked. "If you two continue this game much longer, she will die. Without her, neither you nor the black panther can exist."

"No!" Isabella protested, her face changing color. "That's not true. You're just saying that to confuse me and make me feel afraid."

"Yes, it is true," insisted Babla. "Lion Cub is like me; she is a little Being. You and Panther are like Tantrika, the Nun, and the Slut—you are Inner Beings. If I died right now, Tantrika wouldn't exist, either." Isabella was speechless.

"Babla is right," said Lion Cub. "If I die, you die. For me to continue living, I need this missing part. Please help me find it."

Isabella looked at Lion Cub for a long time. "Okay," she agreed at last. "I will help you." Everyone applauded her decision.

"Well, Isabella," said Humangus after a moment. "What can you tell us about this missing part?"

"Not much," Isabella admitted. "Only that it is part of the light side, that it has to do with the healing of Lion Cub's wounds, and to be seen, it needs several Beings with strong hearts."

"We certainly have that here." The Giant smiled, pointing to the group. All Beings gathered around Lion Cub and opened their pure hearts. Then Humangus guided them into their strong hearts. Babla realized that the heart had to be pure before it could become anything else. In her pure heart, she felt open, soft, receptive, and very loving.

Coming into her strong heart, though, Babla was surprised at the difference: she felt extremely focused and committed. Instead of being soft and flowing, this Love was strong, to the point, and steady. "Wow!" she thought. "This is wonderful! I like the strong heart."

After being showered with strong Love, Lion Cub's heart popped open and a magnificent white bird came out. It had soft fluffy feathers and a long elegant neck.

"Welcome!" said Humangus, bowing to the bird.

"Thank you," she replied, bowing back. "I couldn't have done it alone." Suddenly, the big bird caught Lion Cub's eye and immediately bent over her, stroking her with fluffy white wings. "Oh, sweetheart," she said, making soft noises with her beak. "You are wounded. Let me feather your wounds."

Babla remembered how Mother Hen had healed Scared Rabbit's wounds. Lion Cub gave a sigh of relief, closed her eyes and relaxed, receiving. With the Beings still in their strong hearts and the white bird feathering, Lion Cub's wounds stopped bleeding. In time, the spiral wound in her heart also closed.

The bird took a deep breath and looked around, surprised, as if she had forgotten that anyone else was there. "Oh, by the way," she said lightly, "I am Feather. I'm the missing part of Lion Cub. Without me, Oracle cannot really be born."

"I'm glad you're not missing anymore, Feather," responded the Witch. "We really need you here."

"Yes, yes, I know," Feather replied. "Without me, Panther's energy is too intense, isn't it?" Everyone nodded in agreement.

"Now," she said, focused on Lion Cub, "we can attend to healing that spiral wound in your belly. We'll need Isabella for this."

Isabella stepped forward and sat next to Feather, who plucked a plume from her back and offered it to her. "Simply fan the wound," Feather suggested.

For a long time, the Beings stayed in their strong hearts watching Isabella fan Lion Cub's wound. Then time shifted. They were in Lion Cub's belly, each Being waving a white feather over the enormous wound. They moved to the rhythm of an etheric melody, a sweet smile upon their lips.

Time shifted again. They found themselves around Lion Cub's smooth belly where no wound could be seen.

Feather was pleased. "This is wonderful! Now, to heal the invisible wound in your tummy, we need Panther." The Beings brought the sphere of air close to Lion Cub, not knowing how to proceed. Feather nodded her head and they unsealed it, giving Panther back his freedom.

The black panther shook himself a few times and looked around, his green eyes bright with fervor. Then he saw Feather.

"Hi, Panther," she said lightly. "I'm glad you're here with us. I need your help. Will you put your paw onto Lion Cub's tummy?" Panther obeyed. The energy oozing out of his pores was remarkable, yet something was different. What was it?

"There is no rage now in his intensity," said Wondering Magician, answering everyone's unasked question.

"When the heart is healed," commented Feather, "everything else is easy." She was right. She looked at the Circle lovingly while caressing Panther, who seemed content in holding Lion Cub's tummy.

Lion Cub opened her eyes and said that she felt whole again, after such a long time. She had tears of joy and relief in her eyes, as did the others.

Humangus suggested it was time for the birthing of Oracle. The Beings encircled around the four parts of Oracle. Babla felt a glow around her and, looking up, saw a cloud of iridescent bubbles drawing near. She knew that everyone's Higher Self was arriving to support and celebrate the occasion.

Panther lay on his back, holding Lion Cub and Isabella. Feather, sparkling and light, was caressing all three of them while making mysterious sounds.

Suddenly, the earth opened and the Circle sank into the Underworld. They found themselves in an earthen cave lit by torches hanging on the walls. Except for Feather's humming, no sound disturbed the air. Silence covered the earth and leapt in the flames.

Then they heard the sound of running water and, out of nowhere, a waterfall appeared in one corner. Flowing from the high ceiling of the cave, it touched the earth and was immediately absorbed back into it.

Amid the pouring water, the physical boundaries of Panther, Lion Cub and Isabella started merging into one Being. Feather leaned over this new Being and merged with it. From this union, Oracle was born.

She was solid this time, not like the faint silhouette she had been at first. She had the same pearl-colored dress, long black hair, and huge owl wings. But now, she wore a necklace of fluffy white feathers, reaching down to her chest. She greeted the Circle.

Babla could contain herself no longer. "Oracle, what has happened to the others?"

"They are in me," she glowed. "They can still come out at times, but from now on their home is with me. They are always loved and nurtured here."

Her birthing complete, Oracle took her place in the Circle. Time shifted, and they found themselves back on the Sacred Land.

THE WITCH'S HEART: The Garden of Self-Love

Humangus spotted the Witch sitting in the Circle and smiled, motioning for her to sit in the middle. He told the others that she needed pure-hearted Beings to hold her heart, to allow the fear to melt away so she could own her Essence—Wise Witch, Creator of Sacred Spaces.

Concentrating on the Witch's chest, the Giant made spiraling gestures in the air with one hand. The Witch's heart, the thin layer of ice still around it, elevated out of her chest, expanded greatly, and hung in mid-air for everyone to see and hold.

They all heard footsteps; Frozen Man, holding Gayland by the hand, had arrived. Humangus asked them to join the Circle and, placing Gayland on the Witch's lap, directed Frozen Man to sit back to back with the Witch.

One by one, the Beings came forward and put one hand on the Witch's heart, the other hand on their own. They closed their eyes and focused, giving her the purest Love that there is.

Time passed. Time dissolved. Babla felt like she was floating in the Witch's heart, suspended in space. Finally, there came a sigh of relief as Frozen Man's last layer of ice dissolved.

"Thank you," he said, all brittleness gone from his voice. Then he turned to the Witch and asked, "Will you receive me into your heart? This will open the last closed door."

Holding the Witch's heart with one hand, Humangus came around and put his other hand onto Frozen Man. With tears of gratefulness, Frozen Man dissolved into her heart. And with that, a huge, round golden door became visible inside. On it was written in emerald green: Garden of Self-Love.

Seeing this, Gayland jumped up, opened the door, and entered the Witch's heart. As she walked with delight through the Garden, the group was thrilled. It was warm, moist, and green in there, and fields of flowers spread everywhere.

Gayland turned and looked at the Circle. "This is Home," she said, tears of joy streaming down her cheeks. "This is my Home. Thank you so much for all your help! You, too, Giant. I love you. And I love me!" She ran off blissfully, disappearing into the Garden.

A single tear trickled from the Giant's left eye and touched the Witch's heart, which then quietly shrank to normal size before slipping back into her chest. To everyone's amazement, her body began a steady, wave-like motion that continued for a long time.

The Witch acknowledged these as waves of wisdom and compassion. With her heart fully open, she was able to own her Essence. She saw all the Beings of the Circle looking at her with contentment.

"I welcome you, Wise Witch," Humangus said softly, bowing.

"I'm so glad you're my friend!" Babla smiled, reaching out to hold Wise Witch's hand.

The group spread out for a while, resting and integrating, enjoying the Sacred Land.

KIWI: Delighting in Who We Are

Back in the Circle, Humangus looked at Kiwi. "Oh, I'm fine!" she said in a high-pitched voice. "I'm just here to help. Since I've found Zoran, my Inner Mate, my life has been wonderful. I don't need anything!" Babla wondered why her friend the Fuzzy Brown Bear was fidgeting.

"It's not often that this many Beings with pure hearts are gathered in one place," the Giant encouraged. "Maybe we can do something for you, too." Kiwi averted her eyes.

"If bears could blush, she is blushing," thought Babla.

"Well," said Kiwi after a while, "maybe there is something. I wonder if it's important enough to take up time here, though."

"Just as you enjoy giving," the Magician replied, "so do the rest of us. I would feel deprived if I couldn't give to you from my pure heart. Will you receive a gift?" Everyone else felt the same way and nodded their support.

Kiwi took a deep breath, her eyes misty. "Okay," she said, "I will. Sometimes, especially at night, lying curled up with Zoran, I can't feel my legs or feet. During the day, walking in the forest, it's easier to feel them, and I can feel every other part of my body very strongly."

"Hm," the Giant responded, deep in thought. "What do all of you think?"

Oracle and Wise Witch got up simultaneously, one standing in front of Kiwi, the other behind her, spreading their arms out to their sides, then up toward Kiwi's head, not touching. Their hands were about two feet away from Fuzzy Brown Bear's body.

"I wonder what they're doing," Babla thought.

"They are intensifying Kiwi's energy field so we can see what is happening around her legs and feet," whispered Maya into her ear. Babla left her place and crept toward them to get a better look. Very slowly, Oracle and Wise Witch started moving their arms down, touching only the air. When they came to Kiwi's feet and touched the ground of the Sacred Land, something like a thin fog appeared around the Bear. It was sparkly and transparent, and Kiwi was very clearly visible in it.

Out of nowhere, colors started appearing in the mist: They saw golden white at the top of her head; swirling lavender mixed with dark blue spots around her forehead and nose; horizontal lines of light blue, mixed with vertical lines of turquoise at her throat; swirling pink and green around her chest; bright yellow at her stomach; vibrant orange around her pelvis; and deep, dark red, from her tailbone all the way down to the bottom of her feet. One could see right through the colors.

"Look!" shouted Babla, pointing to the red area. "Somebody is hiding there!"

"It's a fetus," added Humangus.

Lost & Found Man came closer and asked, "Fetus, who or what are you?"

"I am the seed of Kiwi's femininity," came the faint answer.

"That's strange," Babla commented. "I thought that was handled when Kiwi met Zoran."

"Maybe it wasn't enough," replied Fuzzy Brown Bear, perplexed at this whole thing.

Humangus had an idea. "Fetus, are you connected with Kiwi's inability to feel her legs and feet?"

"Yes, I am the reason," Fetus answered. "She needs to totally accept that she is a she-bear."

"Oh, no!" Kiwi cried out. "I don't want to be a she-bear! I hate being a she-bear!" She stomped the ground, furiously waving her arms. Her flashing green eyes met the sea-colored ones of the Giant, and she stopped.

"Yet, you *are* a she-bear," said Humangus in a gentle, but firm voice.

"Yes," she replied slowly, her head hanging low. "I am."

"And a very lovely one," Mountain Lion added.

Kiwi couldn't stop her tears any longer. She sat down and sobbed, her fuzzy brown body shaking. All the other Beings came around and, with their pure hearts, held the Fetus. Wondering Magician started singing of the beauty of being a she-bear, and the others joined in. Somewhere out of time, Kiwi's tears turned into laughter. Singing and laughing merged, and the Fetus started to dissolve.

"Thank you," her thin voice echoed before she was fully absorbed into Kiwi. Having fully accepted her she-ness, Kiwi got up and started walking around, proclaiming, "I am a she-bear. All the universe hear me! I am a she-bear! Yes!"

Back in the Circle, everyone was celebrating Fuzzy Brown Bear as a she-bear. She heard Zoran's loving male voice in her ear, "Hi, Kiwi. Now we can be whole together." Kiwi smiled contentedly.

LOST & FOUND MAN: Uncovering the True Name

Humangus looked around the Circle and asked, "Who is next?"

"Me," announced Lost & Found Man. "I need a new name."

Babla and Humangus told the others Lost & Found Man's story. "And now that he has healed the split, he needs a more appropriate name," the Giant ended.

"I'm smelling air," announced Oracle.

"I'm sensing two big birds approaching the Sacred Land," Wise Witch added.

Babla pulled the eagle feather and the hawk feather out of her pocket. Without knowing why, she had kept them. Humangus took them from her and placed them into Lost & Found Man's palms.

Wondering Magician pointed to the sky. Two black dots from opposite directions were moving toward the Circle. Soon they could see the dots become an eagle and a hawk. Babla couldn't believe her eyes: They were the same birds she had taken the feathers from! This was too much!

Humangus had recognized his friend Hawk and wasn't surprised that Eagle was also there. Both birds landed on the Sacred Land at the same time and stood in front of the Giant. He bowed to Hawk, his eternal friend and Guide; then he bowed to Eagle and said, "I belong to the hawk family. When I was a baby giant, I lost my parents and the hawks raised me." Pointing to the brown hawk, he added, "He is my brother. I do not know you or your family, Eagle, yet I respect your presence, and I have a sense that you will bless me with many lessons."

Eagle nodded almost invisibly, then turned to Oracle. "Expansion is the lesson you will learn from my family," translated Oracle.

Eagle nodded again, then turned to Wise Witch. She closed her eyes for a moment, then said, "Eagle is inviting you to live with her family. Just by being with them, you will absorb their expansive energy and add it to the focused potency you have received from the hawks."

"Thank you," said Humangus, otherwise speechless.

Both birds moved toward Lost & Found Man, stood before him, then turned their backs. What was this supposed to mean?

"Open your heart, Babla," Maya whispered into her ear. Babla did.

"Oh!" she said out loud. "They are talking to me. We need to lay Lost & Found Man upon their backs so that his upper body is on Hawk's back and his lower body is on Eagle's."

Kiwi lifted Lost & Found Man onto the birds' feathers, and after a pause, the birds took off together with their passenger, gliding through the air as if they were one Being. And, they were.

Oracle spoke. "They are telling me that Lost & Found Man is a Being of the air. He needs to receive his new name in and from the air," she said. Then, turning to Humangus, she added, "The air will give his name to you to put into words."

"Good," replied the Giant. They waited, gazing at the sky. Time stopped, then faded away. Out of nowhere a puffy white cloud showed up, floating toward the flying birds and Lost & Found Man. Within moments, they had disappeared into the cloud.

Humangus tipped his head to the left. "His Guides are talking to him," Babla said to herself. She knew that energetically all the pure hearts of the Circle were also in the cloud, holding Lost & Found Man. Humangus closed his eyes.

All of a sudden, the roar of thunder trailed an immense flash shooting through the cloud. Too late, Babla covered her ears. Humangus had opened his eyes and was calling into the sky, his arms outstretched. "Thal! Thal! I got it! Thank you!"

All went quiet. The cloud receded, disappearing into nowhere. Eagle and Hawk flew back and landed in the middle of the Circle.

"Thal," repeated the Giant, engaging the big birds. Both nodded. Kiwi lifted Thal out of his bed of feathers and helped him to a seated position. "Why Thal?" asked Eelprince.

"*Th* for thunder, *A* for air, and *L* for lightning," Humangus explained. "What I heard was 'Thal—Bringer of the Sky Down to Earth.' "

Kiwi turned to Thal and said matter-of-factly, "This means you are a bridge, a bridge between two worlds."

"A bridge," Thal repeated, smiling. "Yes, I like that."

He thanked the birds. They acknowledged Thal in return, then faced the others, looking at everyone. When they came to Babla, they both stopped. Oracle said, "They want you to keep the two feathers." Thal handed them to Babla, who thanked both birds with tears in her eyes.

Eagle and Hawk took off, their piercing cries echoing all around the Sacred Land. Flying in opposite directions, they vanished into the vast, endless sky.

AX-WOMAN, MERMAID, and LITTLE SEASHELL:
The Inner Woman

In the silence of the Circle, Babla could hear the ocean waves—the music of nature. Then she heard the Giant's big yet gentle voice, "Who is next?" This was her time. Babla told Humangus and the Circle of Emanuella's request.

Humangus closed his eyes and tuned in, then got up and asked the Circle to follow. He led them to the far corner of the Sacred Land, to a place they had not seen before, and stopped in front of a dark lake.

"This looks just like the lake at the Place Beyond Paradise," exclaimed Babla in total amazement. "But how can that be?"

"I don't know how," Humangus replied, "but I do know that it is the same lake. You and I are going to go in first, then the others will follow."

Babla could feel her hesitation; what if...? Then, she felt the Witch's hand in hers and all her worry disappeared. They went into the dark lake—down, down, down—and came out to a sandy beach.

Looking around, Babla saw a Mermaid with flowing blond hair sunning herself. Feeling their presence, she sat up and looked at them. Babla was speechless. Looking at the Mermaid's face, she felt drawn into a spiral of something she had never felt before.

"Who are you?" Humangus asked. "Are you a part of Rabia's Inner Woman?"

"Yes. I am her longing, her yearning to be filled. I have to stay down here because neither Rabia nor Emanuella could handle it if I came up to their world. This longing is so profound that I can allow only a little of it to be felt by Emanuella. The rest needs to stay buried in this lake."

Humangus, who had been listening intently, asked her if there were other parts of Emanuella in this lake.

"Yes," said the Mermaid. "On the other side of this beach is the sea. There is another part on its floor."

Thanking her, they left to find the sea. When they had crossed the beach, Babla saw its quiet waters, disturbed only by tiny waves lapping softly on its surface. They immersed themselves in the sea, deeper and deeper to find its bottom. Soft sand welcomed them below, spreading out as far as their eyes could see. Peering around, Babla saw a little seashell resting there, moving gently with the water. It was the only visible thing.

Humangus asked the shell, "Are you the missing part of Emanuella?"

"Yes, I am Little Seashell, and I'm the part that loves and needs to be alone. Just me with all this space around."

"What about Mermaid with her overwhelming longing to be filled?" asked Humangus.

"I don't know," she answered. "I don't know what it's like to long for something. I've never felt that. I just love being here all alone."

In deep thought, Humangus scratched his beard. All good things come in threes. What if there were a third missing part? Looking at Little Seashell, he said, "Even though you love being alone, I believe you still might enjoy some connection with Emanuella and through her, with Rabia. How do you feel about staying right here, yet also being connected?"

Babla looked at Little Seashell; she was so gentle, so little, yet also significant somehow.

"My aloneness is mine," came the proud answer. "What good would it do if I were connected?"

Humangus looked at Babla. She sat down next to the shell and smiled. "Because," she said, "for Rabia to be whole, all of her Inner Beings need to connect with each other and with her."

"Also, the Inner Beings who are restless can benefit from the stillness and restfulness of your aloneness," Humangus added.

Little Seashell was intrigued. "Okay. Let's give it a try. But how?"

Humangus reached into his pocket and took out a thin golden cord. "You hold one end," he said, "and Emanuella will hold the other end. That way, you will always stay connected to her."

Little Seashell seemed to like this idea. They said good-bye to her and left the sea, floating back to find Mermaid.

Mermaid greeted them with a smile. "I don't know what you did down there, but I feel different now. I still carry the deep longing within me, yet it doesn't feel as overwhelming."

Humangus told her about Little Seashell and the golden cord. "Because you are a part of Emanuella, you also are connected to the cord," he added. "Perhaps being connected to Little Seashell's aloneness is making it easier for you to be in your longing." Everyone, including Mermaid, was fascinated.

Babla looked at her; she seemed so fragile, so vulnerable, so open and soft. Mermaid told them she still didn't feel ready to leave the lake.

Humangus walked a bit to the side, putting his hands up to his mouth. He boomed, "Is there a third missing part of Emanuella we haven't yet met?"

With that, the earth began to rumble and shake. "What a time to have an earthquake," thought Babla, covering her head. Then she realized that it wasn't one. Looking up, she blinked several times because what she saw just could not be real! But there it was, right in front of her. A tall woman in a gladiator outfit, holding a huge ax on a long handle, was staring fiercely at them.

"Who are you?" asked Humangus.

"I am Ax-Woman," she thundered. "I am Mermaid's protector. She is too vulnerable and open to leave the lake alone. I need to come with her."

"Where were you all this time?" Babla had found her voice at last.

"Asleep. To wake up, I needed a large and wise Outer Being such as you, Humangus. Now here I am, ready to accompany Mermaid. I will always be standing at her right side, a little to the back." She stood tall, beside the Mermaid, prepared to defend her.

"Wow!" Babla perked up. "With you along, Emanuella can reunite with Mermaid, confident that no Outer Being can hurt her despite her open and soft ways."

Humangus nodded, knowingly. "The souls of all Beings seek balance. Without Ax-Woman and Little Seashell, Mermaid is out of balance, her longing too much to bear. Now, with all of her missing parts found, Emanuella can be with Manuel from a place of balance." Everyone felt this was so.

Ax-Woman stood at Mermaid's right as they floated up from the depths of the lake. Emanuella was waiting for them. She welcomed Ax-Woman and Mermaid, took the other end of the golden cord from Humangus, and tied it to her wrist. She was glowing.

Emanuella, Mermaid, and Ax-Woman left to get better acquainted. So Humangus guided the Healing Circle back to the center of the Sacred Land. Holding hands with Wise Witch, Babla's thoughts went out to Little Seashell at the bottom of the sea. She realized that she wanted to spend time with her, drinking from her aloneness.

After everyone was comfortable again in the Circle, the Giant looked at each Being, his sea-colored eyes shining with quiet wisdom and focused intention. Then he asked, "Who is next?"

BLUE SWAN: Returning to Essence

Elegantly, Blue Swan extended her long neck to indicate she wanted to go next. She had a sad story to tell. After she had repeated it for all the Beings, a mournful silence came over the Circle.

Eelprince broke the mood. "Water is your Essence, and mine, too. Just the thought of not being near it makes me feel like I'm dying."

Blue Swan was thankful for the eel's empathy. "So far," she replied, "I've never felt fully alive. I have no idea what that would be like."

Humangus met her gaze. "Can you tell us exactly what happened right after you were born?"

Blue Swan thought for a while. "I was hatched with other brothers and sisters next to a beautiful lake. After we grew, it was time for us to experience being on the lake. I don't remember anything after that. All I know is that I've refused to go into the water ever since."

"I wonder," commented Eelprince, "what happened right then that you can't remember?"

"Me, too," Humangus added. He looked at Babla, Wise Witch, and Oracle to see whether an answer was coming to them. All three shook their heads no. "I guess," said the Giant, starting to get up, "we'll need to go back to that time and help Blue Swan remember."

The Circle walked to a corner of the Sacred Land they hadn't been to before and stopped in front of a dark brown wooden door. To everyone's amazement, it was standing there upright, not attached to anything, held in place by thin air.

"This is the door to Memories," Humangus explained. "We will ask it to open and show Blue Swan the reason for her fear."

In a loud and clear voice, he stated his request, and slowly the door opened. It revealed a beautiful beautiful landscape with a placid lake in the middle. The Beings of the Circle entered.

When Blue Swan passed through the door, she transformed into a little swan. The lake was big, hosting countless varieties of ducks, geese, swans, and other water birds. The Beings of the Circle realized that because this wasn't their life, they were invisible to those living there, except for Blue Swan.

They watched her be a swan-child with her family. They watched the mother swan lead her young children to the lake for their first swim. Little Blue Swan was a bit behind, trailing the brothers and sisters who had already made their first steps into the water. All of a sudden, a terrible, multiarmed monster arose from the depths, grabbed two of the baby swans, and swept them away along with some ducklings, a few little geese, and a bevy of other young birds.

Before the intruder could return, all the mothers and fathers helped the young ones out of the lake, and fled the area.

The Circle watched the swan family travel to another lake to make a new home. From then on, Little Blue Swan wouldn't go near the water.

Humangus led the Circle back out the door anchored in thin air. Blue Swan, returning to her adult size, was the last one through the door, which closed behind her.

"Now we know," said the Giant.

"And we understand," added Thal.

Blue Swan turned to Humangus. "What is the next step?"

The answer came from Wondering Magician, who was sitting next to Humangus. "There is a moment in life," he began, "when we all are asked to leave our memories behind and start afresh. We must put a period at the end of one page and turn to a new blank page. I think this time has come for you."

"But, how can I leave my memories behind?" protested Blue Swan. "I can't pretend they didn't happen. What if I go into some water and a monster comes up and eats me, too?"

Eelprince smiled. "Leaving a memory behind doesn't mean forgetting it or pretending it didn't happen. My sense is that the first thing to do is to really accept what happened." Everyone agreed.

"And once you've done this, the next step will reveal itself," Humangus added.

The Circle gathered around Blue Swan, their pure hearts touching her feathers, holding her with clarity and the sparkling energy of Love. She started to say, "I accept . . . ," but stopped in mid-sentence, breaking into huge tears she hadn't known even existed until then.

The Beings held her for what seemed an eternity as time stopped and the Circle drifted into timelessness. "This is where healing comes from," Maya whispered into Babla's ear.

When time started again, Blue Swan's tears had stopped. She looked at the Circle and said, "I accept what happened. I accept that some of my brothers and sisters were killed by a monster in that lake." More tears came; deep tears of relief, of acceptance. When they had finished, Blue Swan was ready for the next step.

"Death is a part of life," announced Oracle.

"There is always the possibility that you could go into water and a monster could kill you," Eelprince explained. "Yet, it doesn't mean that you should avoid water. For you and me, avoiding it is like avoiding ourselves, because water is our Essence. Even if you die in the water, you will have died knowing who you are."

"You will have died having lived first," Mountain Lion summarized what had been said. "My sense is that your next step involves making friends with water." Everyone nodded.

Humangus had an idea. "What if," he asked Blue Swan, "we protected you and made sure you were safe, your first time going into water? Would that help?"

"If I could feel safe the first time, it would set an example for all the other times." Blue Swan liked this offer.

Mountain Lion suggested that he stay close to protect her from any possible danger, and Eelprince decided to go into the lake himself first, to make sure there was no danger lurking. Both Beings were eager to assist Blue Swan. Humangus led the Circle to the edge of the Sacred Land, where they saw a lake.

"This looks just like my family's lake!" Blue Swan paled in horror, turning to run away.

"This time it is different, though," explained Babla. "Before, you were tiny and no one was able to protect you. Now you are a grown up and have all of us to help you, if necessary." It made enough sense.

The terror left Blue Swan, and she signaled to Eelprince that she was ready. Eelprince glided in, disappearing into the calm water. After quite a long time, he surfaced to report that all was safe.

Now it was Mountain Lion's turn; he stood close to Blue Swan while she held onto his thick fur. Slowly, she broached a few hesitant steps toward the lake, fear rising in her heart. Babla reminded her that this was a different time now, and her fear gradually dissolved.

Taking her first step into the water, Blue Swan stopped in amazement; it was cool and fresh, almost tickling her feet. Each step took her deeper into the water, her Essence; and then, she let go—she let go of Mountain Lion's fur, and she let go of the memory. She knew she would always remember the story, yet the paralyzing emotions surrounding her past were gone.

Blue Swan was gliding upon the lake, her body rocking to the rhythm of the water. Eelprince swam beside her, being the first to extend congratulations. The others waved from the shore while Blue Swan went all the way to the other side of the lake and back. Coming out of the water, she was noticeably different, her eyes bright, her whole being exuding self-confidence.

"Wow!" giggled Babla. "Your eyes are so deep now!"

"Just like the lake," remarked Humangus.

"Just like your Essence," added Eelprince.

They closed their eyes holding hands, wings, paws, and fins, and rested in timelessness. Their pure hearts connected, blending and merging into one Heart.

UNLOVED PHOENIX: The World of Separation

After a long break, the Circle came back together. Humangus looked around the group, then bowed to Unloved Phoenix. "Tell us your story," he humbly requested.

"I don't know," came a shy reply out of the gray feathers. "I don't think I'm ready. Can't you work with someone else?"

"I could," responded the Giant. "I would like to work with you, though."

"Well, I don't know," the shy voice insisted. "I don't think anything can be done for me here—or anywhere else. I'm just going to have to live like this."

The Wizard, who had not yet spoken, turned to Unloved Phoenix. "How strange," he began. "Each time we were asked to hold one of the Beings in the Circle with our pure hearts, you were the first to contribute. To be in your pure heart, you seem to shift to the phoenix side of you, and your heart is very pure in giving. Right after giving, however, you shift back to your unloved side and stay there until the next Being needs to be held."

"Good observation," commented Humangus. "What does this tell us about Unloved Phoenix?"

"That she needs to learn how to love herself. She can be a phoenix, even when she is not giving to other Beings," Mountain Lion replied.

Humangus turned to Unloved Phoenix and asked what it was like to hear this.

"I'm not sure whether I can trust you all," she admitted, peeking out. "I feel very separate. I know you mean well, but I don't think there's anything you can do for me. So many other Beings have tried to help, but it didn't work. Thank you for trying, anyway."

Armadillo, who had not previously spoken, said, "I came here with the firm resolution that nothing could be done for me. But watching Wise Witch, Thal, and others go through their transformations made me wonder.

"Something mysterious happens each time we open our pure hearts and connect with each other. Even though the events are unpredictable, each time the outcome is magical. I don't see why we can't connect our pure hearts and assist you in your blossoming, too."

"Because I'm different," sadly replied Unloved Phoenix. "I am a phoenix and there aren't many of us around. We have a great mission to fulfill in this universe. We guide all Beings in their journey of transformation. It's a huge responsibility. Because of that, we aren't made like others. What works for all of you might not work for me."

"Yes, it might not," repeated Thal playfully, "or maybe it would. You haven't tried it out yet."

"I haven't," she agreed. "But I know it won't do any good. It's a great burden to carry, but the truth is, I must do it alone, as much as I hate to admit it." And that was that.

It all sounded so very logical to Babla, yet she had a funny feeling that something was missing here. She remembered White Swan's words, "Life is not a problem to be solved; it is a Mystery to be lived."

"Why would Existence create you and give you this big important job to guide other Beings in their transformation, yet leave you all alone struggling on your own?" Babla said passionately, her big blue eyes both curious and daring. "It doesn't make any sense. The Existence I know is benevolent. It gives us challenges so that we can learn and grow, but it isn't so cruel and mean to leave us alone with our pain. It always provides the necessary help along the way."

"I don't see any reason why our pure hearts can't assist you in your transformation, if you are willing to let us in," Wise Witch added. Silence followed.

Humangus looked quietly at Unloved Phoenix and said in the gentlest voice, which seemed but an extension of the silence, "In their very Essence, all Beings are one."

The Healing Circle sat together for a long time holding hands, wings, paws, and fins. Time disappeared, and they entered another world—the World of Separation.

Wherever they looked, there were walls and veils that separated each thing from everything else. In their wonder, the Beings of the Circle didn't realize that walls and veils had come down and separated them from each other as well.

Wise Witch walked for a while, investigating this strange world. When she turned around to say something to Babla, she realized that she was alone. She had no idea where the others had gone. She opened her mouth and called Babla's name, but what she heard echoing back was her own voice saying, "You are alone. You are separate."

"How strange," she thought. "One minute I'm holding hands in the Circle, the next minute I'm by myself in an peculiar world where what I want to say or what I think I've said is not the same as what I hear myself saying. Where am I? What kind of a place is this?"

She sat down and closed her eyes. She heard a faraway voice inside say, "Find your heart." Remembering Gayland and the Garden of Self-Love, Wise Witch found herself immediately there. She smiled. Watching Gayland play with the bees, the butterflies, and the fairies, warmed her heart. Everywhere she went in the Garden she felt immense Love pouring out of the trees, the plants, the waterfalls, and the animals. It was as if all life in the Garden was telling her, "We love you. You are loved."

She took a deep breath and opened her eyes, her hands holding her heart. The walls and veils were still there, yet they were transparent now. She could see through them. She walked up to a veil and stretched out her hand to touch it. But her hand went right through, grasping only the air. She went to a wall and did the same. Her hand passed through as if the wall didn't exist.

"Wow! All these walls and veils are just illusions! They don't exist!" With that, Wise Witch went through the wall herself.

Fascinated, Babla looked at the walls and veils. One could play hide-and-seek in here! Then she realized that she had lost the others. "Strange," she thought. "Where did they go?" She could see only walls and veils. She sat down and closed her eyes. "Inner Guides," she called, "I need your help."

"We are here, Babla," they answered.

She opened her eyes and there they were, sitting all around her. "What is all this?"

"This is the World of Separation," Eternal Friend explained. "These walls and veils separate us from ourselves as well as from other Beings. As long as we believe in the existence of this world, we feel separate and lonely and disconnected."

"It is all illusion," Maya went on. "In Truth, there is no separation. All Beings are one in their Essence."

"Yes," replied Babla. "That's what Humangus said a little while ago. I wonder where he is now, and all the others. White Swan also kept telling me that there is only Oneness in life. And yet, here I am, totally separate from the others, and all I can see is walls and veils. It's hard to believe that this is an illusion. It all looks so real."

"Yes, it looks very real," agreed Alan, moving toward Babla and helping her onto his lap. "Why don't we connect our hearts. I'll send you my Love and you just receive it. Then we'll see what happens."

Babla closed her eyes and opened her heart. A sweet, delightful substance began to enter it. She took a deep breath and leaned back, relaxing. This was fun. After a while, Eternal Friend suggested she open her eyes. She did so and was astonished to see that the walls and the veils had disappeared. She could see the Beings of the Circle all scattered around looking for each other, even though some of them were very close to each other and there was nothing between them.

"Amazing! They believe that a wall is there, so they can't see each other. Not because of the wall, but just because of their perception." Her Guides nodded.

"Now that you know the truth about the World of Separation," said Eternal Friend, "you can simply walk through any wall or veil."

Realizing that some of the walls and veils had come back, Babla felt excited. "I'm going to find Wise Witch." Going right through a veil, then a wall, she saw Wise Witch coming through another one. They hugged each other joyfully and exchanged their stories. Then they decided to search for Humangus.

Humangus looked around; the others of the Circle had disappeared somehow and he was alone in this place. All he could see was walls and veils. He didn't like this. Not at all. He faced the strongest wall and said in a very loud voice, "I am the Giant! I am stronger than you!" Then, with the side of his hand he knocked down the wall. It crumbled to the ground and disappeared.

"Unbelievable," Humangus said to himself. "That wall wasn't as strong as it looked. Yet, stranger still, it just disappeared." He went to another wall, this time knocking it down with half his strength; the same thing happened. He went to a few other walls, repeating his action using less and less strength, always with the same result. Then he went to a veil and reached out to touch it; air met his palm.

"Ah!" He looked triumphant. "This must be some kind of an illusion. These walls and veils are not what they seem to be." He closed his eyes and asked his Guides, the old man and old woman, for help.

"Yes," said the old woman. "You are in the World of Separation, which, in Truth, does not exist."

"It's all up to you," added the old man. "If you believe in separation, that's what you will experience. On the other hand, if you know that Truth holds only Oneness, these veils and walls can't fool you."

The old woman came forward, took the Giant's hand, and continued, "The World of Separation keeps us from the Truth of Oneness. Right now, you are faced with your own beliefs about illusion and oneness, just like the other Beings of the Circle. Phoenix's message, for example, is about the Truth, yet her unloved part believes in separation. But unless all of you experience the Truth of Oneness within yourselves, you cannot assist her in her transformation."

"I see," replied Humangus, his energy very focused now. "I will go find the others." He could feel the old man and the old woman smiling inside of him. As he was heading toward a wall, it opened in the middle, admitting Babla and Wise Witch, who were holding hands and laughing. Then the wall simply disappeared.

Thal realized that he was alone. What had happened? Just a little while ago he had been holding hands in the Circle, and now. . .

There had to be an explanation to all this. But first, he needed to find the others. As the Lord of Thunder and Lightning, he raised his hand and shouted, "Lightning! Knock down this wall so I can move ahead!" No response. He repeated his demand. Again no response. Thal sat down. This was weird. "My thunder and lightning respond to anything that is real," he thought. "The only explanation I can think of for this behavior is that the wall is not real. It sure looks real, though." He decided to give it a try.

When he touched the wall, his hand went right through. Thal smiled, quietly moving past the wall, where he saw Humangus, Wise Witch, and Babla, looking at him, grinning. "What took you so long?" they teased.

Wondering Magician was perplexed. He looked around at all these walls and veils; where did they come from? What was the meaning of all this? Then he realized that he was alone and was even more perplexed. Where were the others? How could he have lost them? He didn't understand it at all.

"What am I going to do now?" he pondered, scratching his head. His hand bumped into his hat which had slid to the left. He put it straight and, holding it on his head, declared, "I am a magician. I am fully capable of handling this situation."

Sighing with relief, he cleaned his glasses, put them on, and went to have a closer look. "I wonder what Humangus would do in this situation," he thought. "The Giant would probably barge through the strongest wall. But I'm not the Giant. I'm just a magician, and even that is questionable." He realized that his hat had slid to the left again. He put it back straight and commanded out loud, "I might not be Humangus, but I am the Magician, and I have what it takes to solve this." He felt better.

Reaching out to touch a veil, his hand went right through. He went to another veil and the same thing happened. After he had tried all the veils, he tested the walls. The result was the same. "Well," he thought, "if my hand can pass through, probably my whole body will, too." And he was right.

Just as he had accomplished walking through a wall, another wall parted and he saw Wise Witch, Babla, Humangus, and Thal coming toward him, smiling.

Oracle looked around. Somehow she had been separated from the others. She took a deep breath and took in her surroundings—walls and veils. She closed her eyes and became quiet. She was sinking deep into herself, to the Place of Truth. When she arrived, she asked, "What is the truth about these walls and veils?" There was no answer.

Oracle knew that no answer from the Place of Truth was actually an answer. If there was no answer about these walls and veils, then there was no truth at all in them.

"All right!" she rejoiced, addressing the walls and veils. "If there is no truth in you, then you are illusion. There is no place for illusion in me. Be gone!"

And the walls and veils disappeared. Right in front of her, she saw Humangus, Babla, Wise Witch, Wondering Magician, and Thal welcoming her.

Kiwi realized she was surrounded by walls and veils. She looked to find the others and saw no one. "I'm alone," she thought, disappointed. "What am I supposed to do now?" The walls seemed very strong.

"If there is no outer help, I guess I could ask for inner help," she said confidently and asked Zoran for assistance.

Zoran appeared and took her in his strong arms. "What you believe in is what you see," he said, looking lovingly into Kiwi's green eyes.

"You mean that if I didn't believe in these veils and walls, they wouldn't be there?" asked Fuzzy Brown Bear, surprised.

"What do the walls and veils symbolize?" prompted Zoran.

"Separation," Kiwi answered. Then her eyes sparkled with understanding. "If I don't believe in separation, if I know that everything is connected, these walls won't be where they are now!"

"Where they *seem* to be now," corrected her Zoran.

"Of course," Kiwi agreed. She walked toward a wall and simply went through it, only to find Wondering Magician, Thal, Wise Witch, Humangus, Babla, and Oracle waiting for her on the other side.

Mountain Lion pranced around in frustration; how did he get to be alone all of a sudden? It had been so wonderful sitting in the Circle, holding paws. Now he was faced with all these walls and veils and didn't know what to do. "If only I had my heart," he thought. It was on the Sacred Land, waiting to come into his chest. He sat down, feeling the sadness of not being whole. He had lived all his life with this sense of loss inside.

Before long, he realized that all this sorrow wasn't helping him find a solution. So he decided to have a closer look at these walls and veils. He was strong; maybe something could be done, with or without a heart.

As the King of the Mountains, he could smell solid rock or stone even from a distance. Solid substance smelled like nothing else. Indeed, something was amiss; even though he was very close to one of the walls, he couldn't smell it.

"Everything that exists has some kind of a scent," he mused. "If this wall doesn't have any scent, then it doesn't exist." This was very disconcerting because he could see the wall so clearly. Yet his sense of smell had never led him astray.

He touched the wall with his nose, and his face went through. "My guess was correct. This wall does not exist." He was pleased.

With that, Mountain Lion went through the wall, which disappeared behind him. He found himself facing Humangus, Thal, Wondering Magician, Babla, Oracle, Wise Witch, and Kiwi.

Armadillo looked around and realized that she was alone. She breathed a sigh of relief. Then she looked further and saw the walls and veils. "Oh, good!" she said out loud. "Now I'm safe. Nobody can harm me. I can rest here." She curled up and relaxed.

Eelprince looked at the walls and veils. "Hm," he thought. "The others must be somewhere behind these. I wonder where." He closed his eyes, imagining that the walls and veils weren't there. Trying to locate the others, he turned toward one of the walls. With eyes closed, he could almost feel their presence behind this wall.

"Strange," he said to himself, "that all of them should be there." He tried again and felt life behind three other walls, yet not as strong. He chose the first one to explore. Eyes still closed, he started walking toward the wall, imagining it didn't exist.

He opened his eyes to joyful laughter. Most of the Beings of the Circle were welcoming him. Astounded, he looked back; the wall had disappeared.

Wizard in the Pumpkin opened his eyes. Where were the others? No one else was around. "Is this a dream? Or maybe the Circle was a dream," he said out loud.

Then he saw the walls and veils. He went closer to a veil and started exploring. It was made out of a very fine material, almost transparent but not quite. It was light blue in color. He stretched out his hand and touched the veil; strange—it felt almost like it didn't exist. But this couldn't be, because it was there right in front of his eyes.

He went to a wall and took his time examining it. When he touched it, he had the same feeling that it didn't exist. But he knew he could trust his eyes, and this wall was as solid as a wall could ever get.

"I don't know what to believe and what not," he thought. "I really am confused."

At that moment, the wall parted and all the Beings of the Circle except Blue Swan, Armadillo, and Unloved Phoenix became visible. To his utter surprise, the wall had seemingly dissolved.

Blue Swan turned her long neck in all directions. It was true, she was alone, surrounded by many walls and veils. "I've lost my friends," she said, alarmed. "What now?"

Fear started to overcome her. Then she remembered Babla's words at the lake and repeated them to herself. "Things are different now," she said to herself. "I'm an adult swan and I can handle this." The fear slowly dissipated.

She realized the first thing was to find out how to get through these walls and veils. Maybe she could pull them down somehow. She opened her beak, trying to pull down a veil, and merely snapped at the air. She tried again with the same result. Then she touched her head to it and went right through it to the other side. There she found the others explaining the illusion of separation to the Wizard. The veil had disappeared.

Humangus looked around and asked, "Where is Armadillo?" Now that all of them knew the nature of the walls and veils, they saw through to where she was curled up on the ground. They went to sit next to her, and with their pure hearts, touched her armor.

"You can stay relaxed, Armadillo," Humangus said gently. "We're not here to harm you."

"You can be as relaxed with us here as you have been without us," Babla soothed her. Everyone smiled. Wise Witch and Oracle explained the illusory nature of separation while Mountain Lion, Kiwi, and Thal demonstrated it by going through various veils and walls. Armadillo understood.

"And now," Humangus announced, "it is time to find Unloved Phoenix."

Oracle moved forward. "Walls and veils! We know you are illusion. Dissolve!" she demanded. The walls and veils disappeared. In front of them and to the right, they saw Unloved Phoenix, all gray, slumped, and crying upon the ground.

She was so involved in her tears that she didn't hear the Beings approach. They created a circle around her, then sat down and opened up their pure hearts.

Humangus guided them into their full hearts. Babla felt an overwhelming Love, like a waterfall gushing out. It filled her from head to toe, then spilled out to Unloved Phoenix. When she opened her eyes and looked around, she could feel the same thing happening with the others.

Soon, Unloved Phoenix was surrounded by Love, like the rays of a rainbow after a rainy day. Iridescent, warm Love was dancing all around.

Now that the Beings had realized the illusion of separation, they could see the walls and veils, very close to her physical form, keeping her separate from them. The rainbow of Love was dancing around these veils and walls, caressing and softening them.

Unloved Phoenix took a deep breath. Then she took another one, and another one. Puzzled, she looked up to see what was happening; somehow, out of nowhere, she had started to feel better. She was very surprised to see the Circle around her. There was so much Love in everyone's eyes that she couldn't stand it.

She closed her eyes and told herself that she was different; these Beings couldn't possibly help her. She had the heavy burden of being a phoenix to carry for the rest of her life. She tried to pull her walls and veils closer together so that their Love couldn't enter; it was making her feel dizzy.

Out of the silence sprang a song.

Babla, starting to feel hopeless, had consulted her Guides. "This Unloved Phoenix seems to be a very hard nut to crack," she told them. "Is there anything else we can do?"

"Sing your Heartsong," came Eternal Friend's answer. So she began and the others joined in:

I love you, whether you know it or not,
I love you, whether I show it or not.
There are so many things I haven't said inside my heart,
Perhaps now is a good time to start.

Nobody knows how it happened, but this little Heartsong touched Unloved Phoenix's heart; it went all the way in and started to spiral, creating a tiny trail. A rainbow of Love followed.

"Just watch now, Babla," whispered Alan. "When the Heartsong is spiraling, it creates space in the heart for Love to enter. Everything that is not Love will be thrown out into the open."

Unloved Phoenix jumped up, flapping her wings about, and began screaming, "I hate myself! Hear me? I hate myself! How dare you all sit here and give me Love. How dare you. You're all blind! You don't see the truth! The truth is that I shouldn't even be here! I shouldn't even exist! I'm all wrong! I don't deserve your Love! Take it back! Leave me alone! You're just wasting your time! I shouldn't have been born in the first place! I don't deserve to be a phoenix! Go away! I can't do anything right! Nobody loves me! Leave me alone! Go away!"

Her voice drowned in her tears. Yet these were different tears. What was the difference? "They are real," whispered Alan.

"Weren't the others real, too?" Babla asked, confused.

"The tears were real, yet the source of them wasn't," Alan explained. "They were coming from a place of desperation and self-pity, which belongs to the World of Separation and is illusion. These tears are opening tears; they come from an inner place of healing and transformation."

The more tears came out, the more Love could penetrate. After a while, the tears stopped.

In the stillness that followed, Thal and Mountain Lion came forward and held Unloved Phoenix's heart. The others touched these three in a way that created a spiral.

Time slipped away and the Beings entered the Wisdom of the Spiral. They were in a circling Universe with no hard edges. Everything around them was spinning in perpetual motion—a slow, winding, wavelike movement that created spirals of all sizes and colors, which then intercepted each other, being created and recreated infinitely.

"Oh, my!" uttered Unloved Phoenix, swirling. "Where are we?"

"We are in the Wisdom of the Spiral," Humangus answered. "This is the Spiralworld beyond the World of Separation."

There was no actual sound, yet the continual motion of the spirals created a certain humming. Babla realized that being here felt exquisite. A light and bubbly joy was exuding out of her. She looked over to Wise Witch and smiled; the Witch's face was radiant. And, so was everyone else's.

Then Babla understood. They weren't just watching these spirals—they were all becoming spirals! She saw the Giant's strong body moving rhythmically. He still had an outline to his form, yet Babla could almost see through him. He was transforming into an iridescent spiral, which held the Essence of Humangus in its Core.

The Eelprince-Spiral was moving ever so slowly and graciously as well. Babla felt more and more ecstasy open up in her, strengthening her own undulations.

The Wise Witch-Spiral touched Babla and the two Beings merged into one another to be recreated again in this endless dance. The Humangus-Spiral joined them, and so did Mountain Lion-Spiral. In eternity, all the Circle-Spirals had joined in, blending in and out of each other, outer boundaries dissolved, inner Essences intact, glowing.

Time returned and the Beings found themselves sitting in a circle on the Sacred Land. Babla looked around and gasped. Phoenix had her wings wide open, the rainbow colors flickering with each breath, her blue eyes clear and present.

MOUNTAIN LION AND BATWOMAN:
Restoring the Lionheart

Humangus looked at the Circle with deep affection. "Who is next?"

Mountain Lion told the Beings his story. He carried the crystal his heart was in to the middle of the Circle. For a long time, everyone silently contemplated what needed to happen next.

"It seems to me," Humangus began, "that the lionheart needs to be taken from the crystal and put back into Mountain Lion's chest. But how?"

"What I'm getting is that if the heart is taken out of the crystal, it will die," responded Oracle.

"There has to be a way." The Wizard and Eelprince spoke at the same time.

"Maybe," suggested Mountain Lion, "this is how I'm supposed to live the rest of my life. It really isn't that bad. I have survived quite well all these years." His voice carried no emotion.

Thal, Babla, and Wise Witch exchanged glances; they realized this was his Veil of Separation. "Surviving quite well" wasn't what life was really about.

"Might there be more to living with your heart than what you have experienced so far without it?" Wondering Magician asked carefully.

"I just don't like false hopes," Mountain Lion replied. "I can deal with concrete things like the mountains. I'd rather accept something that is clear, like my heart in this crystal, than hope for something that might never happen."

"Odd," thought Babla. "It was easy for him to see the veils and walls of separation around Phoenix, yet he seems blind to his own barriers." She couldn't take it any longer. "It seems that what you're doing isn't accepting, but settling for less," she said.

"And I feel that this is your veil of separation, Lion," Phoenix added. The Beings, including the Giant, agreed.

Mountain Lion looked around, not saying a word. Wise Witch walked up behind him and began holding and stroking his chest.

Babla went closer to the lionheart in the middle of the Circle and asked, "What do you need, heart? What can we do for you?"

Humangus also moved forward and put his hands around the crystal, his head bent and almost touching its smooth surface. It was as if he could translate its rhythm into spoken language. At last he said, "We may not be asking the right question. All these questions are good, however, one other question needs to be asked first."

"Well, questions about the present, about what this heart needs now don't seem to be it. What if we asked about his past?" Eelprince suggested. Oracle was nodding her head.

Babla decided to give it a try. "What happened to you, heart?" Immediately the lionheart started beating faster. Within a few minutes it was beating so fast that the crystal started shaking, and the Beings hoped it wouldn't break. Humangus still had his hands on the crystal, trying to stabilize it.

"Tell us your story," Kiwi invited. "We're here to listen." The heart returned to its original rhythm.

"I will," replied a penetrating voice. Everyone turned in that direction; they found Mountain Lion half sitting, half lying down, leaning against Wise Witch, his eyes closed. Both were rocking in slow motion. The voice had come out of his mouth—yet it didn't belong to him.

"I am the lionheart," the voice continued. "I can speak through Mountain Lion now, because you have found the right question to ask, and because his rhythm is matching mine."

Blue Swan moved closer, fascinated.

"Lionheart," asked Thal, his eyes shining with quiet power, "what is the next step? What needs to happen for you to be able to go back into Mountain Lion's chest?"

"He needs to stay with my rhythm," the heart replied. "But first of all, I want to tell you my story." With that, both the crystal and the heart started growing. They grew and grew, until they were even bigger than the Giant.

On one side of the crystal was a door. Humangus reached over and opened it. One by one, the Beings entered. It was cool inside, filled with milky clouds and shooting stars.

Wise Witch opened her mouth to speak. "This is like a different world." She realized that no sound had come out of her mouth, yet the Beings turned toward her, smiling and nodding. This really was a different world—where communication didn't happen through sound and spoken words.

Babla looked up and saw the Sun and the Moon half merged; all sizes of rainbows were appearing and disappearing in and out of the milky clouds. The air felt gooey and she couldn't move very fast.

Alan whispered into her ear that the world inside the crystal was without time. In timelessness, motion slowed. Babla guessed that this world must somehow be connected to the Spiralworld, where fast movements had also been impossible.

The Circle approached Mountain Lion's heart which was pink and smooth, pulsating steadily.

They heard the soundless words of the Wizard: "I've found a door." The Beings proceeded slowly toward him. Yes, he was standing in front of a door that led into the lionheart. Humangus nodded, and the Wizard opened the door.

A bat came flying out, screeching. Or so the Circle thought. Upon a closer examination, Babla realized that the creature had bat wings, but a human face with long dark hair, all messy and unkempt. It perched on the closest crystal wall, gazing at the Beings.

"What are you?" Humangus inquired in thought.

"I am Batwoman," was the soundless answer.

"Batwoman?!!" Mountain Lion exclaimed within. "I vaguely remember a batwoman when I was little."

"I am that," she replied. Phoenix stepped forward and started admiring Batwoman's wings.

The Wizard also moved closer to her and asked in thought, "What are you doing in Mountain Lion's heart?"

Kiwi came close, her eyes twinkling with delight. "Now," she thought, "we're going to hear lionheart's story."

Batwoman looked at Mountain Lion with deep compassion. Then she began. "Long, long ago, long before Mountain Lion was born, his father was the King and his mother the Queen in their Mountain Kingdom. One night, while they were taking a walk in their Kingdom, they heard a strange sound. Going toward it, they found a wounded baby batgirl. They took her in, cleaned up the wound, fed her, and soon she became part of the family.

"After a short while, the Queen gave birth to Mountain Lion, and Batgirl gained a friend. They played for many hours every day, enjoying each other's company. When it was time for Batgirl to become Batwoman, the Queen took her aside and explained that she had to leave and find other batbeings. That is, she needed to die to her Batgirlness to be reborn as the Batwoman. This couldn't be done if she stayed with the mountain lions.

"Batgirl didn't know what the Queen meant, yet she trusted this beloved Mountain Lioness, who had saved her. When she told young Mountain Lion that she had to leave, he became outraged, sprung up into the air in total fury, and said it was all nonsense. He couldn't see any reason for her leaving. This was her home, and she belonged there.

"Seeing that Batgirl was confused, he made up his mind in an instant. He grabbed her as gently as possible, not to hurt her, and swallowed her whole—all the way down into his heart. As long as she was in his heart, he thought, they would always be together.

"When he went home for dinner that evening, the pain in his heart was unbearable. Before he could say anything, his chest exploded and his heart came rolling out. Immediately a crystal formed around the heart, to keep the lionheart alive. During this process, young Mountain Lion lost consciousness and it took a long time for him to open his eyes again.

"In the meantime, the Queen and the King tended to his chest wound, doing their best to help it heal. When Mountain Lion came back to life, he couldn't remember his past—nothing whatsoever, including the time he had spent with Batgirl. He only knew of her vaguely because of the stories his parents had told him about his childhood, hoping he would remember one day. Meanwhile, the King, the Queen, and the Elders decided to leave his heart in the Green Mountain.

"As long as your heart is not in your chest, you will not remember your past," said Batwoman in thought. "And as long as you don't remember your past, you cannot die to it, let it go, and be reborn to the present, to be who you really are."

Wise Witch, Thal, and Babla looked at each other; Batwoman was very wise. Kiwi, who was excited because she loved the heartspace, wanted Batwoman to describe the next step.

"Half of you can hold the lionheart with your strong hearts, and the other half can hold Mountain Lion with your open hearts," she explained in thought. "When both rhythms match completely, the crystal will disappear. Your strong hearts will keep the lionheart alive, while your open hearts will help open Mountain Lion's chest for his heart to enter."

Mountain Lion began leaning against Wise Witch, relaxing. Phoenix, Oracle, Eelprince, Blue Swan, and the Wizard took their places around the lion, holding him with their open hearts. At the same time Babla, Humangus, Kiwi, Armadillo,

Wondering Magician, and Thal went to the lionheart, holding it with their strong hearts.

Batwoman stood in between, her wings outstretched. The Beings, connected in their hearts with the same purpose, went beyond their own veils of separation. Their hearts became one Heart, beating in the same rhythm.

And, in eternity, the crystal around Mountain Lion's heart disappeared and the heart returned to normal size, while simultaneously his chest started opening. At a nod from Batwoman, the Beings, holding the lionheart, carried it to his chest, placing it just so.

With the heart in its rightful place, Mountain Lion's chest gradually closed. Tears rolled down his lion cheeks; tears of remembering. His full memory back, Mountain Lion opened his eyes, walked toward Batwoman, and looked into her eyes.

"Bat or not," he said, "you are welcome in my Kingdom. I would like you to live there with me, if you like. If you want other batbeings around, they are welcome, too. The Green Mountain can be their home, now that my heart doesn't need that space any longer."

Babla loved seeing her Mountain Lion friend as a whole Being. Batwoman was smiling. Deep Love was shining out of her eyes. She flew onto the lion's back, making herself comfortable. As far as Babla was concerned, this was a very clear answer to his offer.

Humangus called for a break, and the Beings spread out in the Sacred Land to rest.

ARMADILLO: Ready to Trust

When the Circle came back together, Humangus looked tenderly at Armadillo and asked, "Are you ready?"

"I hope so. I want to be."

The Giant pointed to the middle of the Healing Circle, and Armadillo rolled herself there. And so she lay there in the middle in a tight ball. The Beings came into their pure hearts.

"I feel that she needs a very soft touch," Oracle cautioned.

It was Wise Witch's idea to come into their open hearts and start touching Armadillo in a spiral form; one of the Beings touched her directly, another

Being touched the heart of the first one, a third Being touched the heart of the second one, and so on. Humangus was at her head, holding it.

At times, he would motion the Spiral to move, and the Being who had just been touching Armadillo would move to the end of the Spiral, leaving the second Being to hold her.

After a long time, Armadillo started taking deep breaths; something was shifting. Sobs of relief came out of her eyes, rolled down, and disappeared into the earth. The gentle, soft touch and open heart of the Circle was allowing her to be vulnerable in a safe way. Wondering Magician started making sounds. Soon the rest joined him, which increased Armadillo's sobs.

Then the Circle-Spiral entered the World of Silence. In this world, the Beings came together as one silent Heart, without veils or walls keeping them apart.

A loud cry broke the stillness; Armadillo's body was straightening out. She was screaming in both pain and delight—the pain of undoing a lifelong pattern as the scrunched up ball, and delight in the new opening. Back in the timeless World of Silence, the Circle held their beloved friend.

Another shift happened and Armadillo turned around to let them touch her soft parts. Through sobs and screams, the Spiral held her, sometimes playing with sounds, other times quiet.

Armadillo gave a sigh of relief and relaxed. She opened her eyes and looked at each Being in deep appreciation. "You were right," she said to Humangus, smiling. "There is another world. I've found it now. Thank you." An atmosphere of celebration filled the air as she got up and walked around, stretching grateful legs that had not been used in a very long time.

THE WIZARD IN THE PUMPKIN AND BLACK MAN:
Healing the Split

When the Circle rejoined, Humangus said, "Our original reason for creating the Healing Circle was to help Wondering Magician lift the curse that was put on him. I suggest that Wondering Magician's process be one of the last ones because the stronger the Circle of pure hearts, the more powerful and effective his transformation will be. To lift a curse takes a great deal of focused heart energy.

"Eelprince will also to be one of the last ones because his mission demands one strong Heart." Turning to the Wizard, he reasoned, "So, I suggest that you go next."

Not expecting this, the Wizard was taken back. "Oh, well," he responded, trying not to show his distress. "I really shouldn't go at all. I mean, I'm doing fine here. It's been wonderful to be a part of all of your healings, but I think we shouldn't waste any time with me. I'm not in great need for healing, you know. Of course, one could always improve and such, but. . ."

"Oh, I see," said Thal, interrupting in mid-sentence. "This is your Veil of Separation. By believing you don't need as much attention as the others, you keep yourself apart."

Babla was relieved that Thal had interrupted because next to her Fireball was going crazy, trying to jump up and slap the Wizard, make him wake up and see reality. So Babla, being the gentle little girl that she was, was glad for Thal's much more gracious approach. But then, what was making Fireball so angry? What exactly was reality?

The Wizard looked blankly at Thal, incomprehension and confusion in his eyes. "I don't understand," he finally said. "I really don't need anything right now."

Seeing that talking about it wasn't getting anywhere, Humangus took charge. "I'm sure you don't," he agreed, patiently looking at the Wizard. "Yet we could still hold you with our pure hearts. Not because you need it, but just for the fun of it."

"Well," replied the Wizard, hesitating, "I guess that is a possibility."

"What I really want to do," Wise Witch broke in, cackling, "is to undulate in your pumpkin."

The Wizard's eyes sparkled. "I would love that," he brightened. "In fact, you could all come and I'll show you my pumpkin." He led the Circle to his pumpkin-house and went up to each door, inquiring whether it was the right one to enter.

Kiwi, who was very practical, seemed perplexed. "Has it ever happened that all the doors said 'no'?" she asked.

"Yes, it happened once," answered the Wizard.

"What did you do then?" Eelprince pursued this idea, trying to look serious.

"Oh," said the Wizard smoothly, "I climbed up and went in through a window. It wasn't that bad."

"I need some help!" Babla said to her Inner Guides. "Otherwise, Fireball is going to get out of hand here."

And help came. She felt Black Panther, Amazon Woman, Alan, and Eternal Friend all around her. She realized she had been holding her breath, trying hard to keep Fireball in check. Now, that she was safe with her Guides around, she breathed deeply again.

"What is going on?" she asked. "Why is Fireball going crazy?" Fireball, seeing Amazon Woman—her hero—ran into her arms, fuming. The Amazon, fully matching Fireball's energy, helped her to calm down.

Eternal Friend explained to Babla, "Fireball feels that the Wizard is not being real, that's why she is so upset."

"I realize he's kind of funny and has weird ideas about his doors, but what does that have to do with being real?" Babla wondered.

"He is hiding his real energy, his real Essence," said Alan. "He spends so much time trying to take care of things on the periphery, like these doors, that he never gets to the Core of Life."

Now Babla understood.

One of the doors accepted them, and the Beings entered the undulating pumpkin. The Wizard was very excited to have guests and began showing them all around.

Wise Witch and Babla went to a quiet spot and sat down, wanting to feel the undulations. Soon they were giggling as the motion entered their bodies and made them undulate, too. The Wizard came around and smiled, the depth in his eyes visible again. "This is why I like my pumpkin," he commented. "It makes me undulate, too."

Humangus, watching with keen eyes, had an idea. He placed the Wizard between Babla and Wise Witch, motioning for the others to gather round. They opened up to their pure hearts and sat in silence, waiting.

The three Beings were soon undulating together, beckoning the rest to join in. Before long, the whole Circle swayed to the pumpkin's rhythm, a new and delightful experience for everyone.

It was very soft and sweet and. . . something was not quite right. "His blood is black," Maya whispered in Babla's ear.

Oracle opened her eyes and stood up. "Black liquid is running through his veins," she announced.

"While I was gray outside, he is black inside," said Phoenix.

"Let's come up to our open hearts," Humangus suggested, "fully open, fully accepting of the way things are right now." The Circle became one Open Heart, holding the Wizard. They found themselves in an open space where time was no more. In the middle of this space, they saw a huge statue of the Wizard. As they approached, they found a door on its left side.

Thal reached over and opened the door so the Circle could enter the statue. It was all black inside. A dark, gooey liquid was running freely everywhere. Humangus led them deeper and deeper into the Wizard's body, until they reached the Core. From here, thick tubes, transparent and empty, were going out to the rest of his body.

"I see," said the Giant. "His blood would normally run in these tubes. For some reason, it has left the tubes and become black. How strange."

The Wizard, who was in his own body with the rest of the Beings, was perplexed. "I didn't know I looked like this from the inside," he commented, visibly shaken. "I just don't understand."

"Maybe what you've just said is connected to what is happening," Phoenix suggested lovingly.

"What do you mean?" asked the Wizard.

"She means that your outer not-understanding and confusion might be connected to the inner black confusion we are witnessing," Thal tried to explain.

The Wizard scratched his head. "That's very possible," he replied. Humangus and Kiwi were busy inspecting the empty tubes. They didn't seem to have any leaks in them, so how had the blood escaped? And why had it changed color?

Babla looked at the Core and pointed; she had detected a leak. Humangus nodded his head; at least one mystery had been solved.

Wise Witch turned to the Wizard. "How have you lived your life so far? What do you believe in?"

He rubbed his head again. In his life he had tried to be fair and nice to all Beings; he wanted others to be happy, so whenever he could, he enjoyed giving out positive attention. He believed in being with other Beings, listening to their stories, trying to make himself available to any Being that needed help.

"What do you do when *you* need help?" asked Mountain Lion.

"Oh," replied the Wizard. "I go into my pumpkin and undulate."

Babla asked Alan, "Isn't being fair and being nice paradoxical?"

"Yes, it is." Alan took this idea further. "If one is really fair, then not being nice sometimes needs to be the outcome. That is, fairness comes out of compassion, and true compassion is not always nice."

"You're just too nice, Wizard," Babla offered. "I think that's your real problem."

"What Babla means," translated Thal, "is that by trying to be so nice you may be forgetting your own needs."

"Yes. And that's why your Core is empty," Humangus added.

"If you want to be true to yourself," said Wise Witch, "you cannot always be nice."

"Oh!" exclaimed the Wizard, looking less confused. "If that's true, then I'll have to change some things here."

"How do we find out what is really true for him?" Eelprince asked. "My truth might not necessarily be his, so how would I know what is his truth?"

"The answer lies in and through his Veil of Separation," Oracle stated. Humangus looked around. Kiwi scratched her head. What was this supposed to mean?

Babla gasped. "I understand! The Wizard's Veil of Separation is being nice and attentive to others, no matter what. In and through the veil would then mean that he needs to go with awareness into being nice, and then go through the niceness to find his truth to the other side."

"But when he goes through the veil," Thal went deeper, "he might not find 'his' truth. He might just find one layer of it, which is what often happens."

The Wizard, with a spark of understanding, nodded. He was ready. He looked at the Circle and suggested, "Being too nice seems to have created a leak in my Core, where my blood oozed out all over. Maybe I need to go into this blood that is totally out of hand."

Yes, this was a good idea. He took a few deep breaths and went into the thick black liquid, followed by the others. It was all dark.

They lost all sense of time as they entered eternity. Half walking, half swimming, they traveled deeper and deeper. The blood was thinner now, and then, they were out. They stood right in front of the leak.

Taking a deep breath, the Wizard went through the leak into the Core with the others close behind. Their faces froze as they met a black man sitting there looking them straight in the eye. "Who are you?" the Wizard managed to say in spite of his shock.

"I am Black Man. What took you so long? I've been waiting for you," he said firmly while motioning them to sit down. As they did so, he told them his story. "I am black, which doesn't mean I am nasty," he said, confidently. "In truth, the Wizard and I are one Being.

"Long, long ago, we got separated by a mean witch, who was afraid of our power. This witch became jealous of our power and played a trick on us, and we fell for it.

"At that time, we were still an apprentice and didn't know how to deal with tricksters. I got pushed into the Core, and each time the Wizard was nice to a Being without being true to himself, I sank further and further. The leak in the Core came from me being pushed in.

"The trick that keeps us stuck is that as long as he doesn't follow his own truth, I can't come out. But without me, he doesn't know how to stay in his power. So, without outside help, there was no way out."

"What part of him are you?" asked Humangus.

"I'm everything that he is not," Black Man answered. "I make decisions very easily. I hold the seed of our power, he undulates and moves with it. I can be firm and to the point, he is wise. He knows when to be soft and lenient, when to question things, when to wait. I know how to start and complete things, he knows how to keep them going, once initiated.

"You may think it is the pumpkin that undulates. In truth, it's his mastery that does it; but because I was missing, the pumpkin would sometimes run wild. It needs his undulating wizardry and my directing capacity to keep steady."

"So as long as you are apart, there won't be wholeness and flow," Wondering Magician said, getting the big picture.

"We'd like to help you get back together," suggested Humangus. The Circle was ready.

"Please take me out of here first," said Black Man.

When he got up Babla realized that he was more like a shadow than a real man. He had the outline of a body, yet he had no substance. Because he was having difficulty walking, the Wizard gave him a hand, but the moment their hands touched, Black Man disappeared. The Beings were stunned; he was gone.

Thal was the first to understand what had happened; he started laughing, pointing at the Wizard, who was standing up, straighter than ever before. Through his eyes shone the depth of wisdom connected with a dark spark of power.

The Wizard nodded. "Yes, Black Man has become one with me again," he said smoothly, yet firmly as well. The Beings celebrated his wholeness and knew that from now on, he would always know which door to take.

Looking around, the Circle realized that they were back on the Sacred Land. It was time for a break.

WONDERING MAGICIAN: Lifting the Curse

The Healing Circle resumed with Humangus bowing to Wondering Magician. It was his turn to tell the others about the curse and his hat.

"The creation of the Healing Circle has a lot to do with the Magician's curse," Humangus added. "A curse is a very powerful thing. It requires a gathering of Beings with pure hearts to lift it. The time has come to release this curse."

"But how can that be done?" asked Wondering Magician in disbelief. "This curse is just the opposite of a pure heart. It won't allow a heart to get near!"

"That's true," replied the Giant. "The heart may not enter the curse, but the curse can enter the heart."

"No, no, no!" the Magician protested angrily. "If it enters the heart it will destroy it. I won't allow any of your pure hearts to be ruined by my curse. I'd rather live this way for the rest of my life."

Babla had never seen such a tender smile on the Giant's face. "Our friend the Magician has a very pure heart himself," he said. "The curse could indeed destroy one pure heart. That's why we are doing this together. I've yet to see a curse destroy twelve pure hearts, joined as One Heart!" Wondering Magician understood.

Next, Humangus asked him to sit in the middle. The Beings came up to their pure hearts and started chanting to the curse, inviting it in. They held the hat and the hands coming out of the Magician's temples. The chanting got louder and louder, deeper and deeper. Then it shattered time.

Upon entering timelessness, the chanting melted, merged, changed its form. In eternity, it became One Spiral.

In the world of time, the curse felt itself drawn to this whirling Heart; it disengaged itself from Wondering Magician's hat and entered the Spiral. Lost

Magician's voice swirled amid the curse. "Noooooooooooo.....!" it cried in utter desperation.

Having entered the spiraling Heart, the curse lost its way back to Wondering Magician. It kept moving further and further down the Spiral, its plaintive echoes becoming fainter. Then it reached the apex of the One Heart. After a long moment of deep silence, Lost Magician's voice reverberated one last time, "Nooooooooo.......!" and left the Spiral to dissolve in the Void and never return.

Humangus suggested that the Circle lie down, their hearts touching the Sacred Land, their heads touching each other. The pure hearts needed to replenish themselves, so the Beings imagined the earth coming into their hearts, offering a place to rest.

Babla thanked the earth for its generosity and graciousness.

When all the pure hearts had been deeply nurtured, the Beings looked at each other. Everyone was refreshed.

"Look!" Babla pointed toward Wondering Magician. The two hands coming out of his temples had disappeared. His hat was firmly on his head now.

Humangus smiled and, bowing to him, said, "The curse has been lifted. And with that, it is time for you to change your name; from now on you shall be Wondering Magician no more. Every Being who meets you shall call you the Magician."

"From now on I am the Magician," he replied, bowing back, with a soft sparkle of self-recognition in his eyes.

EELPRINCE: *The Secret Beyond All Secrets*

The Healing Circle gathered again, holding wings, paws, hands, and fins. Eyes closed, they sat for a long time in silence. Then Humangus took a giant breath and turned to Eelprince. "My Prince," he said, bowing and smiling mischievously, "it is your turn."

"Well," Eelprince replied. "I don't even know where to start searching. The Eel Elders told my father of a secret beyond all secrets. I need to find it and bring it back, but I don't have any leads. My father is ready to give the Kingdom over to me and be a simple eel, enjoying the ocean. So, my becoming the King depends on whether I can find this secret or not." He looked apprehensive.

"The secret beyond all secrets," Oracle spoke. "Do you know what those secrets are?"

"No," Eelprince replied. "I have no idea."

"That's where we shall start, then," said Humangus.

"Oh, I see," said Eelprince. "In order to go beyond the secrets, I must first find out what they are."

"Do you want to be the King?" Babla was curious.

"Of course I do. When I was born, the Eel Elders told my father that I was to be the next King. All my life I was raised to prepare me for this task. It is my destiny."

"Perhaps the first secret is non-attachment, then," suggested Wise Witch, smiling her deep smile.

"I don't understand," Eelprince sounded confused.

"I do!" Thal sat up straighter. He turned to Eelprince and said, "One of the secrets of being good at whatever you do is to not be attached to it. If you can imagine living the rest of your life as a simple eel, being totally content, then if you become King, you will be a compassionate and wise ruler. You will not try to control or manipulate others in order to stay in power."

Eelprince was getting the gist of it now. "How do I do that?" he asked the Circle, hoping for more clues. "How can I not be attached?"

"That's easy!" replied Babla. "Just imagine yourself going back to the Eel Kingdom without having completed your mission."

Humangus suggested that Eelprince come to the center of the Circle, lie down, and close his eyes. Then he guided Eelprince back into the ocean, back to the Kingdom of Eels, not having found the secret that lies beyond all secrets. It was painful. Eelprince could see the sadness and disappointment on the faces of his father, mother, beloved friends, and all the eels who were expecting him to become the next King.

He started crying, sobbing uncontrollably. "I want to be King!" he screamed. "I want to be King! This is my birthright!"

The Beings in the Circle chanted in a low voice, "You are not the King. You are just a simple eel." Eelprince's body was sliding in all directions, in total agony.

Humangus continued to guide him into a possible future as a simple eel. Eelprince went through all kinds of emotions— anger, resentment, bitterness, sadness, desperation, fear, emptiness.

Then he slid beyond emptiness into his real Being, and felt his Essence. Sitting upright, he opened his eyes and said calmly, "I am an eel. Whether I ever become King is not the issue. Being King will not make me a better eel. All eels are the same at heart." The Beings shared smiles of contentment. Eelprince had found the first secret.

Now what? The Beings were looking at each other, not knowing where to go from there. How were they going to assist Eelprince in finding the other secrets? "We need some help," Humangus admitted at last.

"We could invite one of my Inner Guides," Babla offered. "They have helped me whenever I needed it." The Circle decided to give it a try. Babla closed her eyes and asked out loud, "Would any of my Guides like to help us?"

They heard the fluttering of wings, and Wise Owl appeared on Babla's left shoulder. Babla was surprised that all the Beings in the Circle could actually see her. Wise Owl explained that those with pure hearts can see the Guides of others. Babla asked Wise Owl about the secrets. If these things were secrets, how were they supposed to find them?

Wise Owl tipped her head. "Use the first secret you have found," she said. "It is the key to the others." The Beings murmured to each other. Why did all the Guides have to speak in riddles? This didn't make sense at all!

Then Kiwi jumped up. "Of course," she said, waving her furry arms at the obvious. "The first secret is about not being attached. That means we can't be attached to wanting to find the secrets."

Wise Owl was pleased. "Yes. Let go of all desire to find these secrets. At the same time, bring your full intention to the Circle and Eelprince sitting in the middle. Bring your focus to Eelprince and the secrets, without any desire or attachment to do anything about them."

The Beings connected their pure hearts. Then Humangus led them to their full hearts, to feel the fullness of being together. Next, he led them to their strong hearts, where they combined their individual intentions into one strong intention—Eelprince and the secrets. Lastly, he led them into their open hearts and the Circle let go of all desire, opening up to the moment, to the Sacred Land, to everything they were experiencing right now.

Time disappeared and they found themselves standing in front of an open door with the words "NON-ATTACHMENT" engraved on it. They entered and found another door, closed this time. It read: "SELF-LOVE". Eelprince turned the knob and opened the door.

They entered a huge empty hall with stone floors. In the middle a young eel was sitting, looking sad and lost. The Beings approached and quietly sat around him. He looked surprised. Eelprince told him who he was and why they were there.

The young eel looked up with sad eyes and said, "I'm your lost part. A long time ago you put me in here because you thought that with me around you couldn't be a good King when the time came. You told me that I needed too much of your time and attention. As a Prince, preparing to be King, you needed to give it to the Eel Kingdom, not to me. So, you left me here."

The Beings glanced at each other. Why was this place called self-love, then? "Oh, I see," said the Magician. "The second secret is about loving yourself, which means all parts of yourself. If you want to find the secret beyond all secrets, you need to love this little eel first."

Eelprince understood. He came closer to the little eel and took him into his fins. "I want to learn how to love you," he told little eel. "But I don't know how?"

"I don't need much," little eel responded. "All I want is to be with you."

"You could keep him in your heart," suggested Kiwi to Eelprince. "This way, he can always be with you, no matter where you are or what you are doing." This was a great idea!

Humangus reached over and opened Eelprince's heart, and Eelprince lifted little eel up so he could slide in. Little eel slid into the middle of the heart, curled up, and went to sleep. They had found the second secret.

"Use the second secret to find the third," Wise Owl reminded them. The Beings went into themselves, looking for any unloved parts inside with which they could share Love.

In the fragrance of Love, the third door appeared. "COMPASSION" was written on it. When they opened the door and entered, the huge hall was filled with eels. Some were crying, some complaining, some sleeping, some confused, and others were happy and content. What did compassion to do with all these eels?

"The Light of Truth tells me that true compassion doesn't have anything to do with behavior," Phoenix explained. "A Being, full of compassion, loves all other Beings, regardless of their actions."

"Compassion, then," said Eelprince, "is self-love turned outward." Eelprince went from eel to eel, radiating a warm glow from his heart. The eels received it with gratefulness, and soon the whole hall was vibrating with the sacred hum of compassion.

Eelprince turned to the Circle and said, "This is so strange; I feel like the receiver, not the giver. Radiating compassion to others has filled me with it, too. Somehow, I feel very humble."

With that, the hall with the eels disappeared and they found themselves standing in front of a door with the word "HUMBLENESS" carved on it. The door opened by itself and they walked in.

Actually, they walked out. The Beings found themselves outside in a rock garden. There were rocks of all sizes and colors spread out on a sandy ground, with a few trees and bushes in between. "Look at all this space!" Eelprince remarked, "There is so much space here. And, it all looks so simple."

"Effortless ease," replied the Wizard. "When I look around, I feel like taking a deep breath; I'm in awe about the simplicity of life."

Eelprince sat down, and scooping up a handful of sand, commented, "Life is humbling and simple. You know, right now I'm so grateful to be here."

The rock garden disappeared, leaving them in front of another door. Written on it was "GRATEFULNESS." This door also opened by itself, and the Beings entered golden light; they were walking on it, surrounded by it, breathing it.

Blue Swan stretched her neck gracefully and said, "This is beautiful. I've never experienced anything like this before. I'm so grateful to be alive." She spread her wings and started dancing, her fine blue feathers shimmering. In awe of what they had observed, the others joined her. Soon the Circle was dancing in the golden light, or was it the golden light that was dancing around them? The dancing of the Beings merged and became one Dance, one Rhythm.

After what seemed like an eternity, the Dance ended. Standing in golden light, they looked at each other for a long time.

"I know that there is something I need to say, but I don't know what it is yet," said Armadillo, her face soft and open. The Circle stood there, gazing at her in disbelief; was this really Armadillo? "When my healing happened," she continued, "I thought that I had found the other world and that this was all there was for me to find. Now I realize that there is so much more to life, so much more to be experienced. I'm deeply grateful for this opportunity." She was glowing.

Wise Owl appeared on Babla's left shoulder and said, "You have found the fourth secret, that life is very simple and humbling. Now you are in the fifth secret—the secret of gratefulness; through which we enter the Golden Light of Being, of Essence, which is inside of us and all around us.

"You have two more secrets to find after this one. The first five secrets are called 'Secrets of the Light.' The other two are 'Secrets of the Dark.'"

"One finds the Secrets of the Light by totally becoming them, and the deeper secret reveals itself. The Secrets of the Dark are different; you have to use the full integrity of your heart to find them."

Humangus guided Eelprince into his strong heart. The other Beings came up to their pure hearts, holding space for him.

"Golden Light," asked Eelprince, "will you guide me to the next secret?" The golden floor they were standing on opened up and let them through. They were standing in front of yet another door: "LIFE AND DEATH."

"This sure sounds different," the Magician commented. With some hesitation, Eelprince started turning the knob. His fins were shaking.

Mountain Lion moved forward and said, "I can see that you are afraid, Eelprince. When fear appears, integrity disappears. A key to maintain integrity is courage. Find courage in your strong heart, and it will help you open this door."

Eelprince did so. He started breathing into his strong heart and asked for courage. His shaking stopped, and he opened the door.

They entered the deep ocean. The Magician and the Wizard created little orange pills for the Beings of the Circle to take so that they could breathe under water. As they floated deeper and deeper into the ocean, they came across a huge castle made of thousands of shells.

Eelprince, supported by the Circle, led the way into the castle through a large shell-door. But, suddenly, he froze; before him were many types of Beings all being hanged in a variety of ways. Babla moved forward and held one of his fins, Blue Swan touched his other fin, Humangus stood behind Eelprince giving him strength, and Mountain Lion reminded him that courage was a key part of integrity.

Kiwi, as practical as ever, commented, "Yep! We are all going to die." At this, Eelprince snapped out of his frozen spell. He looked around for a long time, trying to understand what was happening.

The Circle started exploring the rest of the castle, swimming through its countless doors. On the first floor, they saw in each room a different way of dying—drowning, suffocating, falling, suicide, diseases.

They found a spiral staircase that went up to the many rooms on the second floor. To their surprise, they witnessed Beings being born in all kinds of ways.

Eelprince was speechless, and Armadillo took it all in. "This is remarkable! Maybe the secret is that Life and Death are connected!"

"Let's go to the third floor," suggested Phoenix. "The Truth must be there." Through another twisting staircase they went further up. At the top was only one door with the words "WAITING ROOM" carved on it.

Eelprince took a few conscious breaths, came up into his strong heart, and opened the door. Standing there, he gasped in utter disbelief. He had entered a huge room filled with ghosts!

"Great!" said Babla, walking in right behind him. "I've always wanted to meet ghosts."

"Me, too," Thal agreed.

"Why is this place called 'Waiting Room'?" asked the Magician. "What are these ghosts waiting for?"

"Good question," replied Wise Witch. "Let's ask them." And she did.

"To be admitted into the second floor," came their answer. The Circle looked at each other in surprise. Oracle moved forward and asked where they had come from.

"From the first floor," the ghosts answered.

"Oh, I see," the Wizard stepped in. "The Beings who died in all those different ways in the first floor are brought here to wait, until it's their time to be reborn. How fascinating."

Humangus turned to Eelprince and took him gently into his palm. "Now it is up to you to find the Secret of Life and Death," he said, looking intently at his friend.

Eelprince took in the Giant's words, then responded, "The Secret of Life and Death is that there is no real death. It seems like life is a part of death and death is a part of life. Death as we know it is just a transition to more life."

"And life as we know it is just a transition to death," Oracle added.

"So, if life is leading us into death and death is leading us into life, this would mean that life and death are part of the same cycle," Kiwi commented.

"Well," asked the Magician, scratching his head, "where is the Beginning then?"

With that, a big trap door on the floor opened and the Circle fell through it down to the second floor, then via another trap door to the first floor, and finally through a third one to the basement of the castle.

They were standing in front of a black door that read: "DARKNESS." Bewildered, Blue Swan asked, "Is this the Beginning?"

Wise Owl reappeared on Babla's left shoulder. "No," she replied, turning to Eelprince, "it is not. It is the last secret you have to find, before you can enter the Beginning, which is the secret beyond all secrets. Remember your full integrity as you enter the Secret of Darkness."

The Beings prepared themselves by breathing deeply. Eelprince, with Mountain Lion and Thal at his sides and Humangus behind, opened the door. The Circle entered darkness.

It was dark. All dark. Darkness everywhere.

"I've never been in a place like this," Armadillo was the first to speak. "There is nothing here."

As the Beings started spreading out to explore the nature of where they were, Eelprince began to shake uncontrollably. Sensing this, Babla stopped, unsure of what to do. Then her pure heart pulled her toward Eelprince. When she followed her feeling, she realized that the others were being pulled by their pure hearts, too. They created a circle around Eelprince and he stopped shaking.

Humangus was deep in thought. He clapped his hands as a light bulb of understanding went off in his head. "Of course!" he said. "We are in Eelprince's darkness as his support. This is his healing journey. Let's all stay with him, in our pure hearts." The Beings sat down circling Eelprince.

"The hearts have to divide, yet stay together," added Oracle.

Humangus tried to grasp the meaning of her wisdom. Then he turned to Wise Witch and asked, "How does Oracle's wisdom translate into our situation here?"

"She means we have to connect our pure hearts with each other. At the same time, this won't be enough support for Eelprince. After our pure hearts are connected deep inside, we need to hold the space for his journey through the other aspects of our hearts, too," explained Wise Witch.

"Great!" said Thal and Mountain Lion together. "We want to be in our strong hearts."

"Me, too," Kiwi added.

"Open heart for me," replied the Magician, followed by the Wizard and Blue Swan.

"I'm in my full heart," Babla and Armadillo both chimed in.

"I will join you," Humangus added.

Oracle, Phoenix, and the Witch said in one voice, "We will stay in our pure hearts."

Sitting in darkness, they all extended their hearts to Eelprince. He went within and commanded, "Secret of Darkness, reveal yourself to me."

The Circle shook as a huge wave of sadness washed over them, hitting Eelprince full force. Huge teardrops rolled down his silvery cheeks, disappearing in the darkness. He became sadness, pure sadness.

At the Giant's suggestion, they connected their pure hearts with each other, extending their full/open/strong/pure hearts to Eelprince.

The wave of sadness subsided but, as the Circle breathed with relief, a giant wave of despair rolled over them, again blasting Eelprince. Now he was in utter hopelessness, writhing in agony, screaming in unbearable pain. There was no way out. He knew he was about to die here and would never see his eel family ever again.

Then he felt the Circle still around him, staying steady for him from the depths of their hearts, the despair gradually subsided as if it had never existed. The Circle relaxed a bit, hoping it was over, when another huge wave enveloped them.

"Watch out everybody!" yelled the Giant. "Stay very strong in your hearts. This is the wave of rage." And, indeed, a red hot wave washed over the Beings, almost consuming them.

Now Babla realized why being connected to each other was so important; this force couldn't be survived alone. The wave left them and hit Eelprince, who was screaming uncontrollably. This gentle, thoughtful Being was cursing and raging at everything and everybody.

Wise Witch moaned, finding this one of the hardest things she had done in a long time—to stay in her pure heart while a Being was in full rage. She closed her eyes and felt her connection to the hearts of the others. Then she took a conscious breath and extended her pure heart to Eelprince.

Armadillo tightened up; all she could think about was rolling into a ball and leaving. Just as soon as she had decided to do so, she felt a tug in her pure heart and opened her eyes, remembering that she wasn't alone; she was part of the Circle and she was safe. She smiled and shared her full heart with Eelprince.

Babla wanted to crawl into the darkness and disappear. "Oh my!" she thought. "What are we going to do now?" She heard Eternal Friend's voice, "This is not your process, Babla. Be as present and as much in your heart as you can for Eelprince." She opened her eyes and remembered where she was. She relaxed into her full heart, feeling the joy of giving.

Humangus was dismayed to see most of the Beings having such a hard time. "The wave of rage is the toughest to hold an open heart space for," he thought. He took several big breaths into his pure heart to strengthen the Circle's connection, then started breathing into his full heart to assist Eelprince.

The first impulse of Phoenix was to fold her wings and go gray. In the midst of this rage, how could she share her beauty and wisdom? Just as her wings started closing, she heard the Light that is the Truth within her, say, "This is not your rage. Hiding the truth of who you are will not make it go away. Shine your Light and be present. You are loved. Eelprince needs your support." She took a deep breath and came back to her pure heart; then, feeling the connection with the others, she offered her pure Love to Eelprince.

Oracle was enjoying every moment of this wave; she loved the hot, potent energy of rage. But because the others were having a hard time, she spread as much joy as possible into the Circle, until it reached all the way to Eelprince.

"Here we go!" Mountain Lion said to himself. "This is hot! Eelprince will need a lot of support with this." He came up to his strong heart even more; but realizing that something wasn't quite right. "Oh, yes," he thought. "I forgot our pure heart connection." When he reconnected to the pure hearts, his strong heart expanded, flowing outward to Eelprince.

While Eelprince was raging, Thal thought, "Anger is such a funny thing." He wondered whether there wasn't a better way to express things. Then he realized that this wasn't his rage. They were in Eelprince's darkness to support him in finding the secrets. He relaxed, deepening his connection to the Circle, and sharing his strong Love with Eelprince.

The Magician was disgusted. To him, rage was one of the most inappropriate things in Existence. He had better things to do and he wanted to leave. Why was he here, anyway? "When a Being is angry, what can one do? Just standing by obviously isn't going to help." he decided. After a while, he felt a tug from his pure heart, which reminded him to stay connected to the Circle. When he did that, he remembered his purpose, came up to his open heart, and extended it to Eelprince.

Eelprince's rage was beyond Kiwi, so she asked her Inner Mate, Zoran, for help. Zoran held Kiwi close and reminded her of her intention: to stay connected to the Circle and to create space for Eelprince. Thankful for the guidance, Kiwi felt a warmth spreading through her and out to the group.

Blue Swan was listening to Eelprince's potent raging. It was so loud. She realized that she didn't really want to deal with this. What could she do anyway? Blue Swan felt very alone and helpless. The tug from her pure heart came as a total surprise. When she realized she wasn't alone she effortlessly came into her open heart to support Eelprince.

The Wizard felt tension in his chest. He wished he was safe in his pumpkin. Rage wasn't safe at all. On a hunch, he started imagining himself in his home, relaxed and comfortable. A deep sense of ease came over him, and with that the remembrance of his purpose. The Wizard reconnected to the other pure hearts and offered his undulations to Eelprince.

Just like that, Eelprince stopped raging in mid-sentence. The wave had vanished as suddenly as it had hit him. He was renewed, feeling the Circle there for him. Just as he opened his mouth to say something, the wave of shame rolled over him. He was in morbid shame about all the rage he had just expressed. How could he have done it? He, the Eelprince. . .

He would never be able to look into the eyes of any Being ever again.

The Circle, stronger than ever, supported him with tenderness and presence. He became shame so totally that there was nothing else left.

At last, the shame subsided, and only the dark remained.

"Let us breathe together," Humangus suggested. "I feel another strong wave coming." He was right. Within seconds, they were engulfed by a wave of terror. Sheer terror.

The Circle froze; so did Eelprince. Connected in their pure hearts, the wave soon left all of them, but swallowed him. As they shook themselves free of panic, they realized that this had to be the last wave. As one Heart, one Being, the Circle kept on holding space for Eelprince in his paralyzed state.

"Integrity. Be in your full integrity." Eelprince didn't know whether he was hearing this from the inside, the outside, or both. It didn't matter. "Integrity. I am in my full integrity." He reaffirmed this statement, first in thought; next, as he could move his lips, out loud. The more he said it, the less frozen he felt. Eventually, the wave receded from his head, then his body. After what seemed like forever, he was free of terror.

Everybody relaxed. Eelprince looked older somehow. There was a gleam of wisdom in his eyes. They all gathered around, holding him as he sank into a well-earned rest.

Eelprince opened his eyes, gazing at the Circle, and asked, "Now what?" In the darkness he could barely see his friends.

Wise Owl appeared and replied, "Now you need to tell us the Secret of Darkness."

He smiled. "The darkness contains the 'dark emotions.' The only way out is to let them pass through. The secret is that the emotions are merely waves, they are not me. If I stay in my heart, these waves will have to pass without harm and disappear. There is no need to fear them."

With that, the darkness parted, and they found themselves standing in front of another door.

"This is the last door," Wise Owl commented. "Behind this door is the secret beyond all secrets." There was no sign.

Eelprince was excited and ready. He was almost at the end of his journey. This was the last door. He opened it and the Beings entered. To their surprise, they started falling. They fell and fell, with nothing around them. Eelprince, remembering his mission, took charge. "We are in a void," he said, trying to sound calm.

The Circle stopped falling. Now they were suspended in—what? "There's not even air in here," Babla added. "We're suspended in the Void."

"Yes, the Void. . . ," they heard Wise Owl say.

"So, the ultimate secret is that the Beginning is the Void," claimed Eelprince. They started falling again, yet very slowly this time.

"Part of the secret," Humangus corrected him. They stopped falling. This was incredible!

"This might be a strange thing to say," Wise Witch said with hesitation, "but this Void doesn't feel empty to me." She was right, because they were staying suspended.

Eelprince closed his eyes and summarized, "We are in the Void. It is not empty. It is not dead. Even though it is a void, it is also alive. It is filled with life."

"It is so totally quiet here," the Magician ventured. "But, I also hear a sound. It's almost like there is sound in the silence." The others nodded, because they could sense it, too.

"And yet when I look around, I don't see any life or hear a real sound," observed Kiwi.

"Maybe the Void carries the potential for all life and sound," said Eelprince almost as a question, as if thinking out loud.

"The seed!" Humangus added, excited. "It is carrying the seed."

Wise Owl appeared once more to ask Eelprince, "What is the secret that lies beyond all secrets?"

Eelprince took a deep breath and sank into the Void. After a moment of stillness, he found the answer within. "The Full Void is the Beginning of all things. It holds the potential, the seed for all life, even though no life is in it."

The Circle looked at each other, astonished; they were back on the Sacred Land, sitting on the ground, intact and at peace. With the healing accomplished, it was time to say good-bye. The Beings hugged each other, expressing their appreciation and Love.

Eelprince felt satisfied; he wasn't attached to becoming the next King anymore; yet if it did happen, he knew he was well prepared.

Kiwi was smiling contentedly, happy to be a she-bear, feeling Zoran's presence and Love inside.

Thal had tears in his eyes, filled with gratitude for his new name. He knew that every Being in the Circle had a place in his heart.

Phoenix contemplated what had happened. The profound healing each Being had undergone was incredible. She felt connected to the Circle, to herself, to all Life. The Light of Truth inside her echoed, "In our hearts, we are One."

The Magician was jumping around, hugging everyone and giggling. "I'm a magician," he sang. "Now I can go back to my people and claim my heritage."

Blue Swan felt light and free. She knew that the Love and support from the other Beings had changed her life. She had helped with their healing, too. She couldn't wait to glide on water.

Armadillo was walking; she knew that what she had learned and experienced on the Sacred Land was only the beginning, and she felt grateful.

The Wizard in the Pumpkin was busy holding each Being and enjoying his wholeness; this had been one of the most healing and transforming experiences in his life.

Oracle was also embracing each Being, anticipating the beginning of a new life. She was thankful to be in one piece, to be able to serve herself and others in need of the wisdom of her Truth.

Mountain Lion roared, "Hear me! I have a heart! What fun!" He had learned the importance of being loved and supported; and he knew that things would be different at home. With his heart in his chest, he was going to make a much better King.

Wise Witch cackled, feeling content and complete inside. She loved her Sacred Land and knew that other circles with other Beings would continue to meet here. She had no desire to be anywhere else. She felt grateful to herself, to the Circle, to all Life.

Humangus and Babla gazed at each other; their eyes touching. Suddenly, Babla realized that she was the same size as he was; what had happened? Had he shrunk or had she grown? She heard Rabia's smiling voice say, "No, little one. You are seeing him through my eyes. In his daily life Humangus is a giant, and I'm not; yet when I open my heart and expand into Love, we become the same size."

After a long hug, Babla saw Rabia take out the eagle feather and hand it to Humangus. "Are you ready for your next step, to spend time with the eagle family?" she asked.

The Giant bowed and took the feather. "Yes," he replied, stroking it gently. "I am ready."

In the silence that followed, Babla knew that even if she never saw Humangus in physical form again, the eternal Love he and Rabia shared would always stay in her heart.

Eagle landed. Nobody had seen her arrive. Her gaze penetrated through each Being, then focused on Humangus. As the Giant approached the big bird, Oracle and Wise Witch explained to him, "For now, Eagle wants you to keep her feather. Yet, once your time with the eagles is finished, you will return it to Babla."

Humangus accepted and Eagle turned her side to him, making a piercing sound. Humangus lay down on her back and she carried him away.

VI.
finishing touches

HUMANGUS: The World of the Eagle

Humangus lost all sense of time. He sank into the eagle feathers and closed his eyes while the air played with his hair and beard. What was his next step? What lay ahead? He did not know, nor did he want to anticipate.

He turned his head toward his left shoulder and checked with his Guides. Old Man and Old Woman both told him to let go, "Trust in Eagle's Wisdom." He took a deep breath.

After a long flight, they landed on top of a huge mountain, the tallest one around. "High mountains," he said out loud. "I've always wanted to live on a high mountain. I guess now is the time."

When he met the rest of Eagle's family, he felt from the quality of their silence that he had been accepted as a temporary, non-flying member. In many ways, life with eagles was similar to life with hawks, yet different also. He knew he needed to focus on what was different; this would be his main task. And so he did.

Humangus found out that the eagles lived a dual life; they were in time and in no-time, simultaneously. In time, they were birds of prey; they hunted and killed for survival. In no-time, there was no thought of survival, so there was no hunting and killing. Humangus knew that discovering more about the nature of no-time was the reason for his stay with them.

During the first part of his visit, he mostly played with the eaglets, watching how they were fed by their mother and how they learned new things. Just as he was born to be a giant, they were born to be eagles. How incredible life was in its endless capacity for creation! His whole being filled with awe.

During the second part of his stay, the eagles took turns inviting him to fly with them. He learned very quickly how to climb aboard, sit on their backs, and hold his balance in the air. As he got more used to being in the air, they went a bit faster, until they were flying at their regular speed.

Once he got used to keeping his balance, Humangus let go of holding onto their feathers and spread out his arms. A profound sense of joy filled his being. It was as if his Essence were expanding beyond his physical body into a realm of no boundaries. Each breath he took intensified this sensation, until there was no breath.

When they landed back on the mountain, however, something very strange happened. Humangus was in a rage, his giant voice expressing anger to the mountains, which echoed for a long time, far and away.

The next time the eagles took him out, he felt the same joy, the same feeling of limitlessness. But, once on the mountain, he broke down in deep sorrow, crying for what seemed like an eternity. When the tears finally subsided, he decided it was time to check with his Guides.

"Trust," they said. "When your energy expands beyond the body, you feel no boundaries. Coming back into the body, you will become aware of every old contraction inside. The expansion allows the tension to surface and be released. Be patient and trust the healing."

Humangus trusted.

After each expansive flight, Humangus continued to feel rage, sorrow, despair, loneliness, fear, or shame. And he let it all flow through him, accepting every emotion as it arose from its long-forgotten place to be felt again.

One day, after a very joyful flight, he was wondering which emotion would show up. None did. He sat down and sank into stillness, becoming aware of a presence behind him. He knew it was Eagle, the one who had brought him here.

The Giant wasn't sure what this meant. Was his time with the eagle family over? Was this another phase of the teaching? Slowly he turned around and faced her. He knew she was ready for him. Was he ready for her?

He climbed onto her back and she took off. For some unknown reason, he didn't sit this time. He lay down, his chest touching her back. She was going neither slow nor fast; he wasn't even sure whether she was flying at all, yet the scenery kept changing.

Eagle flew very high, then dropped very low. Right in between, they entered no-time. Humangus somehow sank down into her. Eagle flew very high again, then very low; and this time, the Giant felt himself becoming the eagle. He now saw the world in no-time through Eagle's eyes and realized that as Eagle, he wasn't just seeing a mountain; he *was* the mountain. He wasn't just flying in the sky; he *was* the sky.

No-time was Oneness—the Oneness of Being.

Eagle landed, and the Giant came back into time as Humangus, yet different. His Guides suggested that he sleep to integrate this experience, and he did. He slept a long, replenishing, and restful sleep.

Eagle took him out on other no-time flights, each of them unique, but the same; very simple, yet profound. When he was comfortable with being in no-time and then coming back into time, she carried him back to the forest.

At the edge of the forest, Humangus and Eagle looked at each other. There was no need to say good-bye; she was him and he was her. For those who have experienced the Oneness of Being in no-time, there is never a need for good-bye.

Eagle flew back to the mountain top and Humangus went into the forest.

LION WOMAN AND CHENG LI:
Babla Learns About Elements, Orbs, and Organs

After a fun-filled and restful time, Rabia and Babla said good-bye to Wise Witch and left the Sacred Land. They knew they would be back. Going deeper and deeper into the forest, one day they came to a lush land with water flowing everywhere, birds singing, and flowers blooming.

Rabia turned to Babla and said, "I'm going to leave you again, one last time. There are a few more lessons to learn, all connected to each other. Just enjoy this beautiful place until the Beings who will teach you arrive. When you are finished, we will meet at the Sacred Land."

Babla spent some time playing with the water, talking to the flowers, and hugging trees. Then, out of nowhere, she heard a roar. A huge lion was standing next to a waterfall, roaring. In slow motion, he began changing his shape.

"Lion Woman!" Babla called out and ran to embrace her beloved friend.

"Babla! How wonderful to see you!" she said, flashing her incredible smile.

Babla was enchanted that Lion Woman was there to teach her things; she couldn't wait to get started. Yet she knew that in Lion Woman's world, patience was key and everything happened in right timing. So she waited, enjoying her friend's presence as they walked through the land. Babla started to feel the earth.

Lion Woman nodded. "Yes. Earth is one of the elements we have inside and outside of us. We also have water, fire, air, and ether. We'll spend our time learning more about these elements."

They came to a shallow pond with the sun shining right on it. Directed by Lion Woman, Babla sat in it, her legs and buttocks firmly on the earth, the water almost reaching her belly.

"This is earth and water," Lion Woman pointed out. "Now feel the sun warming your stomach. The sun is fire. Next, feel the air in your chest and around you as you breathe in and out, expanding and relaxing. The last element is ether; which we can neither see or touch, but only sense.

"Ether element is about spaciousness, about stillness, about balance. By contrast, air element is about movement; air has no boundaries. Fire element gives us direction. The movement of air that is everywhere is directed and focused by fire. Water element is about flow. Within the focused and directed movement, we need to find or create a flow.

"Thus, out of stillness, we can start moving in a directed, focused, and flowing way. Earth element is about form; the flowing, directed, moving stillness takes on a tangible shape. This is how life manifests itself."

Babla could feel the different elements playing inside of her. "Even though each one looks different, they all feel very connected to me."

Lion Woman agreed. "These five elements are all around, as well as inside us," she went on. "Even in nature you can see that each one needs the others to exist, and every living Being needs all five to stay alive. These forces are like brothers and sisters from the same family, the same origin. Inside of you, they exist as moving, rotating, pulsating orbs. Just like the elements in nature, the orbs inside are connected."

"Are there five orbs just like five elements?" Babla asked.

"No. There are seven orbs. The Crown-orb at the top of your head, the Third Eye-orb in between your two eyes, and the Throat-orb belong to ether element; the Heart-orb is air element; the Solar Plexus-orb is fire element; the Creativity-orb is water element; and the Root-orb is earth element. The water element is about flow—sensual, sexual, creative, intuitive flow. Hence, Beings not in touch with their inner flow become very dry and rigid."

"I like flowing things," replied Babla. "I didn't like fire very much, but then I met Fireball and she taught me how to play with it. I'm not afraid anymore."

"Good. Each orb is equally important," Lion Woman continued. "Without the fire we might flow, but we would waste our time and energy, lacking focus, motivation, or the spark necessary to live a balanced life. Or, like in Fireball's case, we could have too much fire and burn ourselves or other Beings. So, fire needs to be balanced with water or earth, or both; or the Pure Heart."

"Is the Pure Heart the Heart-orb?" Babla wondered.

"Not exactly. The Heart-orb is in the middle of your chest and the Pure Heart is a little bit above that. It is in a deeper system than the Orb System, but the Center and Pure Heart belong to the same system. Pure Heart holds unconditional Love. The Heart-orb knows only personal love and can carry our heart-wounds. That is, when your "heart breaks," it is never the Pure Heart." Babla understood.

"The Throat-orb is ether element," Lion Woman went on. "It also is about communication, creativity, self-expression, and intuition. If we do not communicate our truth, we get out of balance and may feel trapped, which means we don't feel spacious anymore. But when we are in balance we can sink into the stillness of ether. Here we can hear our intuition—that is, our Inner Guides. Out of the quiet our creativity explodes, and we can express our Essence."

Babla was loving every moment with Lion Woman. They left the pond and continued walking. Lion Woman led Babla into a funny-looking building made of all kinds of spirals. Babla couldn't decide whether they were spinning or not. The building had one huge hall with enormous orbs in the colors of the rainbow. They were pulsing with a wavelike rhythm in constant, almost invisible motion.

"Reminds me of a jellyfish," Babla joked. Lion Woman looked pleased. The orbs were connected by fine, elastic-like golden threads. Fascinated, Babla went to the middle of this light-and-color show and stood, or tried to. It was impossible to not move; soon she was vibrating, turning, and rotating like the orbs. She felt like a jellyfish herself, expanding and contracting, opening and closing in an ever flowing-rhythm.

Then she got it! In the absolute stillness between the expansion and contraction, and between the contraction and expansion, her body was momentarily suspended. Then the next phase of movement evolved out of the pause.

When she came back to Lion Woman, her friend explained that the stillpoint was a place of deep rest; that's why the orbs could move in their rhythm forever. During that brief yet crucial silence, they received the replenishment necessary for perpetual motion. Babla felt very rested and refreshed after this experience.

As they left the Spiral Hall of the Orbs, Lion Woman said good-bye to Babla by holding her for a long time, her golden-green eyes sparkling with Love. Then she shifted back into the Lion, gave a loud roar, and disappeared behind the bushes.

Babla wandered around, integrating this experience. Then she started wondering whether she needed to learn more.

"Yes," she heard a voice answer. She saw no one, but to her left she felt a familiar warm energy.

"Cheng Li?" she asked. "Is that you?"

In front of Babla's eyes, Cheng Li took form. He bowed lovingly and said, "There are two more lessons for you to learn before you go back to the Sacred Land. One is about the organs. Each organ in the body is related to an element and to an orb. If an organ is not functioning well, it may be sad, angry, resentful, afraid, or ashamed about something. A joyful, happy organ flows in rhythm with the orbs because it is part of the Orb System. Everything in the body is connected to everything else."

"How does healing happen then?" Babla wanted to know.

"I will show you," her Guide offered, leading her toward a huge barn-like building. "AILING ORGANS" was written high above the entrance and inside, Babla saw all kinds of organs. Some were crying, some moaning and groaning, and others looked half dead.

Followed by Babla, Cheng Li walked over to a liver. "The first step," he explained, "is to find out what is ailing the organ." Gently, he put his hand on the liver, which was almost black in color and very quiet, and asked, "Liver, what ails you?"

"I feel so heavy," the liver replied. "It feels like I have more than I can handle, so any new assignment will be too much."

"What is the main emotion connected with this heaviness?" Cheng Li inquired.

The liver exploded in flames, which reminded Babla of a volcano exploding with hot lava. "Anger?" she asked her Guide.

"Rage," he responded, "solid rage. That's why its color is so black."

After a long explosion, the liver started calming down. "Thank you so much," it said to Cheng Li. "I needed your touch. I feel much better now. I'll go back and assume my jobs."

Babla saw that it wasn't black anymore; it had become a beautiful dark red color. "Can you help every organ heal?" she asked.

"Yes," answered Cheng Li. "If it wants to. Each organ will respond differently, of course. And these two steps aren't always enough. Sometimes, even after we find the main related emotion, other steps may be required to assist in the healing."

They came to a heart; it was pale pink, looking dry and shriveled. Cheng Li repeated the first two steps: "What ails you, heart?" he asked.

"I'm tired, I just need some sleep."

"What is the main emotion connected to your tiredness?" he asked further.

The heart thought for a moment, then admitted, "I guess sadness." The heart stayed pale pink and nothing else happened.

Cheng Li said to Babla, "Now we need another step." He turned to the heart and suggested, "Let me touch this sadness. Maybe it will tell us what it is connected to." He reached out and touched the heart.

The heart didn't react at first, then a tiny teardrop surfaced. "The sadness says it comes from the Being I belong to, who often feels quite lonely," the heart replied at last.

"Tell the sadness we welcome it," said Cheng Li, gently. The heart took a long breath and then, tears came. It was like a flood at first, but gradually, the tears subsided. To her surprise, Babla saw that the color of the heart was a healthy pink now, and it wasn't dry and shriveled anymore.

"Tears are wonderful lubrication for the heart," Cheng Li commented. "Yet, if a heart can't let them out, eventually it dries up and dies. This heart, though, is going to live."

"Now you know three steps," Cheng Li said. "However, a fourth step is needed when an organ has endured an ailment for a long time. Even if the emotion is found and released, that organ may need help to resume its regular function."

They walked over to an ovary, which looked like a little egg that was all black and blue. "What ails you?" asked Cheng Li.

"I've been beaten up," replied the ovary. "Poor me. Why does it always have to happen to me? Don't I deserve a happy day in my life? All these other ovaries walk around healthy, it's only poor me who has to suffer. It's not fair."

"No, it isn't." Cheng Li was sympathetic. But the ovary started crying and complaining even more. Then it got very angry and fumed, but it stayed black and blue. Babla couldn't see any change. She looked at Cheng Li, shrugging her shoulders.

Her Guide took all this in stride. "The ovary is stuck in a vicious cycle," he commented. "I call it the self-pity cycle; it goes round and round through different emotions, but no real healing happens. The cycle needs to be broken."

He turned to the ovary and said in a firm, yet loving manner, "Ovary, I know I can help in your healing process, however, you have to want to heal. If you do not, nothing can help you. Tell me now if you want to keep complaining, which is perfectly okay with me. I'll leave you alone and touch another organ that sincerely wants to heal."

The ovary stopped in mid-sentence, startled. "I want to heal, but I'm not sure I can," it confessed at last.

"Let's find out," said Cheng Li. He put his hands on the ovary and calmly spoke, "You know that you are created from a lot of cells. Each cell inside of you has a blue dot, which is its healing potential. Each cell also carries a map of you, the whole ovary in your healthy state. Just go into your cells now and ask them to take out these maps." The ovary did so.

"Now remind your cells of their blue dot," Cheng Li continued. "Ask each cell to connect the blue dot with the map, so that the healing capacity of each cell is connected with the image of the healthy ovary. This will activate the Mystery. We do not understand why things are the way they are, we just know what is so.

"When the blue dot sees a healthy image of the ovary, the cells somehow use the healing capacity of the blue dot to actually create a healthy ovary. Do not ask me why or how, because this is as much as I know."

And that's what happened. Babla watched with fascination as the black and blue marks in the ovary disappeared. In the end, the ovary was breathing, smiling, and looking happy and content. It thanked Cheng Li with enthusiasm and went to resume its job in its owner's body.

Cheng Li turned to Babla. "Now you know what you need to assist the organs in their healing process," he said. "The second lesson is about your place in Rabia's Center. In order to meet the Vultures safely, you must learn how to stay centered."

They started right away. He asked her to sit, her feet touching the ground, and imagine her energy going all the way down from her tailbone into the earth. Then the energy curled back up, split into two, and came up the inside of her legs. The energy became one again where her legs joined her torso, moved into her Center, tumbled a few times, then went back down into the earth.

"The earth is about structure, solidity, stability, and support," Cheng Li explained. "It strengthens the Center. Any shaky or hesitant Center needs more earth energy. Remember this always."

Babla stayed with Cheng Li, learning to bring more earth into her Center. When she was ready, Rabia, Fireball, and Black Panther appeared. This time Babla and Fireball practiced moving the earth energy into Rabia's Center.

"Can't you do this yourself?" Babla asked her Adult Self.

"Yes, I can," Rabia replied, stroking the Child's hair. "But if I center myself while you are afraid or Fireball is angry, it won't work for long because my Center will weaken as a result of the emotions. However, if we do this all together, bringing in more earth and thus more strength to my Center, which actually is 'our' Center, it will stay strong."

This made sense. Babla marveled that Rabia always made sense. It was great to have her as the Adult Self; Babla felt very safe.

The rest of the time with Cheng Li was fun. Fireball and Babla practiced together, learning how to bring earth energy into anger and fear. If Fireball's anger or Babla's fear took over, it was harder to find Rabia and connect with her. However, when they brought more earth into the Center, they could feel Rabia much closer.

After quite a lot of practice, Cheng Li told them that they were complete with their training. He gave them a long hug and disappeared.

Now it was time to find the Vultures; it was time for the final test.

PEACE WITH THE VULTURES: *In Our Hearts, We Are One*

Babla came to the edge of the forest where a huge desert spread out as far as she could see. She sat by a tree trunk, not quite ready to leave the forest. Lost in thought, she jumped at the sound of footsteps. Amazon Woman was approaching with Black Panther by her side.

Babla's face lit up and she knew she wouldn't be alone. To be really honest, she would rather avoid this particular challenge and pretend the Vultures didn't exist, but Rabia and the Inner Guides seemed to have another plan.

Amazon Woman lifted Babla onto her lap, stroking her hair; Babla felt totally protected by her Warrior Guide and started to relax. She had the feeling they were waiting for something, yet she didn't know what it was. A few moments later she found out. At the sound of heavy footsteps, out of the woods Ax-Woman appeared, carrying Fireball on her shoulders.

This was great! Babla started to feel that with all their support, the encounter with the Vultures might turn out okay.

"When you get scared, Babla, Rabia's Center will weaken," Amazon Woman reminded her. "If the Vultures scare you, rather than contracting, reach out for Fireball's hand; that's the key. Then the two of you start bringing more earth energy to the Center. You both will be inside Rabia's Center, and Ax-Woman to her right. Even if she doesn't do or say anything, the Vultures need to feel her presence to respect Rabia. They bow to strength."

"If they need Ax-Woman with Rabia, then why do we have to be here? Couldn't we just go play somewhere else?" Babla asked, hoping she didn't need to face these nasty birds of prey after all.

Amazon Woman smiled and patted Babla's head with understanding. "No. You two are essential, I assure you," she answered after a while. "If you get scared or Fireball gets angry, these emotions will deplete Rabia's Center and come between her and Ax-Woman, leaving Rabia weakened and disconnected. You can imagine that the Vultures would love to dive for her."

Babla could imagine that very well. They all left the forest, with Babla and Fireball sitting comfortably in their Adult Self's Center, holding hands and focused on bringing in more earth energy. So far, this was fun!

As Rabia went into the hot desert, Babla saw two black dots above the horizon and got scared. What if it didn't work? All she could think of was running back to the forest to hide. She felt her hand being squeezed and came back to reality; she was with Fireball in Rabia's Center, Ax-Woman to their right side, Amazon Woman and Black Panther to their left. She was safe. She took a deep breath and tried to relax.

When the dots came closer, Babla recognized the Vultures. They were flying at a record speed. It looked like they were diving for Rabia.

"I hate those awful beasts!" yelled Fireball, shaking her little fists. "I'm going to get them this time! I'm going to punch them right in the nose, if they have one!"

Just as Fireball was getting ready to jump out of Rabia, Babla grabbed one of her fists and held it tight. Fireball froze, looking somewhat dazed. She had forgotten where she was.

"Let's bring some more earth energy into the Center here," suggested Babla, trying to sound brave. Fireball took the hint and drew in a big breath, relaxing her fists. This was tough!

"You girls are doing great!" they heard Amazon Woman's voice. "Leave the rest up to Ax-Woman."

The Vultures stopped in mid-air. They had recognized Babla and were going for an easy prey, yet something was different. Momentarily befuddled, they halted their assault.

"She looks like Babla, or a sort of grown-up version of her," commented one of them.

"Yes," agreed the other. "Not only that, I sense a certain strength around her that wasn't there before. Very unusual."

They decided to check it out and landed in front of Rabia. "Hi, Vultures," said Rabia, smiling. "I am Babla's Adult Self. She told me a lot about you; I'm pleased to meet you."

And Babla, hearing this from inside of Rabia, realized that her Adult really meant it. Securely connected to her Center and to Ax-Woman, Rabia had no judgments or bad feelings; she knew each Being has a place in the Universe and a reason to exist.

Fireball, realizing the same thing, was alarmed. "Does this mean that we need to accept other Beings even if we hate what they do?"

"Accepting a Being not liking the Being's behavior are two different things," Amazon Woman replied. "That is, we recognize that in our Core, our Essence, we are all One. In practical terms, we accept that in the very Essence of things and beyond the Veils of Separation, Rabia and the Vultures are one energy. Remember the Spiralworld we went to during the Healing Circle? The Essence of Being is just like that; one endlessly spiraling energy with many outer forms."

The little girls looked at each other in amazement.

The Vultures, looking at Rabia, were also amazed. This was Babla's Adult Self talking! Something about her told them that she was not prey-material. They looked at each other with nods of acceptance. In Vulture Wisdom, Beings who weren't prey were better as friends than as enemies.

The Vultures told Rabia that they, too, were pleased to meet her —and they meant it. They wished to get to know her better. Rabia smiled pleasantly and rubbed her belly, inside which Babla and Fireball sat, doubled up, giggling.

"Thank you, Ax-Woman," Rabia whispered, turning her head slightly to the right. "Without your presence, this would not have been possible. Let there be no more illusion of separation; in our Hearts, we are One."

the end

dissolving the veils of separation

DISSOLVING THE VEILS OF SEPARATION

Babla reached the Sacred Land that touched the deep blue waters, resting where the waves played with the rocks. She felt tired in a good way, knowing she was finished, and this was the end of her journey. She also felt a sense of relief, as if she had been doing a huge puzzle and there was one last piece to be put into place. She glanced around; all was quiet.

At the very edge of the land, a figure sat on a big rock surrounded by waves. Babla knew that this was her Adult Self looking out at the horizon. Birds, small and large, were flying over Rabia's head, rhythmically circling the rock while a warm breeze tussled her hair.

Babla climbed onto the rock next to Rabia, who was waiting for her. Opening her arms, Rabia swept Babla onto her lap, where the little girl curled herself into a tiny ball, so happy to have completed her journey. She felt Rabia's strong and loving arms holding her, caressing her. She closed her eyes and dropped into a deep relaxation, letting go of all doing and thinking, letting go into being.

Rabia started humming. The sound began at her Center, then spiraled up and down her body, bathing each orb. Babla felt the hum enter her own body, vibrating, pulsating in every pore. She couldn't tell where Rabia ended and she began.

Without really knowing why, Babla opened her eyes. There they were, all of the Inner Beings, all of her Guides, standing in a circle around Rabia and herself, holding hands. Babla looked at the circle—or was it Rabia who was looking? Over there were Tantrika, the Nun, and the Slut; they looked very much like sisters, swaying in the breeze, their unique qualities blending with one another. Zak and Ms. Romantic were arm in arm, their faces glowing with romantic love, looking deeply into each other's eyes.

Emanuella—surrounded by the Mermaid, Ax-Woman, and Little Seashell—was being embraced by Manuel, their bodies moving together in the rhythm of ecstasy. When she lost herself in the blissful emptiness, becoming that with wild abandon, Manuel filled her with his presence, his maleness. And when she totally accepted being full, feeling the ecstasy of it in all of her pores, she experienced herself as empty again. Then, as she let go into the ecstasy of emptiness, Emanuella found fullness once more.

Next to them, Amazon Woman stood strong and tall beside Black Panther, who lay sensuously at her feet, totally relaxed. Fireball sat on her shoulders, intensely present, her aliveness creating a brilliant glow all around.

And there was Inner Judge, very regal in his black robe, looking at the circle, wisdom and fairness shining through his eyes. Loretta and Miriam were by his side, arm in arm. Miriam's caring and giving nature was constantly nurturing Loretta; and Loretta's receptive, soft, and patient qualities were balancing the Judge's mental outlook on life. Maya was behind Loretta, slowly combing her hair.

Golden Queen stood between Mr. Money and Slimy Joe. Her love of and appreciation for money was penetrating Slimy Joe, her respect and humbleness around it going into Mr. Money. Together they created the necessary balance for a constant, abundant flow.

Cheng Li stood in the circle with Wise Owl perched on his shoulder, a rainbow of deep silence emerged from them, spiraling outward to embrace the others in Oneness.

Eternal Friend and Eric were next to Fireball and the Amazon. Holding Fireball's hand, the Cynic felt his doubts and hopelessness lift as Fireball's directed, red hot energy pushed through into action. And Fireball felt her impulsiveness ease off and come into balance when she saw Eric's doubting, questioning eyes. Both knew that it was Eternal Friend's endless, boundless Love and wisdom that sustained this constant dance of energies.

Alan . . . Alan had left the circle and joined Rabia and Babla. As the Inner Mate, he was needed here to create the optimum balance between the Inner Child and the Adult Self. His golden glow, visible through loving eyes and an open smile, showered itself endlessly upon them.

They heard the voice of the Higher Self: "The journey is over. You are done doing. Now is the time for being." Its luminous presence hovered above the circle, embracing them all.

With that, all of the Inner Beings began blending into Rabia; they seemed to step into her, then somehow disappear. The last one was Fireball. As she neared Rabia, she reached over and took Babla's hand, and together they took a step.

Right before Babla merged with Rabia, she thought of the graceful White Swan and wondered what had happened to it. She heard a voice saying: "I am here, Babla. I am a White Swan no more. I have dissolved into the sky. Now I am the whole sky, the whole Galaxy, the whole Universe."

Babla didn't know whether the voice was coming from inside or outside of Rabia. She sensed that it was both.

As time came to a stillpoint, Rabia realized that she was being drawn into the Higher Self. Or was the Higher Self being drawn into her? This time she was ready to receive it fully, completely, and to be received equally by it.

Just like the waves of the deep blue waters entering the Sacred Land, the Higher Self entered Rabia, and Rabia was one with the Higher Self. The One Being dissolved into the Sacred Land.

Yet, a presence, a different fragrance was also in the air now. This was the unique Essence of Rabia-ness, which added to the sacredness of the land and to the depth of the waters.

When the mind is at peace,
the world too is at peace.
Nothing real, nothing absent.
Not holding on to reality,
not getting stuck in the void,
you are neither holy nor wise, just
an ordinary fellow who has completed his work.

Layman P'ang (c. 740–808)

Adapted by Stephen Mitchell

Afterword

I met Rabia in 1992 and began working intensely with her, discovering who I am. Working with Rabia over the years has led me to Veils of Separation. Each time I approach this fairy tale, another piece of my spiritual journey is revealed. In the face of life's challenges, I am always reminded of the simplicity of life and the joy of my inner work. Indeed, life's experiences are an opportunity to look deeper within.

Many times while reading this book, I have asked, How does this situation fit into my growth process? How can I use this portion of the story to transform my own unfinished business? The clarity each process ultimately brings is so complete, that my Inner Beings are able to recognize their own veils. By using this book, my desire to find wholeness has become stronger than holding onto separation.

I find it especially beneficial to explore Rabia's examples involving at least two polarized Beings who do not know the other exists. Stuck in their belief systems, they need both to find their positive qualities and to accept each other to come into balance. Rabia shows how opposing inner forces can meet and work together as they learn new roles.

There is a possibility for change every time two conflicted Beings come together. In this way, all veils of separation diminish, allowing space for Oneness. I am grateful for the many levels of teaching in this book. It is a cherished jewel in my collection of tools for inner work. Rabia's commitment to following her truth no matter what has been a guiding light for me to embrace each moment.

Jodi Korpi
longtime friend and apprentice

About the Author

Rabia Erduman was born in Istanbul, Turkey and later spent ten years in Germany before arriving in the United States in 1983. She has traveled extensively in Europe, India, and Bali and is fluent in English, German, and Turkish.

Rabia's B.A. in psychology is the foundation of her private practice, in which she uses the Clarity Process, Alchemical Hypnotherapy, Craniosacral Therapy, and Polarity Therapy to assist clients in their process of self-discovery. Rabia also teaches tantric and spiritually-oriented workshops. An inspiring lecturer, she has given talks on tantra, hypnotherapy, past life regression, and living a life in ecstasy, among other topics.

Her search for the ultimate Truth led Rabia to India. There she met an awakened being, Osho, which totally changed her life. Years later, when she was ready for her next step of self-inquiry, another awakened being, Gangaji, opened the door.

To those wishing to understand her work, she says, "I have found working with the combination of mind, body, and energy to be highly effective in reaching optimum balance. My life and work are about being in the moment, free of fear and the feeling of separation. Deep joy is a natural outgrowth of this process."

Tapes

For ordering information: www.WuWeiWu@earthlink.net
Available tapes by Rabia are:

Relaxation

Side A, <u>Parts of the Body</u>, moves the listener into a deep state of relaxation, where the body can rejuvenate at a cellular level. It includes a color healing for relieving tension in specific areas of the body.
Side B, <u>Journey to the Beach</u>, is a guided journey into the rhythms of life, including discovery of the still point, from which all action arises, and to which it all returns.
$14,-

Sit & Be

This guided meditation, which focuses on a relaxation of all parts of the body, invites the listener to gently peel away distractions, release tension, and set the self free to be fully present in the moment. Side A is with music, Side B without.
$14,-

Inner Silence

Moving through the layers of thought and emotion, this meditation guides the listener beyond duality into the core of Being. Side A is with music, Side B without.
$14,-

Chakra Meditation

Side A is a journey through the chakras.
Side B is a manifesting visualization down the chakras.
$14,-

Higher Self Meditation / Core Meditation

Side A guides the listener to a meeting with the Higher Self.
Side B is a journey into one's core to meet the Wise Old Woman / Wise Old Man.
$14,-